UNRAVELING THE SPECIAL EDUCATION MAZE

An Action Guide for Parents

BARBARA COYNE CUTLER

RESEARCH PRESS
2612 North Mattis Avenue
Champaign, Illinois 61820

Work on this book was supported by HEW under Grant MH 14761 awarded to Boston University, Department of Sociology, by the National Institute of Mental Health, Division of Manpower Research and Demonstration.

The chart in Appendix B is reprinted from *Insight*, Vol. II, No. 6, by permission of The Council for Exceptional Children. Copyright 1980 by The Council for Exceptional Children, 1920 Association Drive, Reston, Virginia 22091.

Copies of this book may be ordered from the publisher at the address given on the title page.

Cover design by Jack W. Davis

Composition by Omegatype Typography, Inc.

ISBN 0-87822-224-3
Library of Congress Catalog Card Number: 80-54006

This book is dedicated to parents
searching for services
for their handicapped children;
but, most of all
to my own parents
who have supported me
during my search.

Contents

Foreword

Articles in professional journals happily report marked success in research-oriented programs for educating special-needs children. The federal government awards millions of dollars in grants and contracts to state agencies, school systems, and educational organizations for the development and implementation of more effective educational programs. Special education receives favorable reportage in newspapers and magazines and is the subject of hopeful and heartwarming television programs. In my experience, however, few persons in the system for delivering services to special-needs children, who have the daily and long-term responsibility for the welfare of the children, are very happy.

School boards, for example, complain about the expense of special education programs and about the needs of the other children. Special education administrators describe their jobs as having too many conflicting demands, too little direct authority, and too little access to enough money for enough time to deliver comprehensive, high-quality services. Teachers describe themselves as being isolated in a large system. They assert that the demands of their jobs are not well understood and that their hard work is often not appreciated. Parents argue that there is little recognition or understanding of what they have been through, and that they have little opportunity to have an impact on the planning and administration of the services their children receive. Parents also note their dissatisfactions with services being delivered:

the poor curriculum, the lack of therapy (speech, physical), and the insufficient communication with teachers and administrators. Children, finally, express their discontent in worsening patterns of physical aggression, truancy, teasing, self-stimulation, inattention, and tantrums. The bottom line, then, is that in spite of the concern, energy, and money expended, a number of children are not getting the education which they need and to which they are entitled.

Unraveling the Special Education Maze examines this situation and offers a method for change. Three main ideas run throughout the discussion. The first is that parents do occupy an important position in the special education delivery system, but they are either largely excluded from participation, or, through passivity or fear, simply fail to effectively participate when the system is open to them. The relationship between parents and the school system is understandable in terms of the sequence of experiences undergone by many families.

The parents of a special-needs child experience sadness, bewilderment, and anxiety regarding their child's condition, his or her future, and their own sense of self-worth. Typically, parents spend many years making the rounds from one professional to another in the search for understanding of their child's condition, a prognosis, and recommendations for practical actions which they and others can take to help the child. In the process, they may spend a great deal of time, effort, and money and often obtain conflicting opinions and recommendations which do not seem to produce much beneficial change in their child. Moreover, as time goes by, the parents may feel (and may be) isolated from their own families, from neighbors, and from the community—yet the daily effort of rearing and coping with their child continues and perhaps becomes more difficult.

In the long run, the parents may become very sensitive to the opinions of others and afraid to assert themselves with professionals because they see themselves as incompetent or because they believe that by doing so they may lose what services are being made available. Or, they may be so burned out that they wish to leave the whole job to those who are legally mandated to educate their child.

Some parents, on the other hand, become very angry or at least assertive. They may demand that certain services be delivered and may escalate the intensity of their demands when they feel frustrated. In this case, a cycle of increasing hostility between the school personnel and the parents is maintained, often to the detriment of all parties, especially the child.

The second main idea is that most of the shortcomings and problems in special education are the result of the inadequate *organization* of services rather than a lack of commitment on the part of workers in the system. The organizational sources of difficulty are numerous. For instance, the service delivery system has *multiple, conflicting goals* or functions. It is designed to simultaneously train students in basic skills, educate them in more academic skills, enculturate students so that they can become members of the larger social system, baby-sit for children while their parents work away from the home, and take custody over and control children whose behavior is difficult or impossible to manage. On the other hand, workers may expect or want the system to provide a livelihood, a sense of self-worth, and an opportunity to acquire skills enabling them to move onward and upward.

Although there is not the space here to fully address each one, other organizational sources of shortcomings in the delivery of special educational services include the following: (1) the wide range of children's needs to be served; (2) the relative isolation of special education in the school system; (3) the unclear or conflicting lines of authority among teachers, aides, special education administrators, school principals, and directors of pupil personnel; (4) the relative absence of criteria for evaluating the quality of instruction provided independent of changes in students (perhaps stemming from disagreements among theoreticians and researchers); (5) the difficulty of altering the behavior of teachers (because of

unionization, tenure, or absence of evaluation criteria);
(6) the use of services provided by persons and organizations with virtually no commitment to the school system
(such as cab companies, consultants, private schools, or
diagnostic clinics); and (7) the often antagonistic relationship, or, more generally, the lack of a productive working
relationship between the school system and the parents.

In general, long-term results of these types of organizational problems include difficulty in planning and
delivering a comprehensive set and sequence of services
to meet the needs of all the children; the development
of behavior patterns among workers which contradict
many of the goals of the organization; difficulty in
evaluating both the process and outcomes of the educational program in a way that prescribes changes; difficulty
in making fundamental changes in the organization itself;
and increasing frustration and despair among workers,
leading to half-hearted efforts and staff turnover.

The third idea that pervades the book is that parents
can make important contributions to the system and can
help to change it for the better—both for their own child
and for the children of others. In spite of the organizational and personal problems, they can learn to understand the organization of the special education system, to
evaluate services as well as their child's strengths and
needs, and to develop the skills and will for communicating effectively with special education personnel.

This last idea is not wishful thinking. Both Ms. Cutler
and I have found that, during the course of our training
programs for families, many parents are able to transform
their intimate and previously unarticulated knowledge of
their children into precise descriptions and prescriptions.
They learn to evaluate their children's strengths and
needs and to plan comprehensive, long-term educational
programs. They learn to evaluate the quality of an
educational program and to make recommendations for
change. And they become angry when their suggestions
(often easy to institute) are not adopted (and sometimes
not listened to) by school personnel who feel threatened,

harassed, or overworked. Some then become advocates for special-needs children, working very hard to produce change in the system.

The past decade seems to have shown that substantial improvement in the effectiveness of special education services will not be produced merely by the addition of money and personnel to existing systems. Perhaps what is needed is a productive relationship with parents, through which feasible and acceptable goals can be established, the knowledge of the parents can be integrated in the school and the knowledge of the teachers can be disseminated to the home, and services can be continually evaluated and revised.

This book was written primarily for parents, to help them to institute and maintain a productive relationship with special education systems, or, in the case of organizational resistance, to work to obtain the services their children need. However, the book will be equally useful to caring educators and to other professionals. It will help them to understand the position in which parents find themselves; to enlist parents as partners in developing appropriate educational programs and obtaining needed services; and to teach parents advocacy skills as part of training programs and support groups.

And no one could be better suited to portraying the points of view of all those involved in special education than Barbara Cutler. Simply stated, Barbara Cutler has been there. She is the parent of a twenty-three-year-old autistic son. Because of his unmet needs (educational, social, and therapeutic) she became involved in AMIC, an organization of parents of autistic children in Massachusetts, and has twice served as its president. Her first serious experiences with systems came about through her advocacy efforts on behalf of autistic children. From a quiet and compliant parent, she became a leading advocate, assisting key Massachusetts legislators in reviewing and revising the document which was to become the state's model special education law. She has served on the Task Force on Children Out of School, and the Massachusetts

Special Education Advisory Council, and currently serves on the Massachusetts Developmental Disabilities Council.

At the same time she was learning to become an outspoken and competent advocate, she earned her master's degree in education from Harvard University. After she trained in a special education classroom in a public school setting, she went on to direct a small model program for very handicapped adolescents. As Regional Mental Retardation Coordinator for the Massachusetts Department of Mental Health, she gained insights into the operation of still another service system.

From 1977 to the present, Ms. Cutler has been the Head Trainer on my project, Community-Based Training Programs, which is funded by the Experimental and Special Projects Branch of the National Institute of Mental Health. In her capacity as Head Trainer, Ms. Cutler has been able to employ her knowledge of the service delivery system and of parents' experiences in it, her educational skills, and her advocacy skills to the task of helping parents educate their special-needs children.

Over the years, Ms. Cutler has earned the trust and admiration of a large number of parents and professionals who have come to value her insights and experiences, and appreciate her determination to deal publicly with issues which affect the welfare of handicapped children and adults and their families.

Martin A. Kozloff

Preface

Many parents are quite literally in the dark about the rights of their handicapped children to a decent and appropriate education. Others may have heard something about the new special education law for all handicapped children, but they believe that their children are too young, too old, too handicapped, or too difficult for the public schools to educate. Yet all children, with or without handicaps, are entitled to a free public education.

Some public school systems, in their indifference to the needs and rights of handicapped children, are like mazes that bewilder parents trying to reach the goal of appropriate and beneficial services for their children. These parents find their efforts leading them to dead ends or through the same paths they have wandered in many times before. They have no way of judging how close or how far they may be from the goal. They need something to guide them.

Public Law 94-142, the Education for All Handicapped Children Act, is the map that can straighten the winding paths of the maze and lead handicapped children to the brighter future which the right educational services can bring. It provides parents with ways to avoid the dead ends and to keep moving forward.

For parents who are now frustrated by or uninformed about the educational system and its obligations to their children, this book offers the chance to learn how to use Public Law 94-142 to get to that more promising future their children deserve and to which they are entitled.

Acknowledgments

This book has been derived from a great sharing of experiences and ideas among parents and professionals over the past ten years. In the beginning, we mostly shared frustration and failure. Occasionally someone would report that through insistent and continuous contact with a school system, some parents were able to get something more for their children. The rest of us would listen carefully and try to use or adapt their techniques in the hope that our children could benefit too. In this way we inched along. It wasn't until state and national education laws were passed, guaranteeing our handicapped children the right to education, that we were able to take a giant step.

The terrain we travel is still rough, but with the resources and allies we have found, we can keep moving to reach the goal of an appropriate and adequate education for every handicapped child.

Along the way I found a number of resources, and the most important resources were people. *Parents* have been my first, special, and continuous resource. Over the years some of these parents developed into professional or paraprofessional advocates; others, of necessity, could only advocate for their own children, but they were always willing to share their needs, hopes, and experiences with others in any way that could help.

Leading the list of people to whom I am indebted are the Directors of the Parent Information Centers (PICS), Martha Ziegler (Boston), Charlotte Des Jardins (Chicago),

Judy Raskin (New Hampshire), Bernadette Merluzzi (South Bend), Betsy Britten (Ohio), and Barbara Scheiber (Washington, D.C.). A bouquet of thanks must go to the impressive parent advocates at the Federation for Children With Special Needs: Pat Bausemer, Evelyn Doherty, Joanne Driscoll, Beverly Graham, Janice Mallett, Eileen Souza, Phyllis Sneirson, Pat Theroux, and many others in that office who sometimes sought my advice, and ended up by giving me more than I had given them.

Charlotte Aladjem, Bernice Brown, Frank Donnelly, Roz Forsyth, Cynthia Gilles, Louise Hackett, Eileen and Jerry Kramer, Regina McLaughlin, Stu Robinson, Carol Stevens, and Edith York have kept me informed, motivated, and on task as I developed an understanding of parent advocacy and its potential power.

The *legal advocates* were the first to openly stand beside parents. Without them our special education laws would be weak or nonexistent. I am personally indebted to Paul Dimond, Larry Kotin, Bob Crabtree, and Reed Martin for showing me the power of the law. Two Massachusetts legislators, David Bartley (the former Speaker of the Massachusetts House) and Mike Daly cared enough to sponsor and push the best state special education law in the nation, and to submit it to a concerned legislature and a caring governor, Francis Sargent, who signed the bill into law.

Professor Gunnar Dybwad, who has been in court speaking out for the handicapped more times than anyone can count, is the supreme and most vocal advocate for the handicapped; he has served as my model for understanding issues and for speaking up.

People inside the educational system were getting ready to join parent and legal advocates in our efforts to improve services for handicapped children. We had no trouble finding them. The foremost was Dr. Robert Audette, former Massachusetts Commissioner for Special Education. At the federal level we found Harvey Liebergott. In the cities and towns we found special education directors who cared, like Jim Underwood, Mabyn Martin, Ray Bohn, and Joyce McClelland.

In the classrooms (that is, on the front lines) I found exceptional teachers like Dr. Barbara Bruno-Golden, who first taught me that a good teacher knows how to use, work with, and support a caring parent, and Larry McIlroy, Bruce Pemberton, Diane Sullivan, and many others who have shown that they can and want to work with both students and parents.

And at the *university level,* working on understanding and changing the system, there were people like Al Murphy, Frank Garfunkel, Larry Brown, Hubie Jones, Sue Gordon, Don Maietta, and Sol Levine to provide support and advice; and since the days of my fledgling advocacy there has always been Helen Kenney, who valued the parents' contribution long before the laws were written.

Of course there are a few people who defy categorization, like Dr. Mary Jane England and Ann Connolly, who have remained strong advocates for children as they moved from service in one public agency to another; and Milt Budoff, whose determination to remain in the private sector as critic and evaluator of the educational system has allowed him to act as advocate free of the constraints that public service can impose.

Mary McKinnon, Chevy Martin, and Leela John have their own special place in the field of aggressive, and sometimes outraged and "noisy," advocacy; when I have faltered or weakened, their examples and prodding have helped me to raise my voice that one more time.

All of these people have contributed to the shaping of the ideas and experiences that form the basis of this book. Others, especially parents, who are not named because there are so many, or whose names I never knew, have shared their problems, experiences, and insights over the years. Some will recognize their stories and their contributions; others will agree with the substance; and a few may wonder how I managed to come to "that conclusion!" The applications and interpretations are my own. But I am grateful to all the people who said "Right on!" and "The book is needed. Do it!"

The "doing it" involved endless hours of turning handwritten text which was crossed-out, scribbled over, and arrowed, into a beautifully typed manuscript that began to look like a book, thanks to Sue Arnold.

It would have been difficult, if not impossible, to write a book without the support, caring, and patience of family and friends. My special supports came from Carol McDonough, George Cutler, Marty Sawzin, and Elaine Sullivan, and most of all from my children, Robert and George, who over the years have suffered with me through those difficult times which prepared me to write this book. I hope that they have benefited from my learning experiences and have not been harmed by my failures.

Of all the caring and contributing people, Marty Kozloff is the person who made this book possible. He insisted that I had something to say that people needed to know; then he gave me the time and the space to do it.

One

You're Entitled . . .

Elizabeth is eight years old but can say only a few words to express her needs. She can't dress or wash herself without a great deal of help from her parents. For three years she has been in the same class, where she spends almost two hours each day working on puzzles. Her parents want her to learn more language and self-help skills.

Ms. Graham is a special class teacher who is trying to get more help for her students from the speech therapist and the occupational therapist. But they are scheduled by the special education director for only one hour each week. She is equally frustrated by the denial of her request to move her classroom to the floor where the cafeteria is so that a physically handicapped student can eat lunch with the other students. When her students' parents ask about therapy or relocation, she merely shakes her head.

Sam is eighteen but is not easily understood when he speaks. Last year he started to act out. One day he threw a book across the room and struck the teacher. The principal expelled him because the school can't deal with him. His parents can find no other programs for him, so Sam just sits at home and waits.

What do these stories have in common? They are all about children with handicaps who, in spite of requests by teachers and parents, are not receiving the educational services they need and to which they are entitled under Public Law (P.L.) 94-142.

WHAT P.L. 94-142 MEANS FOR
YOUR CHILD AND YOU

By now, most of you have probably heard that P.L. 94-142 (the Federal Education for All Handicapped Children Act) guarantees a free and appropriate public education to all handicapped children. But many of you may not yet be fully aware of the important role which you, the parent, have to play in helping your child derive the maximum benefit from the law—an educational program designed and delivered to meet your child's unique needs. P.L. 94-142 gives you the right to actively participate in the process of developing an educational plan for your child. You can have a voice in determining your child's educational career by becoming your child's advocate, which means demonstrating your concern for your child and your commitment to his future by giving as much time and energy as are necessary to help him obtain those services to which he is entitled. It can be hard work, but it can make the difference between a good program and a poor one.

"Why," you want to ask, "if the law says the school systems must educate my child, do I need to become a parent advocate? Isn't the school staff responsible for finding the right program?" The answer is that of course they are responsible! However, school systems serve many children, and may overlook some of them, especially handicapped children, when priorities are being set. When the school finance committee orders the superintendent to keep costs down, who will insist that your child get the speech therapy he needs so badly? It won't be the special education director or the teacher or the speech therapist. No matter how well-intentioned, concerned, and competent they are, they still take their orders from the superintendent. If you don't advocate for the service, your child's needs may be forgotten.

P.L. 94-142 is a declaration of your child's educational rights and of your right as a parent to participate in the educational process. It is a guarantee like any other guarantee: It is something you use when the product or service fails to meet the claims of the maker or service provider. For example, if you buy a toaster that doesn't work as it is supposed to, you take action. You get out your sales slip and guarantee, and take the item back to the shop, call the company, or, if necessary to get satisfaction, write the company president about your complaint. You don't wring your hands and wait for the company to find you. It's the same with P.L. 94-142. You check out the product (your child's education) to see if it is working (your child is making progress). If you find that it is not working, you use your guarantee to get a good education for your child by calling and going to the school system, and, if necessary, to the state Department of Education.

There will be some parents, especially of older or more severely handicapped children, who will say, "I don't think the law will help my child because there are no programs for him. The school doesn't have the right kind of trained people or facilities, or enough money. The law won't make any difference to us." These parents have not looked at the terms of the guarantee provided by P.L. 94-142. The law applies to all handicapped children, even the most severely disabled, and has been extended in some states to include nineteen- to twenty-one-year-old students (see p. 11). In fact, one of the reasons the law was written and enacted was because there were one million students in the United States with no education at all. The law refers strongly and specifically to the severely handicapped student, the older student, and the student who is excluded from education. But if parents don't use the guarantee of P.L. 94-142, then, for some handicapped children, the law will make very little difference.

The full implementation of the law depends on parents. Knowledgeable and active parents can and do make a difference in the quality and availability of educational services for their children. In the few years that P.L. 94-142 has been in effect and for the longer periods that some states have had special education laws, we have seen the results of parent action. We know for a fact that the children of parents who are effective advocates do get more and better services than they would have received without their parents' efforts. Many conditions have been improved because of parent action:

- There are handicapped children who were going to school in church basements (because there was no room for them in the public schools) who are now in respectable special education classrooms in public school buildings.

- There are students whose former classrooms were located next to the school boiler room who are now located in classes on the main floor.

- There are other students, formerly isolated from contact with regular education students, who are now enrolled in regular gym, music, and art programs and sometimes in social studies, reading, and math classes.

- There are adolescent students who would have been pushed out of school when they turned sixteen who are continuing their educational programs.

- There are physically disabled students of all ages who are seeing the inside of public school buildings for the first time because the schools have installed ramps and widened doors.

- There are other handicapped students who are being seen for the first time in their school careers by language therapists, physical therapists, and other specialists.

- There are children, once denied any form of education, who are receiving year-round (twelve-month) educational programs.

- There are many children who are beginning to read, write, talk (or communicate by signing), participate in recreation, take care of their own personal needs, and demonstrate other skills once considered beyond their reach.

In many cases, parents were the first to raise the issue of providing education for their handicapped children, and most of them used the law to back up their claims. They acted as advocates for their children, and they made the difference between no program, or an inferior one, and a good program which would allow their children to take their rightful places in society. You can make a difference for your child if you are willing to face up to the school system by becoming the spokesperson for your child's education.

Of course, you are thinking, I want to help my child get the education he needs and is entitled to. But don't you have to have professional skills and special knowledge to be an advocate? Don't you have to be some kind of recognized expert to do the job? How can I, a mere parent, become an effective advocate? After all, I've often heard lawyers referred to as advocates, and they are experts in interpreting the law.

It may help you to know that there have been lawyers who have looked to skillful and knowledgeable parent advocates for advice in dealing with school systems. These parents were not professionals, just good advocates who learned through hard work and practice how to do the job well. Any parent can become a good advocate.

WHAT IS AN EFFECTIVE ADVOCATE?

Let's discuss and list the basic characteristics of a good advocate:

1. greater *concern for the child's best interests* than for the concerns or interests of the school system

2. *long-term commitment* to the child's welfare and to being the child's advocate

3. *knowledge of the present needs* of the child or the ability to recognize those needs

4. *assertiveness* in pointing out the child's needs to the people responsible for meeting those needs

5. *ability to work with others* (professionals, para-professionals, and other parents and advocates) to develop appropriate and beneficial educational goals and plans for the child

6. *ability to find and use information, allies, and resources* to put the needed educational plans to work

The list may seem overwhelming, but note that there is nothing in it which says you need to be a lawyer, an educator, or a doctor. It includes only personal characteristics which you may already have, can strengthen and adapt, or can acquire with some self-instruction and practice. Measure yourself against this comparable list:

1. Who cares more than you about what is happening to your child and what the future will hold for her? Yes, there may be many professionals and other outside advocates who care about your child and who are on your side, but they probably have tens or hundreds of other students or clients to be concerned about. As a parent, your love and concern is deeper, stronger, and more enduring.

2. Who has been and will be around your child longer than you? Professionals come and go, sometimes yearly, and they sometimes leave when you feel you need them most. That teacher who was so kind and interested has just moved to another part of the country, or that sympathetic psychologist has opened a practice a hundred miles away. You, however, will be there with your child throughout her educational career, and beyond if she needs you.

3. Who knows more about your child's growth, personality, special needs, and special skills than you? You know how hard she tries to do certain things, how well she gets along with the neighborhood children, or how lonely she feels watching life go on around and without her. You are the best source of information about your child: You are the expert in residence. As useful as medical and school records are, they explain only part of your child's experiences. You are the best available expert with the broadest overview of your child.

Stop here for a moment to recognize that on these three points (caring, constancy, and information) you lead the field of potential advocates for your child. You come by these qualifications naturally because you are the parent. Parents are the logical and natural advocates for their children—they are the first and last resource. Others can help you do the job (and you will want their help), but no one is as qualified as you in these three basic requirements for being an effective advocate.

Now for the last three qualifications you probably need some help. Most people do, including professionals. You can give yourself the help you need through reading (Appendix A lists helpful books on parent advocacy, assertiveness, and other topics), planning, and practice.

4. All that being assertive means is speaking up and hanging in. Some of us are better (and bolder!) than others. But even if you are shy or lack confidence, you can learn to be more assertive. You may already be feeling a little surge of confidence from realizing that as the natural advocate, you have some powerful qualifications that no one else can match. With the guidance of the later chapters of this book you will work on developing more confidence and learning to state your child's case more assertively. You need not learn to be mean or unpleasant, just firm and constant.

5. Working with others is something you have done before, but you may have yet to work as equals with school personnel. Luckily, school people react in the same way as anybody else to praise, diplomacy, or persuasion. Your ways of dealing with pleasant and unpleasant co-workers will help you work with school people of both sorts. After you have rid yourself of some ideas you may have about "mere" parents and about experts who have all the answers, you will become comfortable in your working relationships with professionals. You will be drawing on your everyday experience and skills to learn how to cooperate with, disagree with, and, once in a while, even manipulate school people.

6. Some of you may feel sure that you are especially weak in obtaining information and discovering allies and resources, but all of you have some skills in this area even if you haven't applied them to getting educational services for your child. For example, you used the directions and guarantee for the toaster; if you couldn't understand these papers, you probably asked the right friend to explain them to you; and if your friend suggested that you write to the company or the Better Business Bureau, chances are you followed up on the idea. These are your everyday skills which are the basis for developing special advocacy skills for finding and using information, allies, and resources.

It will take some time, effort, practice, experience, and more practice for you to become skilled in these last three items, and, for some parents, more than a little courage. But you will be doing what other parents have already done. In a short time you will be able to say, as this parent has said:

I couldn't believe myself at the school meeting! I just told them what I wanted for Mike and why he needed it. I sounded so calm even when we had this long, involved discussion about getting more speech therapy for Mike. I thought I was losing, but I stuck to my guns. By the time they agreed to give him the extra time with the therapist, I was exhausted. But did I feel good! It was worth it. I think the next time we meet I won't be so nervous and it will be a little easier for me.

As you use the skills which you will be learning or improving, you will keep getting better at using them. You will become more relaxed about or at least less frightened of your meetings with the professionals. It will never be really easy, and you can never become casual about any meetings that will affect your child's education. You will, however, derive great satisfaction from your personal successes as an effective advocate, and even greater satisfaction from the improvements in your child's education that result from your advocacy.

RIGHTS ARE NOT FAVORS

Now that you are beginning to believe that parents can become good advocates for their children, let's begin your practical training by defining rights. The first thing you need to understand about legal rights is that *rights are not favors*. They are not gifts of administrators or teachers; they are not windfalls which have come because there's a little extra money left over in the school budget; and they are not special privileges given to the children of parents who are pleasantly accommodating and who don't make any "trouble" for the school people.

Legal rights are entitlements granted by legal processes such as acts of Congress and decisions of federal courts. Having rights under the law means that your child is entitled to certain treatments and services, that you are entitled to participate in the process of determining the amounts and types of services he receives, and, most importantly, that you cannot legally be denied these things. You need never argue with anyone again about whether your child should have a public education. People who withhold services and treatments from your child or deny you the opportunity to get involved in shaping his program are themselves breaking the law. School systems are now obliged to take the rights of handicapped children very seriously.

In fact, school systems should have been serious about special education long before the enactment of P.L. 94-142, because your child has had the right to a public education all along. Public education, by definition, is a service that the community provides to its citizens—all of them, without discrimination. Think about other public services which your town provides, like police protection. If your house was broken into, you would expect the police to come, not to tell you, "We only investigate incidents on the east side of town. It's too bad you live on the west side." If you got a response like that, you would probably complain to some higher authority. And if that higher authority told you that there was not enough money in the budget to serve residents on the west side, you would carry your complaint to a still higher authority.

You would not passively accept this treatment because you know that as a resident of your community you have an equal right to protection.

Unfortunately, parents of handicapped children have looked at their children as special cases and, even worse, have allowed public administrators to treat their children as special cases, which often meant with discrimination. Yet parents of handicapped children have been paying taxes to support public services which are provided to other children while their own children have been denied some or even all services. A reminder that you too are a taxpayer is in order when someone tries to justify withholding services to your child by telling you that "the taxpayers won't stand for any increase in school costs." The situation for parents of handicapped children was both unjust and illegal.

What was needed then was a statement on the national level to finally make it clear to everyone that public education was a service which must be made available to all children of school age, regardless of handicap. The government decided to make a new and complete statement after its inspectors looked at education across the country and found not only that many handicapped children were placed in poor programs, but that millions of handicapped children were in no programs at all. They also saw that many people from schools and other agencies were working on the assumption that there was nothing wrong with excluding certain children from public education. What the government did then was to state in strong and precise language that the rules must now be rigorously followed. The government did not say, "Let's give these poor handicapped children some new services." Instead they said, "These children have present rights which are being violated, and these illegal exclusions must stop here and now. No longer can school systems get away with practicing discrimination. These children, like all other children, have been entitled to education, and now they must receive it."

P.L. 94-142 has confirmed without question and without exception your handicapped child's right to an education. But who will make sure that the law is carried out? Schools will do some of the work; citizen organizations will do some, too. But when it comes to implementing the law for your own child by developing and providing the right program, the responsibility for action will rest heavily on you, the parent. P.L. 94-142 recognizes the need for parent participation and requires that school systems seek the assistance of parents in developing programs for their handicapped children. Let's look at some of the important parts of the law.

WHAT P.L. 94-142 GUARANTEES YOUR CHILD

1. All handicapped children between the ages of five to eighteen are entitled to a free, appropriate public education designed to meet their needs. The law has made possible the extension of the age of service from eighteen up to twenty-one, and from five down to three, as of September 1, 1980, in certain states. (Ages of service for each state as of May 1, 1980, are in Appendix B. For the most recent information, check with your state Department of Education or organizations which provide help or information to the handicapped.)

2. The law states that its highest priorities are in serving, first, those handicapped children who are currently in no educational programs, and, second, the most severely handicapped children who are presently getting services which do not meet their needs.

3. The law requires that each child be placed in the least restrictive environment, which means that each child should partake of normal settings and activities to the best of her abilities. It does not mean that all children must be educated in the regular classroom.

4. The law requires that each handicapped child be provided with an Individualized Education Program (IEP). An IEP is developed in cooperation with the par-

ents through clearly specified procedures which include sufficient notice to parents for meetings scheduled at mutually agreeable times and places, and active parental participation in these meetings so the child's educational program may be developed, discussed, and agreed upon by the parents, as well as the school system. (The IEP process will be discussed in chapter six.)

5. The law provides safeguards for both the child and parents by assuring that the child will have continuous educational services, making the child's school records available to the parents for their review, providing certain opportunities for independent evaluations for handicapped children, and providing parents with the right to request a due process hearing if they feel that their rights or the rights of their child are being denied.

These are the basic provisions of P.L. 94-142. For the time being, this should be enough information to convince you that your child is clearly entitled to a public education, and that both you and your child have rights recognized and protected by the law. As you learn, chapter by chapter, how to become a parent advocate who will be effective in dealing with the educational system, you will want to know about the fine points of P.L. 94-142. Reed Martin's *Educating Handicapped Children: The Legal Mandate* (Champaign, Ill.: Research Press, 1979) will give you a clear explanation of the details of P.L. 94-142 and will make it easy for you to quote the law, chapter and verse. This can be a very effective tool when you are dealing with reluctant, timid, or even uninformed school people. If you use the Martin book for specifics and substantive supports, and this book for skills and strategies, your child will be represented by a strong and capable parent advocate.

Remember that P.L. 94-142 assures you, as a parent, that you have a central and powerful role to play. Through its insistence that schools make every effort to involve parents, the law invites parents to become advocates for their children. It clearly gives parents the power and freedom to act in behalf of their children, and the responsibility to take action and to do it well.

HOW A PARENT BECOMES AN ADVOCATE

If you are beginning to feel a little nervous or even a bit overwhelmed about becoming an advocate, you are on the right track. In advocacy, the stakes are high and the outcome is crucial, so you need special assistance to achieve better services for your child. Knowing about P.L. 94-142 is a major step in the right direction, but it is not enough to create a successful advocate. You must also know how school systems operate and what you as a parent and a nonprofessional, concerned spokesperson for your child can do to bring about changes that will benefit him. In short, you need to know how to deal with the system. This book is designed to help you understand how the school system operates and how to get it to provide the services your child needs.

In chapter two you will learn how school systems control parents through the perpetuation of myths which keep parents at a distance and in awe of the professionals, and which have sometimes kept handicapped students in inadequate programs, or even out of programs.

You will look at the power structure of school systems in chapter three, see how school politics can limit the performance of even the most competent teachers and administrators, and learn how to recognize the educators who can and want to help you and what to do with those school people who stand between your child and a better educational program. You will learn how to separate fact from fiction, and what you must do to counter the effects of myths and snow jobs.

Just when you are beginning to feel that the politics and pressures of the school system are assuming unmanageable proportions, chapter four, the longest chapter in the book, will help you discover *your* hidden assets— your daily living skills and your potential allies and resources. This chapter will show you how to turn those everyday skills into effective advocacy tools and turn yourself into a confident and competent advocate.

In chapter five you will learn how to use and test your personal skills and common sense when you visit your child's classroom. You will be guided step by step through the program evaluation, from your very first request to visit up to the time you sit down to discuss your questions, concerns, and careful observations with your child's teacher. Your developing skills and sound judgment will not equip you to take over the classroom (that is not your intention!), but you may find for the first time in your life that you are actually taking part in a discussion with a teacher, if not as a potential partner, at least as an equal participant who knows that he has valuable information to share.

At this point, you will have in your repertoire enough information, experience, practice, and preparation to sit down with the school people in the IEP process. The IEP is the very heart of P.L. 94-142: It is the blueprint for your child's daily school program. Without an IEP, your child has no guaranteed educational services; without a good IEP, your child may be cheated out of some of the services he needs. Your job is to get that good IEP. Chapter six will walk you through the whole IEP process, from the first notice you receive (perhaps at your request), through the hammering out of the specifics of the educational program, to the final resolution, which will hopefully result in a good IEP for your child.

"Hold on!" you are about to say. "What's this 'hopefully' business? Doesn't all this work I'm about to do promise me a good program for my child? Why should I do all this work for nothing?" Although in the majority of cases active participation as a parent advocate will bring about a good IEP with more and improved services for the child, there will be a small number of parents who will not reach agreement with the school people and who will feel forced to reject the IEP. What can they then do to help their children?

Chapter seven addresses the problem of the rejected IEP. Parents in this situation still have options such as mediation and appeals. All the work they have done and all the information they have collected will be used to their advantage when they have to confront the school system. Confrontation is a difficult experience for parents (as it is for many school people) and is not to be entered into casually. But when there are serious deficiencies in the IEP and irresolvable differences between the school people and the parents, then the parents must be determined to go all the way. Chapter seven will tell you how to use confrontation to your child's advantage, what kind of help you need and where and how to find it, and how to survive the difficulties of confrontation.

When you achieve your goal—an appropriate IEP designed to meet your child's educational needs—and are looking forward to a well-deserved rest, the final chapter will prepare you for monitoring the implementation of your child's IEP. The hardest and most time-consuming work will be behind you, but your long-term commitment and concern for your child will require you to continue as advocate and participant in the educational process. You will want to assure that the IEP is not merely a paper product but a daily working plan for the teachers and specialists educating your child—that your child is in fact receiving all the services written up and agreed upon in the IEP. Chapter eight will tell you how to watch over the program and what to look for in your monitoring of it.

As you use this book, you will read about the experiences of other parents who decided to take on the system and learned how to deal with it. Some parents learned how to become effective advocates on their own through trial and error, success and failure; others, thwarted by their lack of confidence and information, gave up after some valiant but brief attempts. You will have the benefit of their experience as you prepare to deal with the school system and make it work for your child.

This book won't promise you that your child will have an ideal IEP, be given a private school education, or have unlimited access to the services of a dozen different specialists. It can promise that your child will at the very least have a better IEP and school program because you took advantage of your legal right as a parent to advocate for your child's educational needs.

Now let's begin by taking a good hard look at the school system.

Two

Managing Myths: Substituting Fact for Fiction

"It's hard for parents to be objective."

"Let's just leave the teaching to the teachers."

"A full school day is just too much for your child."

"The principal is a very busy person with many responsibilities. He will get back to you when he has more time."

"The methodology of this teaching program is quite complex and would be hard for you to understand. Trust the professionals to do the job right. Just sign here please."

Many parents have heard statements such as these when they have tried to obtain services, gain admittance to their children's classrooms, offer suggestions for change, or simply get information from school people. There is one thing that these statements have in common: They are all based on myths, that is, they are half-truths which are accepted by the majority of people and which are used by a minority of people to control the behavior of individuals who would question the workings of the system.

When parents question the school system, those school people who feel threatened by them use just these kinds of statements to keep them from "meddling" in school business. Many parents submit to such statements without any attempt to defend themselves and their special value in being participants in their children's education.

Some are so intimidated that they find themselves nodding in agreement to end a difficult situation. Others are uncomfortable or even resent these remarks, but, because they do not have the necessary facts or skills to correct or counter the statements, they may retreat in silence. In this way, parents allow themselves to become victims of myths which have been used by school systems for too many years.

Fortunately, P.L. 94-142 clearly states and protects the rights of parents to participate (or "meddle") in the educational process. But in order to fully contribute to the process, parents must discover some of the hidden meanings in the myths and acquire the skills to dispel myths that can undermine their effectiveness or even prevent them from helping to shape their children's educational future. Parents must understand why the myths have survived in order to be able to deal with them.

THE PERSISTENCE OF MYTHS

Why do these myths persist if they tend to prevent or limit the involvement of concerned parents and if they do little to improve the education of handicapped children? They persist because there *is* an element of truth in every myth; yet that truth is only partial. Of course the educator is a specially trained expert, but parents know their children best and have seen what they can do outside the school setting. Yes, it is sometimes hard for parents to be objective, but experts aren't one hundred percent objective either. And a child may indeed have trouble with a full school day, but it may be the content of the school day that is the problem and not the length of the time spent in school.

Myths also persist because they seem to work. They are effective in keeping a smokescreen around the human and everyday limitations and imperfections of the people who work for school systems, and, to the extent that they silence or confuse parents, they provide security to "threatened" school personnel. However, the myths do not really benefit anyone—children, parents, or even school personnel.

THE WAY TO DEAL WITH MYTHS

Dealing with myths is a little like cleaning house: You have to keep doing it. Unlike housecleaning, however, each time you confront, counter, and dispel myths, you will find yourself doing less and less. In this chapter we will identify and discuss the types of myths about parents, about teachers and other professional educators, and about children with handicaps. We will examine a number of specific myths drawn from the experience of many parents, focus on the behaviors of both parents and school personnel which support the myths, offer some explanations of why the myths are wrong or counterproductive, and then develop some ideas about things parents can do to overcome the harm done by the myths. You will learn to recognize and understand the myths in operation, make statements to yourself which will strengthen your resolution to counter these fictions with facts, and make statements to the school people which will demonstrate to them that the myths are in error.

THE MYTHS ABOUT "MERE PARENTS"

The "mere parents" myths have their foundation in a collection of beliefs held by some school people that parents always know less and are less capable than professionals (because to them a lack of professional training means a lack of objectivity and good judgment), and that parents will waste hours of the professionals' valuable time if they are allowed to participate in their children's education. This kind of thinking puts you on the receiving end of professional expertise and in a defensive posture when you try to deal with the school people. Thus, you may feel that you must argue for your ideas and requests while the professional simply passes judgment. Measured against the professionals (and *by* the professionals), you, the parent, are always found wanting.

All parents and educators are affected by the "mere parents" myths, and to some degree all believe them (this includes assertive parents and well-intentioned educators). It is important to keep in mind that both parents and educators are victims of these beliefs—parents because they are prevented from fully stating the case for their children, and educators because they deprive themselves of a necessary source of information about the children. (Keep in mind that you have a great deal of factual information about your child and that the school people need your information now and throughout your child's school years.) Here are the primary "mere parents" myths which have been keeping parents in their place:

- Parents are naive laymen who can't and shouldn't teach.

- Parents are too emotionally involved to evaluate their children.

- Parents are still obedient school pupils who should be seen and not heard.

Parents Are Naive Laymen Who Can't and Shouldn't Teach

The thinking behind this myth goes like this:

Parents don't know anything about teaching. They have not had professional training. Yet some parents are always trying to give the professionals advice on how to work with their children and even how to run the classroom, in spite of the fact that they are totally ignorant of the sophisticated instructional and evaluative methods which modern teachers and specialists employ. Usually a reminder that the teacher has had special training, years of experience, or an advanced degree will put an end to their questions and demands. Parents may mean well but they just don't know anything about teaching.

A number of teachers and other professionals feel very strongly about this myth. Their training is very important to them: for some, because they have unquestioningly followed the dictates of methods which may now be considered outmoded or at least in need of some thoughtful revision; for others, because of their personal need for a social and professional status which puts them at least a notch above the average guy.

The open and competent teacher, on the other hand, welcomes questions from all quarters to help in his ongoing search for new educational methods and directions, and, while proud to be a school professional, is more concerned with doing the job well than with personal prestige. Although very few parents are also trained educators, the secure teacher recognizes that parents are the child's first "teachers" and continue to teach their child throughout his growing years.

Let's look at the myth in action. In her parent-teacher conference, Beverly Jackson brings up the subject of reading with some excitement. She tells the teacher that her severely retarded son, Dennis, is able to select his favorite soup, Chicken Zucchini, from the many soup cans on the kitchen shelf.

Mrs. Jackson: I know he can't read, but he always picks out the right can, even though all the soup cans look alike. He must be recognizing some of the letters. Do you think he could begin to learn to read?

Teacher: Mrs. Jackson, Dennis is now fifteen. If he hasn't learned to read by now, it's highly unlikely that he will ever learn. I can show you in his folder that when he was twelve, his former teacher tried him on a new reading readiness program which he couldn't do at all. We have used the most up-to-date methods. Reading is simply beyond Dennis's ability.

Mrs. Jackson: But how do you explain the fact that he can pick out the right can every time?

Teacher: Well-meaning parents often give help to their children without even be-

ing aware that they are doing it.
You probably smile at him when he
touches the right can. We have tested
Dennis and we know that reading is
beyond his level. You really should
leave the teaching to the teachers and
not torment yourself with unreasonable hopes. In a few minutes I have
another meeting. I would like to use
this time to discuss Dennis's inatten-
tive behavior in class.

Mrs. Jackson: (Sighs) What's wrong with Dennis's
behavior in school?

This parent has presented vital information to the
teacher, but since the teacher hasn't seen it himself, he
discredits it. The open and responsive teacher would ask
for more information and plan to check it out in school
on the chance that Dennis is just ready to read, even if
only a small list of words.

Roy Williams is another example. He is explaining to
the IEP team that he thinks his son, Stephen, is ready for
a full school day.

Mr. Williams: . . . and my wife tells me that when
Stevie comes home he's after her to
take him to the store or to let him go
to the playground. But we can't let
him go to the school playground because school is still in session. It seems
to me that he has plenty of energy for
a full school day.

Teacher: Energy is not the issue, Mr. Williams.
Stephen is not yet ready to handle the
strain of a full school day. He becomes
increasingly frustrated after two hours
in school. Three hours is the maximum amount of time he can manage
in school without being disruptive.

Mr. Williams: I know he can get restless because I've been helping him at home with his homework. He's only good for fifteen minutes at a time. So we alternate. Fifteen minutes on his school work; then we may go outside and shoot a few baskets. We'll come back in and work for another fifteen minutes. I don't know why it works, but it sure seems to help. Is there something like that on-and-off stuff you could do in school?

Teacher: What would you suggest, Mr. Williams?

Mr. Williams: I don't know. I thought you might have some ideas.

Psychologist: These emotionally disturbed children, Mr. Williams, have to learn to accept limits. Stephen is just now learning to slowly manage the classroom according to its rules. If we make special rules for him, he will become confused and we would have a lot of testing behavior in school which would be detrimental. (Smiles) After all, he can hardly play basketball in the classroom, can he? Maybe next year he will be ready for a full day. His progress is slow but steady. You don't want to disrupt that, do you?

Mr. Williams: It seems awfully slow to me and I worry that he's missing so much school.

Principal: I understand your impatience, but rules are important.

Mr. Williams: Nothing more you can do now?

> *Principal:*   All in good time, Mr. Williams, all in good time. We'll let you know when we feel he's ready for more.

This parent also has some important information for the school. He doesn't have all the answers, and he is looking to the professionals to use the information he has provided to help his son. If the team had been receptive, Roy Williams might have heard this reponse:

> It sounds like you are having some success in working with Stephen at home. Of course, we don't have the same freedom and flexibility you have at home, but we should look into ways we might adapt your approach. If we could schedule some gym activities for late morning, he might be able to stay into the afternoon. We want to be cautious, but we need to be thinking about ways we could expand Stephen's day.

Unfortunately, the present team believes they have all the answers. Their frequent reference to the rules may reflect the concern that this parent is breaking one of the unspoken "rules": Parents shouldn't interfere by trying to teach or make recommendations for teaching. In their efforts to control this parent, the team members discard information which could help them do a better job.

When parents present the kind of valuable information illustrated in these examples, the team members should make use of it to review and improve the school program. Dennis Jackson may be ready to read at last, even if he is fifteen. And Roy Williams seems to be working well with Stephen. In fact, the parents may be having more success at home than the teachers are having in school. Open and responsive teachers would be asking the parents for more information, rather than cutting the parents off (or down!), and would be planning ways to test out and use the information. For example, Dennis's teacher might try some meaningful (to Dennis) sight words on cards or even collect soup labels for a start (perhaps the earlier reading readiness program held little meaning or was too babyish to keep Dennis's interest), and Stephen's teacher could be thinking about alternating desk work with a physical activity such as erasing blackboards, getting milk, or carrying notes to the office, to see if this pattern of activity could help.

When parents' information is simply ignored or discredited, they feel bewildered and frustrated. They may respond by assuming that the knowledgeable professional is right, that their information is unimportant. This "mere parents" myth survives because it is based on the statement that parents have not been trained as professionals. But parents aren't asking to run the classroom; they only want the professionals to pay some attention to what they have seen, heard, and experienced with their children. Yet some school people interpret parents' lack of professional training as evidence that parents know nothing about teaching, and can't or shouldn't teach at home or offer suggestions to teachers.

What educators forget when they engage in this kind of thinking is that parents were the first "teachers" their children had. They taught their children language ("doggie," "car"), concepts ("go bye-bye," "stove hot"), manual skills (using a spoon, a fork, and a knife, in that order), social skills ("thank you," "I need help"), and even some "academics" like colors, counting, and table games. Depending on the child's handicap(s), parents may have varied in their rates of success, but they did teach. When their children reached school age, the parents expected the schools to provide education, but they did not forget how to observe and how to help.

In many cases, parents of children with handicaps must do more teaching at home than parents of nonhandicapped children. They do this out of necessity to help their children overcome some of the obstacles presented by the disabilities and the denial of educational services. Most of these parents do a remarkable job, but their extraordinary achievements go unrecognized by school people. Parents of handicapped children may even be seen as less able or "defective" because they have produced a disabled or "defective" child. Of course, this kind of thinking and treatment is nonsense and grossly unfair to both parents and children, but it exists. Parents can deal with these attitudes by asserting their children's rights and by reminding themselves of their past achievements with their children.

If you are treated in any of the ways discussed, you may begin to doubt your own reason, ears, and eyes. When you find yourself asking, "Who am I, a mere parent, to question the statements of experts?" or if you find yourself retreating, think about the good things you have helped your child achieve. Make some self-statements to strengthen your determination to keep everybody on the right track, dealing with the educational issue you have raised. To yourself you might say things such as these:

It is my right to be here actively participating in my child's education.

I don't have to be a professional to know what I have seen my child do.

My information about my child is valuable and should be useful.

It doesn't take a mechanic to tell someone they have a flat tire.

My requests are reasonable.

If they want more information, I am willing to get it.

These statements are the basic ideas to keep in your head. Whenever you have any reason to expect difficulty, you might practice saying these things to yourself (using your own words) before the meeting, and maybe even write them down to refer to for support and encouragement during the meeting.

For example, to the professionals Beverly Jackson might say:

I honestly believe that Dennis is ready to learn to read; I have seen him choose his favorite soup from cans with identical labels. If it would be helpful, I am willing to observe him more carefully in the next week. My spouse and other children will help me check my observations. In the meantime, I would like you to look at Dennis to see if there are ways you can further help him in school through other methods or materials you know about. Then let's meet again to see if there's something more that can be done to teach him to read.

When you make these kinds of statements to the professionals, you are doing several things:

- demonstrating your ability to work cooperatively and in a businesslike way with the professionals

- involving them actively by referring to what they can do (they can seek methods and materials which will build on your successful efforts or meet your child's needs)

- demonstrating your objectivity by seeking more information through your own efforts and by asking the professionals to check out the information you have presented

- letting the professionals know you intend to stay with the problem or issue until it is resolved

Note that you do not allow the professionals to dismiss or belittle your requests: Giving in would only confirm their belief in their own absolute expertise. However, in spite of your feelings of frustration, you never argue and insist they do it your way. Arguing gives them a reason to label you an "emotional" parent and ignore your requests. The myth of emotional parents who do not see their children objectively is another powerful prejudice you must overcome.

Parents Are Too Emotionally Involved to Evaluate Their Children

The thinking behind the myth goes something like this:

Parents can't be objective because they are so emotionally involved with their children. They can't get

enough distance from their children to gain a realistic perspective and evaluate the real problem. Only
someone who is outside the family and professionally trained can be truly objective about the problem
and about what needs to be done. Teachers and
specialists know more about the child's actual educational needs than parents.

For example, Alma Jones, at her conference with the
teacher, is asking if her daughter, Lucille, who has
cerebral palsy, could leave the classroom five minutes
before lunchtime in order to get down the stairs before
the lunch bell rings. Lucille has told her mother that it
has been difficult for her to get through the milling
students to the cafeteria, that she always arrives last, and
that she has only enough time to eat half her lunch. The
teacher smiles and says, "Now, Mrs. Jones, we shouldn't
baby Lucille. I know mothers do like to protect their
children, but Lucille shouldn't be getting special treatment. Don't you want her to be treated like the other
students? If she is going to learn to be self-sufficient, then
let her take her knocks with the other children instead of
asking for special favors. Lucille is just trying to get your
sympathy." Mrs. Jones is confused. She tries to let Lucille
do as much for herself as possible, but is she still being
overprotective? She drops the subject.

Roger and Glenda Backman are another example. They
ask at the IEP meeting whether their son, who is mildly
retarded, can be accepted on one of the intramural
basketball teams. The guidance counselor responds, "Ray
would have a difficult time keeping up with all the other
players who are not handicapped and so much faster and
smarter than he is. He seems to be doing well in school,
and the normal children are just beginning to accept him.
I know that you would like him to be as able as your other
children, but he is handicapped, after all. You shouldn't
be pushing him too hard." Mr. Backman answers, "But
you should see him play with the other kids in the
neighborhood. He's as good as any of them, at least in a

basketball game." There are some knowing smiles around the table as the guidance counselor says, "Perhaps his friends make allowances for him. I think we should stick to Ray's educational plan so that his teacher will have time to talk about his work in arithmetic, which is quite poor." Mr. Backman looks angry, turns to his wife, shrugs his shoulders, and is silent.

In these two examples the parents have been seen by the school people as being too emotionally involved with their children to be able to make valid judgments or recommendations. For example, Alma Jones wants to "baby" her daughter and hold her back. Roger and Glenda Backman, on the other hand, want to "push" their son into situations for which he is not ready. Sometimes the perspective of the school people shifts, depending on parents' current requests: Last year's pushy parent may become this year's overprotective parent. No wonder some parents are confused about their ability to be objective; they try, but for one reason or another they never quite seem to make the grade.

Often professionals patronize parents by making assumptions about parents' motives. When asked to explain or support their assumptions, they will sometimes dredge up the worst possible example of parent behavior they can remember, such as the parent who insisted on driving his able-bodied ten-year-old child two blocks to school any time it threatened to rain. Of course, there are parents who are pushy or protective and who are determined to do things their way without considering the effect of their actions on their child's growth and welfare, but they are in the extreme and should not be cited as examples of average parents. Most parents are primarily concerned about their children's welfare, and give long and serious thought to how much protection ("babying") their children need and how much challenge ("pushing") the children can successfully manage.

In both examples the parents have allowed the myths to go unquestioned. Instead of pursuing the discussion with the teacher, Alma Jones begins to question herself.

Although Roger Backman is angry and frustrated by the patronizing way the group treats his request to have his son take part in school sports, he feels people aren't really listening to him, and so withdraws in silence. His wife goes along by saying nothing. The myth remains effective in keeping parents in their place.

How might parents respond to the emotionally involved parents myth in a positive, practical, and productive way? First they must examine the myth to discover the element of truth on which the myth is based. Then they must question the conclusions which have been drawn from that element of truth. The truth here is that parents are emotionally involved with their children. Of course they are. Imagine what it would be like raising children if you were not emotionally involved! Your emotional involvement is your antenna that tells you when something good or bad is happening to your child. It is your love for your child which keeps you interested in the many small steps of your child's growth and development (making you the rich source of information that you are) when others, less involved, would lose interest or forget. Sure, sometimes you have hesitated or been too eager for your child, but you weren't too far off the mark, and when you discussed it with someone who was interested and treated you as a competent person, didn't you decide to ease up or be a little more cautious? Your emotional involvement is not only a good thing for you and your child, it is essential for your child's development.

Unfortunately, professionals sometimes assume that parental emotional involvement is a drawback, a set of blinders parents wear, and a hindrance to professionals in their efforts to help parents see their children more "objectively." They may discount the value of the information presented by a parent without at least checking it out because of one past experience with a truly "emotional" or biased parent. Roger Backman has seen his son play basketball; Lucille has told her mother that lunchtime is difficult for her. Yet what these parents have seen and heard is being ignored. They are understandably frustrated and angry.

When parents hear professionals devalue or ignore the information or requests that they are making, they should react in the following ways:

- recognize the value of their emotional involvement
- learn to make statements to themselves such as "Of course I care. Where would my child be if I didn't care?"
- keep the professionals on task by not allowing the discussion to be closed ("Yes, we don't want to give her more help than she needs, but we still have to figure out how to get her to the lunchroom on time. What can we do?")
- continue the discussion by asking what more information is needed by school personnel to make the request acceptable or for them to begin to consider possible solutions to the problem the parent is presenting

Let's go back to Alma Jones. Here is a possible scenario:

> *Teacher:* . . . instead of asking for special favors. Lucille is just trying to get your sympathy.
>
> *Mrs. Jones:* Yes, I do appreciate the effort Lucille puts into keeping up with her classmates. But I am concerned that we may be asking too much of her in this case. Is it possible for her to leave class five minutes early for lunch?
>
> *Teacher:* Well, yes. I suppose it is. But it would make the other students even more aware of her differences.
>
> *Mrs. Jones:* Can you think of any ways to minimize these differences or perhaps other solutions that might be better?
>
> *Teacher:* Give me some time to think about it.
>
> *Mrs. Jones:* Would you call me in a day or two to let me know what you have done? I'm

especially concerned because Lucille isn't finishing her lunch. Could you let me know how much of her meal she is actually missing?

Teacher: But, Mrs. Jones, I'm not in the lunchroom. We have aides for that.

Mrs. Jones: I didn't know that. (Stifles a groan and takes a deep breath) I know teachers need their breaks. But you know Lucille better than the lunchroom aide. I'm sure, with your experience, if you monitored the situation for a day or two, you would find the right solution to the problem.

(Mrs. Jones then arranges to talk with the teacher by phone toward the end of the week.)

Notice that the "new" Alma Jones acknowledges her emotional involvement ("I appreciate Lucille's effort"), ignores the teacher's assumptions (the parent is babying Lucille), and keeps the discussion going by asking questions that involve the teacher in monitoring the situation and solving the problem. Instead of being put off by the teacher's remarks about babying Lucille, Alma Jones perseveres, politely and firmly, and arranges for further consultation. By presenting herself as a rational, on-task, and caring parent, the "new" Alma Jones refuses to play along with this "mere parent" myth. If Roger Backman can stay on task by asking the IEP team to have the gym teacher check out his son's basketball playing skills before allowing the discussion to be closed, then he too can become an effective advocate for his son.

If it sounds easy, it isn't, at least not the first time. If you have any reason to expect the "overly emotionally involved parent" treatment, then you must practice dealing with the myth before you go to the school. Practice with two sets of statements—those you may need to make to yourself ("I am a good, caring, and concerned parent. I

know my child. I am here to find solutions"), and those
you make to teachers and others ("I am asking to meet a
real need my child has. What information do you need?
How can you find out? What solutions can you find or can
we find together?"). If necessary, write statements down
in your own words and refer to them at the meeting. With
practice and experience you will become more confident
about your own contributions and eventually encounter
fewer people who will attempt to use this myth to put
down your efforts. When they do try, your calm and firm
manner will force them to set the myth aside.

For those of you who have successfully maneuvered in
situations involving this myth, or for those who have been
fortunate in dealing with educators who feel that parents
are reasonably objective, and, therefore, useful as sources
of information, there is another myth waiting in the
wings for you to face and manage.

Parents Are Still Obedient School Pupils Who Should Be Seen and Not Heard

Most parents stand in awe of school people and systems
because schools represent our childhood images of authority and mystifying expertise. We are all products of
school systems and we still retain a number of childlike
school behaviors based on the old rules: "Stand in line,"
"No gum chewing," "No talking out of turn."

The school building brings out these old feelings and
behaviors in practically everyone who doesn't work in a
school. School people who feel most secure in authori-
tarian roles tend to exploit this habitual response to shore
up their status with almost everyone who is not a regular
part of the system. They may use a commanding tone of
voice, keep people waiting in the outer office or halls,
require silence as you walk the corridors, and generally
treat parents as children and intruders. They make it
clear that everyone in the building has a particular place,
and the parent's place is that of the child.

Parents who are in a school building advocating for
perhaps the first time may feel threatened and see them-

selves as disruptive. Old habits like school behaviors do die hard. Years of training as school pupils develop a knee-jerk kind of response in parents when they find themselves in the setting which trained those behaviors. Whether it's five, ten, or twenty years since you were in school, those old habits stand ready to resurface. But your days of being an elementary school student are gone forever. You can't be sent to the office or to detention: The school's former power over you is gone. They do, however, have a new power—the power to decide your child's future. When concern for your child makes you nervous, you may find your old school habits emerge to make you even more nervous. Fortunately, you can learn to recognize these behaviors and feelings as old and excess baggage, dismiss them as silly, and get on with the grown-up business of advocacy.

When you find yourself becoming uncomfortable in the school setting, you must learn to examine your discomfort: "Am I sitting here quietly waiting in the principal's office because I am a courteous adult who will allow a reasonable delay before my appointment, or because I am the old school child who dares not speak up?" "Am I hesitant to visit my child's classroom because I want to carefully review the educational program first, or because I am fearful of being in a place I don't 'belong'?" When you examine your feelings you will learn how your behaviors support the myth and how school people can use your discomfort to keep you from becoming involved in your child's education.

Put the burden of being an old school child behind you by saying some of the following things to yourself:

As a concerned parent I have a right to be here for this visit.

My presence here is not disruptive. I am here for important reasons.

I expect to act and to be treated as an adult.

Statements like these will weaken the old, unnecessary behaviors which make your job of advocacy more difficult. When you understand the effects of the myth, you will become more assured and effective when you present yourself at the school as a concerned adult acting in behalf of your child. It will take practice and experience to strengthen your ability to advocate, but other parents have done it, and you can too.

You may find yourself facing any one or even all three of the "mere parents" myths at any given meeting. It will help if you know what you are up against so that you can adapt and strengthen your own positive behaviors. Asking yourself these questions can help you determine which myths are operating in the situation:

Am I being treated like a naive or ignorant person or like one whose information is meaningless or even worthless?

Am I being treated like a sentimental, overindulgent, or unreasonable parent?

Am I being treated or feeling like an old school pupil?

When you identify which myths are creating the problems at meetings with the educators, search your memory for helpful self-statements you can use. If you are especially nervous or expect things to be difficult for you, prepare yourself by writing down in a notebook those bolstering self-statements you may think you need, then refer to them when you feel uncomfortable or pressured. In this way, you can carry your supportive slogans with you. Each time you think them or read them, you will be a little more assured about your ability and right to advocate.

This assurance will enable you to present yourself as a calm, rational, and strong person who is determined to be the best advocate for your child's education. Your attitude will help to shatter the myths held by educators. Nevertheless, the first time you deal with a teacher or group of professionals you may feel you botched it ("I gave in too easily," "I forgot to mention some important things," or "I let myself get upset"). Even if you are new at being an advocate, you did some things right: By meeting with the school people you shared your concern about your child's program and you presented important information. If you prepared yourself with self-statements, you probably found you were doing well for at least some of the time. Next time you will do better because you are becoming aware of how the myths operate and learning how to defend yourself against them. But you will need to be aware of other myths that may be present along with the parent myths and may control the behavior of the school people in their dealings with you.

THE MYTHS ABOUT EDUCATORS

In addition to parent myths, there are persistent educator myths which can limit the effectiveness of teachers, specialists, and others involved in the education of children with handicaps. The ones which most frequently undermine the establishment of a parent-educator partnership which could benefit the children are the following:

- Educators are super experts in their field.
- Educators are totally objective.
- Educators are free agents.

If these myths sound familiar, it is because they are the other side of the parent myths. As parents are expected to behave in emotional, naive, and dependent ways, educators carry the burdens of the opposite expectations— total knowledge of the field, complete objectivity, and full freedom to act. Since it is simply not possible for any one person to have all these qualities, educators can feel threatened when unrealistic demands (society's, parents', or the professional community's) are made on them and may insist more strongly on the truth of the myths.

Educators Are Super Experts in Their Field

Education is not unique in maintaining the myth that the professional has all the answers and that laymen not only are lacking in knowledge of the profession, but are also incapable of understanding explanations given by the professionals. Unfortunately, many professions perpetuate such mystiques.*

Although it is true that educators have special skills and understanding which have been acquired through years of training, the field of education is so broad that no individual or even several individuals can know every method or technique. Because they work with various numbers of students, the educators' time for observations may be limited, and, therefore, those observations of students' needs may also be limited. It may be impossible for educators to know every facet of every student—strengths, weaknesses, and most effective teaching methods for each individual. Parents can add their observations to those of educators, thus enlarging the amount of information available about the individual needs of handicapped students. If in an effort to appear expert and competent to laymen an educator ignores information which the parent offers, everyone loses, including the educator. To be a competent educator requires not only a foundation of special skills but also an active involvement in seeking educational solutions by using personal observations and information from parents, who are also "experts" with regard to their own children.

Professionals caught in the super expert myth try to maintain the appearance of knowing all out of fear that otherwise parents or colleagues will question their com-

---

*Members of the medical profession often support a super expert myth. Many parents have presented questions or information to their children's doctors only to be told that they are just being anxious parents. In a number of cases, a year later the doctors announce their "discovery" of a serious condition to the parents, who were concerned all along. Like educators, physicians should pay attention to the information that parents have about their children. The most famous example of doctors and parents working together led to the development of PKU (phenylketonuria) testing and early treatment, which followed doctors' interest in mothers' reports about symptoms such as unusual urine odor in their seemingly normal infants.

petence. Furthermore, the need to appear super competent may become more imperative as school budgets are
tightened and more people vie for fewer permanent
school positions. School personnel may feel financially
and professionally threatened if they confess that they do
not have all the educational answers at their fingertips.
They may sometimes overstep the limits of their own
field of expertise in an effort to appear knowledgeable, as
in the following example.

Molly McDonald is concerned because she thinks her
young, mentally retarded son has problems with his
vision. At the school meeting she asks the professionals
about Andy's performance in school and whether they
think he is having any problems with his vision. They
answer, "No," and go on to develop Andy's educational
plan for next year without suggesting diagnosis by a
medical expert. Fortunately, Molly McDonald continues
to observe on her own. Two months later she takes Andy
to an eye doctor who tells her that her son has a serious
visual problem and will probably need to wear strong
glasses for the rest of his life. When Andy starts wearing
the glasses, he becomes less clumsy and can do more
things successfully.

An alternative scenario, in which the educators are interested in the parents' information, might be as follows:

Mrs. McDonald:	Do you think Andy has any visual problems?
Sp. Ed. Director:	Why do you ask? Have you noticed anything different in his behavior?
Mrs. McDonald:	He seems to be getting more clumsy and he squints funny at his fork when he's eating.
Teacher:	I haven't noticed anything, but I'll watch more carefully now that you have raised the issue.
Sp. Ed. Director:	I hope you two will keep in close communication (to teacher and parent). If either of you feel there is a question

about Andy's vision, I think he should
be tested by an ophthalmologist. The
IEP can be delayed if you want to
wait for the medical report, or we can
proceed and revise it later if needed.

In the first scenario, the school people played "expert"
beyond their limits and crossed over the line of educational expertise when they "diagnosed" Andy as having no
visual problems. Their expertise should have helped
them recognize, on the basis of Andy's performance in
school, that he was facing some new difficulty. Instead
they assumed that Andy's problems of clumsiness, odd
gestures, and poor performance were all part of his
mental retardation. Fortunately for Andy, his mother was
concerned and wise enough to follow through on her own
observations, and eventually to seek out the right expert
for this job—the eye doctor.

What could this mother have done at the IEP meeting
instead of accepting the school people's opinion? She
could have given a fuller explanation of what she had seen
at home. If that did not arouse the suspicion and interest
of the educators, she could then have insisted that Andy
be tested before she would sign the IEP. To support herself in this undertaking, she would have made self-
statements such as "I don't have to be a pro to know what
I have seen my child do" or "If I'm going to help Andy, I
have to be persistent."

The burden of being an all-knowing expert is as unfair
to the educator as it is to the parent. Sooner or later the
expert will be found out, and will then appear to the
parent to be untrustworthy or incompetent. Many parents are more comfortable and more trusting with the
professional who can occasionally say, "I don't know." It
has been the writer's experience in working with parents
in training programs that the "I don't know" answer can
help to establish a cooperative and trusting relationship
between parents and professionals. Too many parents
have been given absolute or definitive answers in the past
which have been proven wrong over time (for example,

Dennis did learn to read with a new teacher, and Ray now plays on a regular team at the Community Center).

When parents suspect that they are dealing with educators whose behavior seems to be controlled by this myth, it is important that they do not insult the training, experience, or intelligence of the educators. Since parents have to work with these same educators to develop a good IEP, they must stick to the facts about what they have seen and heard their children do, and make it clear to the professionals that they, the parents, are not trying to assume a professional role. Rather, they are caring parents who are acting as responsible advocates for their children by keeping the important facts before the professionals as services are being planned, developed, and reviewed.

Parents must be ready to support the educators who can say "I don't know the answer" by appreciating their honesty and by cooperating with them to find the answers. Real experts know their resources and look to parents as a powerful and special resource for information about their students. But educators who present themselves as all-knowing experts may be convinced that they are more qualified than parents because they are completely objective: This is another myth.

Educators Are Totally Objective

Many educators and other professionals believe that parents' statements about their children are to be taken with a large dose of salt because parents are emotionally involved and lack the special training that develops the objective judgment which professionals have. The parents see the tree, but the professionals see the forest.

Of course, it is true that most parents are more emotionally involved with their children than teachers are, and that occasionally their emotional concern can cloud their judgment, but educators are not as free of emotional involvement as they would like to believe. Their "objectivity" can be distorted by their personal need to support and justify their years of specialized training and work with students. If a parent questions a teacher on the use and effectiveness of a particular method with his child, that teacher may be faced with a dilemma: If this isn't the best method, then maybe I have not effectively taught a number of students or even failed to teach some students because of my reliance on this method. It may be easier for a weak teacher to believe that the parent is wrong and the method which has been used for so many years is still the right one.

A strong teacher, on the other hand, would be able to accept parents' suggestions of information or even criticism of a given method because she knows the effective methods will stand the test of parents' questions and because she expects to be learning more every year about new methods, theories, techniques, and ideas which will help meet individual students' needs. The strong teacher accepts the responsibility for searching out new methods and answers in order to teach more effectively, unlike the weak teacher who tries to defend her past performance and protect her present position by emphasizing her years of training and denying the value of parent input.

Let's look at an example:

Mrs. Costa: I know Rudy has had a hard time with arithmetic. He sometimes gets very upset doing his homework, even though it's only a few problems. I try to help him. Yesterday I had him using his fingers to count, and it really helped him.

Teacher: I do not allow him to count on his fingers in class, and I would prefer that he not do it at home. He must learn to do the sums in his head.

Mrs. Costa: But that way he can't get the right answers, and he's so unhappy when he makes mistakes.

Teacher: He can't go through life counting on his fingers. He will have to learn like others with his kind of disability—

through practice, practice, practice. You know, I have worked with children like Rudy for many years and I know what they need. They learn by rote; they must do things over and over until they learn to do it right.

The poor parent is in a bind. If she helps Rudy by letting him use his fingers, Rudy will be in trouble at school. Yet without that extra help, Rudy is condemned to practice failure over and over until he learns to hate arithmetic.

The secure teacher might have said:

I know Rudy is having a hard time with math, and I appreciate getting this information from you. If using his fingers helps him get the right answers, maybe I should be trying it in class. Let me check it out. Also, there may be other materials in my files that might help me give Rudy the extra help he seems to need. We'll stay in touch on how he progresses in math.

or

You know, there was a time when we discouraged children from using their fingers to do math, but now we feel differently. In school Rudy has used blocks to do his work, and right now he's using lines drawn next to the numbers to help him do his sums. I'm impressed that you noticed he needed something to count and let him use his fingers. He needs the success of doing it right. And I'm pleased you spend time with him on his homework. Don't worry that he'll use his fingers forever. As he makes progress, he'll rely less and less on learning aids like fingers and lines.

In this case the information is well-received by the teacher who is willing to either try another approach suggested by the parent's experience or acknowledge the value of the parent's observations and efforts.

There are other times when educators' objectivity is on the line. The teacher or specialist may see a need for more individualized instruction or some special therapies, but he is in no position to ask for more services or help from the system, which claims to be short on money and staff. The educator experiences a conflict between his professional judgment and the resources available to him. Since it is hard for anyone to live with conflict day after day, soon the educator may begin to believe that perhaps the need is not so great after all, and eventually may come to dismiss the student's need for additional services. In this way, the educator can escape from the uncomfortable realization that the student has serious needs which he is powerless to meet, and can maintain the feeling that he is providing a good program or service. Consider the following example:

> *Mr. Harrison:* But last spring you said Mona needed more speech therapy.
>
> *Teacher:* Well, I have given it much more thought. You know, there are a lot of pressures on children like Mona, and she is a very sensitive child. If we stress her speech problems, she may become more socially withdrawn.
>
> *Mr. Harrison:* I think her poor speech interferes with her social development. Because the other children have difficulty understanding her, she is often left alone or, at best, is the last one to be included.
>
> *Teacher:* Let's give her time to develop at her own pace and see what she can do naturally and without pressure.

This type of switch is not made to meet the child's educational needs, but to sustain the teacher's own feelings of self-esteem and self-worth: He needs to believe that his job is worthwhile and his efforts are not wasted. This kind of mental gymnastics or adaptation is used by everyone, including parents. For example, one family may make financial sacrifices for a child's braces because they feel that orthodontia is essential for her physical and social well-being, while another family may be so poor that they have nothing to sacrifice and come to believe that their child doesn't really need braces: Yet both children may have the same need. And sometimes parent advocates, in efforts to get the right services for their children, may find themselves beginning to believe that the professionals are doing a good job because believing that is easier than continuing the frustration of the struggle to get services.

It is important for parents to understand that educators may also unintentionally make these kinds of mental adjustments to preserve their sense of professional worth, and to recognize that educators are not always free to act solely on the basis of their professional judgment to pursue and develop the programs they once realized were needed.

Educators Are Free Agents

Many parents ask why, if the school personnel know a program is needed, they don't just set it up. Since it is the school's job to educate all children, parents expect that school people will do what is necessary.

What parents need to know is that people who work for school systems are not free to pick their resources—people, time, space, or materials. The school system sets limits on what is available to any employee and on what means school personnel can use to request or pressure for more resources. Parents don't realize that they may have more freedom to act than school people often do. When parents understand that educators are limited by the rules and structure of the system and that parents can more freely speak out, act, or even badger for services, then parents will realize that their advocacy efforts can help competent and concerned educators get needed services. Chapter three takes a close look at how the system operates and what kinds of experiences parents may have when they try to deal with the school system.

All these myths about educators persist because many parents and professionals would like to believe that educators are all-knowing experts, clear-sighted and clear-headed, free of bias, and free to act on the children's needs as they see them. These myths place enormous burdens on educators, who, like everyone, have both skills and shortcomings, who also need and want the resources necessary to do their jobs well, and who may need parents as allies to get the needed resources from a resistant school system.

THE MYTHS ABOUT HANDICAPPED CHILDREN

Parents can also help educators, themselves, and their children by learning to recognize and dispel some common myths about handicapped children. Here are some important ones you may have come across:

- These children's handicaps are the source of all problems.
- These children can only learn by rote.
- These children can't handle a full day.

These Children's Handicaps Are the Source of All Problems

This myth is used to explain anything that goes wrong in school or with the child. It's as if the child is no longer a person but has become the disability. There is no need to search for new understanding or teaching methods because the child is retarded, learning disabled, cerebral palsied, autistic, or some other label. Whatever the child does, the educators can point knowingly to the label. For example, Andy, the mentally retarded boy with an undiagnosed visual problem discussed earlier in this chapter, does not warrant attention from the educators as he becomes more clumsy because he is retarded; the assumption is that his retardation is the cause of his clumsiness (until mother brings him to the ophthalmologist). If Andy were a nonhandicapped child, his behavior might have prompted concern and action from the educators, who would be asking the parent about his vision and the need for testing. But, like Andy, children with other handicaps may have their problems simply blamed on their disabilities.

Danny, who is labeled emotionally disturbed and learning disabled, has had his new baseball cap stolen in school. He bought the cap with money earned for doing chores at home. His loss is dismissed by the teacher, who makes no effort to get it back for him. Every day for a week Danny asks the teacher, "Where is my hat?" and is told not to talk about it. The following Monday he asks again, but now the teacher forbids him to mention the hat again or he will have to leave the classroom. Danny swears at the teacher and is sent home. Danny now has no hat, no understanding, no justice, and, for a few days or more, no education. The teacher explains that Danny is distressed because he is "emotionally disturbed"; she does not see that his distress is an appropriate response to the loss of something he valued and worked to obtain.

Jenny, who is nonverbal and "autistic," is working on her usual morning puzzle which she has already done twice and is expected to do three times. The teacher prods her to keep working and tells her to finish if she wants her gold star. Jenny, making noises, looks away and claps her hands rapidly. The teacher takes the puzzle away, says, "No star, Jenny," turns to the aide and says, "These autistic kids can't do any work for very long. Now she's going to keep up this weird clapping behavior." Jenny smiles a little and begins to clap again. Jenny's behavior is considered weird. But her refusal to do the puzzle still one more time might make sense to the teacher if she were asking the right questions: Is Jenny's behavior telling me she doesn't want to do the puzzle? Are puzzles still a useful activity for Jenny? Instead, the teacher makes the assumption that Jenny's "weird" behaviors grow from her autism and not from her boredom, which is a normal, human response to a lack of stimulation.

Whatever problems these children encounter in the classroom are explained away by the educators on the basis of the children's primary labels: Andy is clumsy because he's retarded, Danny is upset because he's emotionally disturbed, and Jenny won't work because she's autistic. Instead of searching for more or new information to solve the problems, the educators locate all problems squarely in the child. In this way, they absolve themselves of the responsibility to do more careful observation, look for new approaches, and develop new solutions.

Of course, these children have disabilities (that is the kernel of truth behind the myth), but, like all children, they have human needs for recognition, understanding, support, stimulation, and novelty, and these needs are often overlooked or minimized by the educators. Since many school systems are just now beginning to serve a broad range of children with special needs, providing the right supports and programs may not be easy; educators must search out new methods, information, and insights to do the job. They must avoid assumptions that go with labels. Parents must continue to observe their children, looking for strengths, weaknesses, and supports which work. They must share (and even insist on sharing) with the educators information about their children, keeping the educators aware that their children have basic human needs which require attention in addition to their special disability-related needs.

These Children Can Only Learn by Rote

Unfortunately, some educators believe that children with handicaps must be subjected to endless drill and practice to achieve any gains in their educational programs. They believe that rote learning is the answer; thus, the more handicapped a child is, the more likely that child is to have learning drummed into her.

While it is true that the more difficult a task is, the more practice is needed for mastery, it is also true that any child, no matter how seriously handicapped, can become bored or frustrated through repetition of meaningless tasks. Every child needs not only to be supported, but to be stimulated as well. For example, after months, maybe even years, of doing puzzles, Jenny is just possibly bored. This task may have once been interesting when she was gaining mastery in a visual-motor (coordination of eye-hand) skill. But seemingly endless repetition* may have reduced her motivation and even tolerance. On some occasions she is compliant; on others she may be expressing her reluctance through "inappropriate" behavior. Perhaps it's time to introduce some new visual-motor activities to get her working again.

Rudy's failures in math when he is not allowed to count on his fingers should be signaling his teacher that simple rote learning is not effective; his parents have already recognized the importance of successful attempts based on counting aids. The answers he is trying to learn by rote are probably meaningless to him since he is so often wrong. Unlike Jenny, he continues to try, but for how long? A child's behaviors—failure, frustration, or boredom—are messages that the materials or methods are not working and that the teacher should look for other ways to help. There are tasks Rudy could do to support and stimulate his math learning, such as counting out food cans or setting the table at home, building structures and counting the number of floors or pieces to make a new floor, or playing math games using dice and counting moves (at home or in school). The possibilities are endless: counting and sorting balloons of different colors for a party, sorting socks (basic two table for addition or multiplication), and even using regular playing cards for counting, sorting, matching, and games. These activities can be fun, at

---

*Autistic children have a reputation for disliking change and for being highly repetitive themselves. However, in a structured program with planned change, even autistic children benefit from and enjoy the novelty and stimulation of new or higher-level learning tasks. Structure does not mean lack of stimulation.

least some of the time, and should seem important to the child because he is really helping at home or at school.*

Too often both teachers and parents feel so over-whelmed by the burden of a child's disability that, in efforts to overcome or limit its effects, they fall back on drill and routine practice (forgetting that writing or do-ing something one hundred times used to be a form of punishment). They try to drum learning into children's heads, as if battering would do the job when children need stimulation and normal activities which they can enjoy and can feel are important (even grown-up) and make sense. Parents or teachers may fail to take advan-tage of the normal opportunities which can aid in the development of early academic skills.

What can a parent do? Do not be afraid to test out your child's developing skills around the home. In this way, you can learn about your child's strengths, weaknesses, and the kind of help or modifications needed to promote active learning. You should, at the same time, keep a simple record of your observations which you can share with the educators. Your information can stimulate them to question their assumptions about how various handi-capped children learn. It will require effort on your part and perhaps a little repetition to get the educators to take a careful look at your child's performance and needs; however, once they realize you are really concerned and serious about your child's program and that your observa-tions are accurate, they may begin to investigate new materials and methods.

These Children Can't Handle a Full Day

Many people equate disability with fragility or a lack of stamina. They expect that children with mental and

---

*If you are looking for ideas on teaching basic skills or "testing" at home, consult the 1979 issues of the bimonthly magazine, *Excep-tional Parent*, which have several articles written for parents (and teachers) by Dr. Barbara Bruno-Golden and Barbara C. Cutler.

physical handicaps will require less activity and considerably more resting periods than nonhandicapped children.
They tend to become protective in ways that can limit the
learning of handicapped children, for example, planning
classroom naps for trainable retarded adolescents who
might benefit more from the regularly scheduled gym
periods provided to nonhandicapped students.

Because of the myth, parents and teachers may see
weakness where none may exist. They may see evidence of
weakness in children's boredom, frustration, or disruptive behavior, all of which may result more from the program's inability to meet the children's needs than from
any lack of stamina in the children. When students are
bored, frustrated, or disruptive, it is harder for the
teacher to work with them. Sometimes it is really the
stamina of the teacher that is called into question: He may
be the one who needs the shorter day with the more
challenging students.

Certainly there are some handicapped children who,
because of certain disabilities such as heart and respira-
tory problems, are less able to maintain a constant level
of activity or to engage in strenuous activity. The energies
of these children should be conserved in school. For
example, an educator may tell a parent, "I just feel so
badly for poor little Lisa when she starts getting cranky. I
know the school day is just too much for her." Lisa's father
shares the educator's concern about his child's heart condition and the fatigue he sees in her at the end of the
school day. But he also notes that her classroom is on the
third floor and the lunchroom and recess area are on the
ground floor. He raises the possibility that his daughter is
exhausted from climbing stairs. He plans to ask if the
school can accommodate Lisa's needs by relocating the
classroom on the first floor to spare her the unnecessary
physical effort of mounting so many flights of stairs.

If you are in doubt about a full day of school for your
child, think about your child's performance at home. Is
he raring to go out to play as soon as school is over? Is he
still awake for the eleven o'clock news, or up at the crack
of dawn when everyone else is still sleeping? If you don't

see evidence of fatigue at home, on school days or week-
ends, the problem at school may be something other than
lack of stamina.

But if you still have questions about your child's ability
to withstand a full day, you should consult your child's
physician. Like the educators, the doctor also needs the
facts which only a parent can provide. Since every child is
different, and you know more about your child than
anyone else, share with the doctor your observations of
your child. If the fully informed doctor says that your
child requires more rest for medical reasons, you should
then explore with the educators the options for your
child to have rest periods at school so that he may
miss as little schooling as possible. If the educators feel
the school program is too mentally or physically taxing
for some students, they can gear the classroom to the
learning and activity level of the students by using the
appropriate materials, methods, and activities, and by
adjusting the pace to fit the students.

When you are told your child is not strong enough to be
in school all day and you know his physical health and
energy levels are good, you may rightly suspect that it's
the teacher who can't handle a full day. He may not be
skillful enough or may have too many children with not
enough help in the classroom. Ask for an aide for the
teacher. Perhaps the program isn't the right one for your
child, and therefore your child reacts out of frustration.
You have the right to ask to change the program—totally
or in part.

This myth of "weakness" has in the past deprived a
number of handicapped children of full educational
opportunity. Your information, questions, and insights
can help the educators develop new ways of thinking
which can lead to a better program for your child (and
possibly for other handicapped children as well).

THE SHATTERING OF MYTHS

We have discussed some common myths about parents,
educators, and handicapped children. The myths persist
because people believe them. Shattering myths is tough

work and can only be done by consistently giving the lie to the myths through your businesslike presentation of yourself as a concerned parent, your statements of observations you have collected about your child, and your determination to see that the important issues you raise are not ignored or forgotten.

If reading about these myths has not yet struck a familiar chord in your experience, when you begin to deal with the school system you will see how pervasive they can be. As a parent advocate, you will not let a myth slide by in silence; your silence could be interpreted as acceptance of the myth. On the other hand, you need not argue; you dispel the myths by demonstrating that you are a reliable, informed parent who deals in facts, and that your child (one of "these children") can in fact benefit from a full educational program designed to meet her needs.

When you find yourself in a situation where several myths appear to be operating, try to deal with one at a time. For example, Margaret Olson responds to the educators at the IEP meeting:

> I appreciate your skills and experience, but I have seen Bert perform at home. His attention span is longer than two minutes.

She then takes out her notes and describes Bert's behavior. (Her opening statement deals with the myth of educators as super experts. Her behavior, statements, and notes deny the myth of emotional parents who can't be objective.) Mrs. Olson continues:

> I don't know everything about children like Bert, but I do know my son. This is the way we help him at home so he can do the work. When he is having difficulty with his homework, his father or I stay close by to offer him help when he asks for it. But after he understands the problem he will work on his own for as long as fifteen minutes.

(Once again, she acknowledges the expertise of the educator without denying what she knows about her son and the help she has given him. She also refuses to play the game of "these children" by telling the educators that whatever they know about children like Bert, at least he can work independently for fifteen minutes when he understands what is expected of him.

After a while the educators stop talking about "these children" and stick to Bert. They may start listening to Mrs. Olson's information because it is factual. She continues to participate in the planning process as an effective parent advocate. Her son may need more of this and less of that, but he doesn't need any myths to interfere with planning his program.

Obviously, this is hard work. Chances are in your first meeting you will not be successful in dealing with all the myths that arise or even in recognizing them, since you too are learning to disbelieve them through understanding and practice (using supportive self-statements). As you improve, however, the myths will appear like red flags to call you to action. Your careful and thoughtful responses will begin to educate the educators to the erroneous assumptions the myths embody.

We have presented some examples of the myths in operation and of the kinds of things you can say to yourself and to the educators to advance the development of your child's education. You now are beginning to understand some of the things that may have gone wrong in the past when you dealt with the school system. Perhaps you are thinking about making that first phone contact. But don't rush out yet. There is still more that you need to know about dealing with the system before you become the cool, controlled, and effective advocate.

Three

A Closer Look:
Systems, Services, and Snow Jobs

Elsa Morgan is always ready to help at the school Christmas fair, to go on field trips when teachers need an extra parent, and to volunteer in the school library. The principal has told her she is a caring and concerned parent, a real asset to the school. He has been working hard for three years to get extra speech therapy for her handicapped son, but the budget is getting tighter all the time. Mrs. Morgan waits patiently.

Donald Turner got fed up with waiting for the school to provide a full day for his daughter. He went to the PTA meeting to corner the principal, who had not returned any of his calls. In the school halls, he loudly threatened that he would pull his daughter out of school if she did not get better service. Afterwards he felt worse because his daughter loves to go to school and he never intended to keep her home.

These parents may understand their children's needs and the meaning of P.L. 94-142, but they do not understand how to work with school personnel. Let's take a closer look at the day-to-day operation of the school system, at the behavior of the individuals working for it, and at your own behavior when you approach and try to deal with that system to get services for your child. If you intend to be an effective advocate, you will need to know how to ask for services in ways that get the system moving, how to tell the "good" guys from the "bad" guys, and how to modify your own behavior and acquire new skills so that you get what you ask for (or at least most of it).

A LOOK AT SCHOOL SYSTEMS

School systems, like other bureaucracies, tend to be conservative: They are not quick to change nor are they noted for their flexibility. Their mottoes could be "We've always done things this way" or "Business as usual." The business of schools has generally been to provide a standard service (education) to a standard group of people (average children) at a standard cost. The quality and cost of education may vary from community to community, but within each community the school system tries to educate children in the same way. If a child fits the mold, fine—he gets an education. "Misfits," however, tend to get pushed out of school, or, if they are well-behaved and don't look too different, pushed to the back of the classroom.

Of course, you have met individual school people who have cared about the children who don't fit the mold, and who have really tried to help, but who found there was only so much they could do. You may even have known teachers who weren't offered a new contract or who chose to move on after a year because they asked too many times for more support services, for new ways of doing things, or for moving the special class out of the boiler room. They didn't fit into the system either.

When you asked why these people were no longer with the system, the standard system response was probably that they were not able to work well with others. Translated, this means they could have been good teachers and good administrators, but they asked for change—new methods, new services, or more services. Change is not a goal of school systems; they want to deliver the same old service with maximum efficiency and a minimum of fuss. All systems tend to resist change: Otherwise, P.L. 94-142 would be fully implemented because it is the law of the land, every handicapped child would be in a program which meets his needs, and you would not be reading books on how to get services. While systems don't like change, they can be changed by pressure from the community, by strong advocates who assert their rights and their children's rights under the law, and by the threat or initiation of legal action. Making waves works.

The Hierarchy

In order to make waves with success, you need to know who to approach in the system and when. Like all bureaucracies, the school system has a hierarchical structure: Everyone working in it is working directly under someone else. The teacher answers to the special education director (or principal), and the special education director answers to the pupil personnel director, who in turn answers to the superintendent, who answers to the school board, which must account to the elected officials or directly to the voters. Every person has a certain status with particular responsibilities, powers, and limitations.

The teacher can choose classroom activities, but she must arrange with other teachers and specialists for times when children are to be mainstreamed, receive support services, and have access to facilities like the gym, arts and crafts rooms, or cooking room. She may have to get approval through the principal's office, just as she does for classroom materials and equipment. However, special education teachers often have a lower status* than regular education teachers and may have less access to facilities, which is why special education classes may have physical education only twice a week, while regular classes have it three or more times per week. Status and stigma, rather than the children's needs, often determine the availability of services and facilities. Therefore, the committed parent advocate can become a trusted ally of the teacher whose power in the classroom evaporates in the school halls and front office because of such discriminatory attitudes.

---

*Unfortunately (and unfairly), society often views our handicapped children as different, inferior, and even less deserving of service than nonhandicapped children. This view is also extended to the people who work with them. Teachers are deemed inferior by association: "If she were really a good teacher, she'd be teaching the bright kids." Special education teachers, in fact, require more skills than usual to deliver the individualized instruction most handicapped children need. When you meet this kind of prejudice, you should counter it with remarks like "Doesn't it take more skill and brains to do a hard job than an easy one?"

The principal, who is responsible for all the children in her school, has the power to make decisions about how to use personnel and space in her domain within certain limits, and those limits are primarily financial. The general rule is to stay within the budget and not ask for more money. But, at times, you will also see personal relationships determining the use of staff and space; for example, a teacher favored by the principal may get a nicer classroom.

Not every school principal believes in or supports special education ("I have three hundred kids to be concerned about. I can't spend half my time worrying about ten"). You can generally expect problems for special classes (poor support for teachers, isolated space, a separate wing, a basement classroom) and unavailability of facilities at suitable times with principals who feel they have had special education thrust upon them. A fair principal will try to provide at least equal access and time to children with handicaps; a caring principal will supply more to meet the children's special needs.

The special education director works with the personnel who provide special education in the school. He may supervise the special teachers and support staff, set up a method and format for developing IEPs, share in the hiring and firing of special education staff with principals, develop budgets which must go to the director of pupil personnel (or pupil services) for approval, and generally plan for and coordinate special education services with other administrators who probably have more power. The special education director is knowledgeable about the education of handicapped children, but, since the number of children he serves may be fewer than those served by a principal, he may have less authority or impact on decisions than other administrators. Although this is the administrator with whom you will deal most often, you should recognize that his power is limited. On the totem pole of administrators, he may be at the very bottom.

The director of pupil personnel may be responsible for all hiring and firing of teachers and specialists, and for preparation of school personnel budgets. She has direct access to the superintendent of schools, although in large systems there may be assistant superintendents for elementary and secondary education who present budgets, based on all the program plans developed, to the superintendent, who then brings everything to the school board for approval, cuts, or disapproval.

The diagram below shows how the administration interacts with the personnel and children in a single school. Note that most of the power to make decisions is located at the top, and that the children and services are at the bottom. The unbroken lines denote active, working relationships between school people. The broken lines show you the people who may or may not work together. For example, in one school the principal rules with an iron hand and has only a nodding acquaintance with the special education director, while in another school both regular and special teachers meet together and plan regularly for the mainstreamed handicapped students who are their joint responsibility.

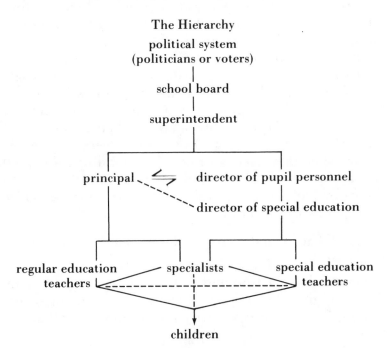

The Hierarchy
political system
(politicians or voters)

school board

superintendent

principal　director of pupil personnel

director of special education

regular education teachers　specialists　special education teachers

children

Your school system will probably differ a little from this basic diagram. It may be smaller (two or three principals and a superintendent), and therefore easier to maneuver. You may know the administrators and school board members personally. Or it may be even larger, and you will need to add a few more rungs and titles to the ladder. But this diagram of a hierarchy can serve as your basic map of how to get from the bottom of the system to the top when you need to. Most of the time you will be working with your child's teacher and the special education director. However, there may be times when your child is not getting the services she needs, and you will want to reach someone with more clout. Know who's who in the hierarchy.

This discussion must seem like a long way from your child's classroom and your request for some extra speech therapy or gym time. But understanding the hierarchy of a school system can help you be a more effective advocate by giving you a sense of the lines of authority and the checkpoints for information and power. That way, the next time a request disappears between administrators' offices or is transformed into something different in the budget, you will know who to contact.

This does not mean that you must concern yourself with the school budget in order to get an appropriate service for your child. But sometimes you will want to remind the school administrators that special needs of your child and other children are not being met, and at other times you will want to support concerned administrators when they need your help in defending the special education section of the budget. Your familiarity with the structure of the hierarchy will help you to recognize who wields the power of the purse.

The "Good" Guys and the "Bad" Guys

Besides a map of the system, you will need a script to understand the action and to tell the "good" guys from the "bad" guys. As you work with people inside the school system, you will discover very few, if any, real villains—

people who genuinely dislike you or your child, who put in their time only to collect their paychecks, or who enjoy having the power to make decisions that can make the lives of other people (parents, children, or school personnel) miserable. Most people are well-intentioned. But people who work in a system are usually not free to act on their good intentions: They must play certain roles, say certain things, and perform certain actions. Within the limits of these system requirements, some school personnel will be effective resources in getting good services for your child. Because your goal is an educational program that benefits your child, you can define these people as the "good" guys. People who interfere with or prevent you from getting good services for your child are, by definition, the "bad" guys. Some school people will shift back and forth from being resources ("good" guys) one time to being obstacles ("bad" guys) another time. In order to decide who will be your best resources, you need to understand a little about the experiences and motives of school people.

Most people, especially those who go into special education, begin their educational careers with good intentions and lofty ideals like the following: Every child is unique; all children (no matter how handicapped) are learners; schools should help children to acquire the skills they will need to function as adults in society; schools can help children develop good self-images and feelings of competence; and learning can be an exciting and rewarding experience. Somewhere between "go" and the time when you encounter them, school people may have lost some of their idealism, energy, commitment, and feeling of effectiveness. But what happened to them and to the ideals they started off with?

If they are teachers, they may have been responsible for too large a class, found too few support services (speech and physical therapists who were not available or who were available for so little time that it didn't make much difference), or worked under a principal who viewed special education as his special cross to bear. These teachers may have asked many times for more services and space, only to be refused, ignored, or intimidated through subtle messages that their contracts might not be renewed if they continued to bother people. When they compared notes with friends, they found other school systems were not really different. They grew tired of asking and getting nothing in return for their efforts. If the disillusioned people are administrators, their experience may have been the same, with too much work, too few resources to build effective programs, too many requests for personnel denied, and too many attempts to create new ways of doing things which were frustrated by a system insisting that "we've always done things this way."

It helps you to understand that most people start out with good intentions, but when their efforts are continually thwarted by the system, many of them learn to adjust to the system's demands. They become "well-adjusted," and this conformity—this giving in or up—results in an education for your child which may not meet her needs. Some of these well-intentioned people are still hopeful or even still requesting more in spite of getting very little; they can often be revived by the appearance of a parent who means business about education and advocacy. Others will need more cordiality, convincing, and even coaxing on your part to trust you as the ally they need and may have been waiting for. But there will be some who are burnt out and will be no help to you at all. In fact, they may even stand in the way of your getting services for your child. Unfortunately, they have become the "bad" guys—they are in the way.

Let's look at some examples of "good" and "bad" guys talking to parents:

> *Mr. D'Amico:* (Finishing a long talk on child's language needs) . . . and I really feel Lola needs to be evaluated by a speech therapist and get some regular speech therapy.
>
> *Teacher:* Well, I do see a lot of what you're talking about in the classroom.

Mr. D'Amico:	Don't you think she needs more help?
Teacher:	Oh, boy! (Hesitates) Well . . . frankly I do. But I've asked several times and there's only one speech therapist for the entire school.
Mr. D'Amico:	What can I do? Is there someone I can ask? I'm going to do anything I can to get help for Lola.
Teacher:	Good for you! My asking won't help, but maybe I can tell you who you should be talking to and help you plan what to say. Let's start with . . .

This teacher is a "good" guy. He's been waiting for someone like this parent for too long and is ready to offer the benefit of his knowledge and experience. Together they will go after the service.

But look at another example:

Mrs. Wu:	. . . he doesn't seem to remember a lot of things you tell him, and I think he really tries.
Teacher:	Robert is often inattentive. He isn't motivated to do his work.
Mrs. Wu:	But I was reading about something called "auditory memory" problems, and the article said . . .
Teacher:	I'm quite familiar with the concept, Mrs. Wu. You'll simply have to face up to the fact that your child is lazy. Have you talked to him about trying harder?
Mrs. Wu:	Yes, I have. Thank you for your time, but I have a dentist appointment in ten minutes.

This teacher is a "bad" guy. Notice how the problem is shifted back to Robert and his parent. "Your child is lazy" and *you* should "talk to him." The learning problem (auditory memory) is not even considered.

The following is an example of one kind of principal and parent interaction:

> *Mr. Howard:* . . . and Walter really needs more work in his physical education program. I looked in and he was just wandering around the gym.
>
> *Principal:* He's getting gym time twice a week. What more can you expect?
>
> *Mr. Howard:* His IEP says three times a week, and the program is supposed to be set up and supervised by a physical therapist.
>
> *Principal:* We don't have a physical therapist any more. She's on maternity leave. And given the fact your son doesn't do much in gym, I see no point in giving him or others like him more time when all these *normal* kids can benefit more from time in the gym.

The parent could continue the discussion by arguing that if Walter had more time and teaching, he might benefit more from physical education. But this principal is bad news; she sounds like she's doing Walter a favor by letting him into the gym at all.

Another principal might be more responsive:

> *Principal:* Well, Mrs. Foster, our therapist is gone. And I've asked the pupil personnel director for a replacement, but she's so frantic about the budget that I've gotten nowhere.
>
> *Mrs. Foster:* Isn't there something you can do?
>
> *Principal:* I've tried. But you know, sometimes a parent can make more waves than a principal . . .
>
> *Mrs. Foster:* Are you suggesting that I should go over your head?

Principal: What do you think? I'd like to have that therapist too.

This principal is a "good" guy because he's admitting that he's powerless and that maybe a person outside the system can do more. He is not wasting the parent's time by pretending that the service may or may not be provided at some vague future time, which is definitely a help in this situation.

When you meet someone who is willing to say "I can't get the service. Go to my boss," you will need to protect that person who has shown you that he is willing to feed you information which you need to do your job well. When you go to the pupil personnel director, you will say *only*, "I am coming to you because I spoke to the principal and he said he cannot give my child the service which is in the IEP." Then you will explain to her why it is essential that your child get that service now.

Other administrators (special education directors, superintendents, etc.) and specialists (who, like teachers, give direct service) will fall the same way: There will be "good" guys and there will be "bad" guys. You will learn to sort them out through their words and efforts, through their good advice and direction, and through their up-front and behind-the-scenes actions on behalf of handicapped children. Did you get the needed service? Yes? That's a "good" guy!

When you first begin to work as an advocate, some people will confuse you. They will warmly greet you by name when they see you, and sooner or later they call you back on the phone. But did you get the service or are you on your way to getting the service? That is the measure. The warm smiles and handshakes you get will not educate your child.

Now and again a "bad" guy falls into the position of a "good" guy by mistake, default, entrapment, or even change of heart. For example, you may overhear the principal at a PTA meeting telling another teacher or parent that there is a new speech therapist on board. You can jump in with, "I'm so glad you were able to get the therapist. Now Harold can get the extra help he needs. I appreciate your efforts." You know about the therapist, the principal knows you know, and your praise is hard to ignore. Or the principal may have seen a film at a conference and returned to school convinced that physical education is the answer to the problems of handicapped children. He pushes and gets the necessary personnel. Your child's services improve. The principal is now your "good" guy, even if he wasn't on your side last week.

It is important that you continually evaluate the effectiveness and the assistance value of the school people with whom you are trying to work because first impressions can be misleading, individuals do have bad days, people do change their attitudes, and when there are personnel changes in the system, the power of an individual may increase or decrease. Yesterday's "friends" may be today's hindrances but tomorrow's supports as they respond to the pressures and priorities of the system. Sure, it would be great if school people were always friendly and consistent in their support, or even consistently difficult so that you could know what to expect. But they aren't. You will have to deal with them where they are at any given time.

INEFFECTIVE WAYS TO DEAL
WITH THE SYSTEM

Parents deal with school systems in a variety of ways, some effective and some not. Either their work with schools is productive (they get what they want) or counterproductive (they get little or nothing, or they even lose something). Let's look at the counterproductive patterns of exchanges first.

Isolation

This exchange is no exchange at all: The parents never see or rarely talk to the school people. Some parents do this because they have complete trust. They say that "the school system has the child's best interests at heart and is doing all it can." These parents may not be aware of the pressures school boards and finance committees apply to school personnel. Or worse, they may not understand their children's right to education and may actually believe the school is doing them a favor in educating their handicapped children.

Then there are the parents who have no confidence in what they know about their children (the "mere parents" people). They will tell you that the teachers and specialists are professionals trained to do the job. What can a mere emotional and ignorant parent do but let the professionals do their job without bothering them? Some parents give up (if they ever started) because they believe that "you can't fight city hall" or that "one person can't change the system." Such apathetic parents take what they get without gratitude and without hope. They probably know their children should have more.

Other parents, who are afraid of rocking the school system, work hard at being "good," quiet parents who don't bother school people. They take what they get out of fear that, if they complain, their children will get worse service, less service, or even no service. Unfortunately, people who expect nothing generally get nothing. When services are being cut back, the children of "good" parents may suffer the most.

These parents—the trusting, the apathetic, and the fearful—take what they get because they don't realize what their children are entitled to, what power and competence parents have or can develop, and that even the most difficult system can be changed by strong, committed advocates.

Co-optation

Some trusting and fearful parents do have contact with school people. Because they believe that the school system can do the best professional job without any meddling from the parents, or that their speaking up might jeopardize their children's services, many of these parents tend to become servants of the system; that is, they become co-opted by the system. They accept what their children get without question, and they are grateful. They will do what is asked of them, from baking cakes for the sales and helping out in the lunchroom to signing the IEP. Their actions are based on proving their gratitude by demonstrating their respect for the professionals and their constant willingness to be helpful. Co-opted parents are also "good" parents.

Besides trusting and fearful parents, the "good" parents may also be "seduced" parents, ones who may have started out as advocates and who have become co-opted through attention and friendly gestures. Their struggle for services makes them grateful for kind words and special relationships. Over time, they too become the "good" parents of the system.

The "good" parents give the system no trouble. Some schools are experts at recognizing these parents and do just enough to keep them in an ingratiating posture: a few kind words ("It's nice to have a parent who understands the problem"), a little threat ("Let's not rock the boat by making too much noise about Aaron's speech needs. They may cut back on what he has now"), or a special concession ("I'll try to get more, but you know how tight the budget is this year"). These parents are grateful for crumbs, and their children get educational crumbs instead of services.

Be wary of the teacher or administrator who tells you that you are not like other parents (because you are so understanding and realistic), who shares her problems with you, who is always in when you call, and who is unusually prompt about returning your calls. She may be trying to make you a "friend" for her own purposes: Aren't friends sympathetic and helpful? Don't they make allowances for each other, give each other more time when needed, and not criticize, at least not in front of anybody else?

In the beginning of a personal relationship with a school person you may get a slight improvement in services and a well-massaged ego. As time passes, you, the understanding, "rational" parent, may find yourself sympathizing more and more and getting fewer services.

While this parent seduction or co-optation is going on, your child is in limbo. You have made a "friend," but you may also be sacrificing your child's services and future for personal attention.

Co-optation is a hard pattern to change because the seduction of parents is a gradual, even insidious, process during which you have many occasions to develop the habit of supporting and sympathizing with the school person. However, you can learn not to personalize your relationships with school people through some careful planning and role playing in which you rehearse as the child's strong advocate instead of the school's pal. You are out to influence people and gain services, not to win friends. When co-opted parents learn about their children's educational rights, they can begin to disengage themselves from "personal" ties with the school system and to look for methods and skills to help them become the strong and independent advocates that their children need.

Reactive Confrontation

Sometimes when parents first learn about their handicapped child's right to education, they react with bewilderment, anger, and frustration. In an attempt to right the wrong done to his child, an outraged parent may go with fire in his eyes and heart to confront the teacher or administrator, and shout, "What are they paying you for? You ought to be out sweeping streets for all you know about these kids!" or "You never liked my kid anyway, you jerk!" The reactive parent, in venting anger upon the first representative of the system he is able to contact, sometimes blames an individual who may in fact be powerless to meet the parent's demands to correct the school system's failure. Parents who flare up like this think the school people will move now because they really told those people off.

Occasionally, this may bring immediate but short-range results; most of the time, however, what happens is that these parents have given teachers or administrators good reason for not dealing with them anymore. The school people, being on the receiving end of such fireworks, will often, with some justification, react with anger of their own. Although they may attempt to placate, threaten, or ignore the parent at the time of the confrontation because of the parent's "irrational" behavior, they feel they now have good cause to reject the parent as a participant in the planning of educational services for his child, or they conclude that with a parent such as this, no wonder the child has problems, and schools can't be expected to do much to help a child from an unstable home situation. If the school people are justified in avoiding the parents or even refusing to see them, how can parents be effective?

When school people avoid parents after such a confrontation and do not improve services for the children involved, parents become more frustrated and demoralized; they have done their worst and still the system didn't budge, so they feel that they might as well give up. Obviously, "we can't fight the system."

School systems, which have years of experience in dealing with all kinds of parents, know that most parents who use reactive confrontation are not likely to continue because of the emotional drain and exhaustion involved; such parents usually give only one performance and then return to isolation. They reason that "if we can ride out the storm, these parents will eventually leave us alone."

If you are a parent who has used reactive confrontation, you probably know that fireworks behavior is a mistake. It is a mistake, however, that you can repair. It may require an apology on your part: You can say that you are sorry for the things you said at the meeting, that you don't know what came over you, but that you were really worried about Maria's progress, and, in addition, you are having problems in your job, all your children have been sick, or the pipes burst. You may still believe the person is incompetent or heartless, but you are not going to say it to his face. Besides, you can't prove the person doesn't like your child, should be sweeping streets, or is a jerk. Do not say anything you can't back up with specific information or data. However, you can, if necessary, eat a little crow for a good cause—your child's future.

If you can't get past the secretary, leave a message that you want to apologize for your behavior the other day and hope the teacher or administrator will get back to you. If necessary, leave a note. It's hard for school people to refuse an apology, especially when they are bent on showing how rational, cool, and objective they are in contrast to your emotional behavior.

Once contact has been reestablished, you can set about the business of advocacy through preparation and planning. If you know you have a short fuse or tend to get easily excited, your preparation should include more role playing, possibly reading a book on relaxation (and learning how to do it), and perhaps taking someone with you who will keep you on task and under control.

EFFECTIVE WAYS TO DEAL WITH THE SYSTEM

Remember that you can change your behavior and direction at any time; in fact, to be a good advocate, you are always acquiring new behaviors, changing old ones, and increasing your advocacy skills. When parents learn skills and strategies, as well as rights, they can start to act in more productive ways with school systems.

Productive Assertiveness

Parents who have been fearful, who have been naive about their children's rights, who have been trusting (but are now disillusioned), and who have been drained by emotional confrontations, must start their self-training program by developing productive assertiveness. (The outraged parent was assertive but that kind of assertiveness is not productive. He burnt out quickly and the school system returned to business as usual.)

What does productive assertiveness involve? First, it means knowledgeable parents. You know what the law says and what it means for your child; you know what is in your child's IEP, what evaluations have been done on your child and what they show, what specific kinds of services will benefit your child, and what sources and resources for information and support are available to you. You have done your homework.

Then, because you are well-informed, you prepare yourself to present your case to the school people. You examine your strengths and weaknesses, including some assumptions like "I'm only a parent" and "I don't know any other role but pupil." You note that you are good with groups, or you get nervous when you have to speak up; you are good on details, or you can't remember a thing under pressure; you are a person who remains cool under fire, or you tend to get very emotional when people are pressing you for answers; you think well on your feet, or you think of the right response after the meeting or when you're falling asleep.

As you plan for the first contact or meeting, make a list of your strong and weak points. Then write out what you need to do to correct your weaknesses.

1. You are nervous about speaking up, so write down your questions and demands.

2. You can't remember a thing; again, write it down (everything you will want to say and use at the meeting or on the phone).

3. You tend to become emotional or lose control; then have someone on your side with you who can help you stay on target, or take over for you when you need moments to calm down.

4. You're afraid you won't give the right response; the person you ask to accompany you to the meeting, if well-informed by you, can help. Furthermore, your advocacy is not a one-shot deal. You will have contact after contact with the schools and other opportunities to use your "right response."

Your preparation probably includes role playing. Try to think in advance of what the school people might say to your requests, including the worst. Let your fantasy loose. Make up your own responses and rehearse them:

If the principal says . . . then I'll say . . . and if he says . . . I'll tell him . . . and then I'll bring out the evaluations . . .

By preparing yourself for the worst, you may not need to use all your practice responses, but you will be in control when questions or statements are made because you have immediate answers and actions at hand.

As part of your role rehearsal, include ways to close the meeting or phone call if you feel it is becoming unproductive. Yes, you can end a meeting by requesting an evaluation, asking that another person attend the next meeting, or just saying you need time to think about the important issues that have been discussed.

A very important component of productive assertiveness is your understanding that advocacy for your child is a long-term job, and you are making the full commitment to that job. This commitment will affect and strengthen your manner and delivery when you are dealing with school people. You are embarking on a journey which can bring good services to your child through her school years (and in some states even beyond the usual high school years).* You will find that there are ways (people and methods) to strengthen your weak points. And, as you gain in strength, you will become a better advocate.

To complete your preparation for productive assertiveness, you need to begin keeping your records (chapter

---

*P.L. 94-142 allows each state to set its own upper age limit for special education as long as the limit is consistent with the state's own special education laws and with the age limits for regular education. For example, in Michigan, handicapped people are entitled to special education if they are under twenty-six; in Massachusetts, special education is provided to students from age three to twenty-one; but Ohio and North Carolina have a cut-off age of eighteen for both special and regular education students. In no case can a school system legally deny service to handicapped people until they have reached the age of the oldest-attending regular student in the system. See Appendix B for a chart which will tell you both the upper and lower age limits for special education in each state as of May 1, 1980.

four gives more details). Develop your file by collecting information about your child's past and present program, beginning a list of school meetings and calls with space to record results, listing your concerns and requests, and having a notebook or clipboard to take with you to meetings. Your file can be fancy or simple; a shoe box or shirt box will do nicely. The important thing is that you have your notes and records where you can find and use them. Prepared in this way (you have reviewed and collected the needed information, you have assessed your strengths and weaknesses, you have practical responses), you can now attend your first meeting with confidence. You arrive on time, organized and with a list of questions and issues. The way you present yourself (calm and businesslike) tells the school people you are serious and there to stay as long as your child needs services.

Productive assertiveness is necessary for the first step in working with school systems, but it is neither a first step nor a stage. It is a quality you will develop and use in all your dealings with the school system. You will maintain the ability to be productively assertive by keeping up-to-date information and resources, and by rehearsing for situations which may look difficult.

When parents have initiated the process of working with the school system by asserting their children's rights and needs, they will find available to them three methods of dealing with the system.

Collaboration

Collaboration is the ideal method to develop good educational plans for children with special needs. In this process, the school people accept the parents as legitimate and equal partners in planning services, and respect and value the information and concerns that parents present.

To be an effective advocate in this case, you need first to value your own ideas and questions. You are not "a mere parent": You are a valuable source of information about your child. Second, you need to be informed (through your own efforts) about your child's past evaluations and educational plans, and of his performance in the current school placement. When you are informed and confident, you will no longer be timid about contributing to the development of good services.

In speaking up at meetings, you will present your information and requests in simple but specific language:

Not—Peggy needs more services.

But—Peggy's progress in speech has been slow. Can we increase sessions with the speech therapist from two times per week to every day?

or

Not—Michael can't read.

But—Michael's reading doesn't seem to be improving. Wouldn't he benefit from some individual tutoring?

Your request is clear and straightforward. The teacher or therapist may agree with your concern and respond with another suggestion. Their responses should also be simple and specific so that you both know you are talking about the same thing; the professionals should avoid jargon. At certain times, jargon is used to put parents down by reminding them that they lack professional training. In the collaborative setting, however, jargon may be a momentary lapse, and a simple request from you for a clearer explanation will remind the professionals to use everyday language. Since professionals do talk to each other more than to parents, a confident parent can overlook these occasional lapses as long as the professionals are making an effort and the messages, if not clear the first time, are understood on the second try. When you have asked about more speech training and you hear things you may not understand, like "apraxia," "syntactical," "cvc's," etc., it's time to ask for a translation.

Since collaboration is a process of sharing, you will want to remain open to suggestions from the school people, as in the following exchange:

> *Teacher:* I understand why you want more speech sessions for Peggy, but I have

been working on an idea which might
be better. The speech therapist has
agreed to spend an hour in my classroom to set up programs I can do with
my kids. I had hoped to work with
Peggy and Mitch, who have similar
speech problems, every day.

Mrs. Sullivan: You mean that she will continue twice
a week with therapy and work every
day with you for practice? That means
more speech work and less time out
of the classroom. Sounds reasonable.
I want to hear more . . .

This parent and this teacher are sharing and developing
new ideas, and Peggy can be the beneficiary. This kind of
give and take is the mark of collaboration. There is no
put-down, no pressure, no freezing of roles ("I am the
teacher; you are only a parent"); there is rather an openness, a sharing of ideas, and a common goal of improved
services for the child. There may be disagreements, but
differences are expected and respected.

Happy is the parent who can advocate through genuine
collaboration; sometimes parents find themselves in a
process that looks like collaboration, but is co-optation in
disguise. You begin to sense that you are giving in or
giving up more than you are getting. (The successful
advocate is one who gets more for her child than she gives
up.) It may be that the school people wanted to collabo-
rate from the beginning, but pressures to keep costs down
have increased within the system, and, in spite of their
good intentions, they feel they must hold back on new or
increased services. Or it may be that subtle attempts at
co-opting parents were there from the start and have
increased to a level where you find yourself asking, "Just
what is going on here?" When that question comes up,
take some time to assess the situation. Is it just smiles and
handshakes, or is it the services you want?

When collaboration fails or turns out to be nonexistent,
you will shift to a process which involves not only infor-

mation and assertiveness, but which requires the continued use of strategies and the frequent presence of someone who is willing to back you up at meetings, either as a witness to the proceedings and a silent supporter, or as a contributor of suggestions.

Negotiation

If the mark of a good parent advocate in collaboration is the ability to share information and remain open to suggestions, the mark of a successful parent advocate in the process of negotiation is the skill to obtain more than you give away, through the judicious use of strategies and compromise.

"But wait a minute," you might be thinking, "we're talking about education—my child's and that of other children with special needs. It's hard to believe that school systems play these games with parents. It's their job to educate, after all." Remember the discussion of the system and the pressures within it: the school budget, the limited number of specialists, and the limited amount of time teachers or administrators may have available for you and your child. Handicapped children may well be a priority of the system, but they may be priority number three or four or even number ten or twenty.

How can handicapped children become a high priority in a school system? Through parents who bring their children's needs to the educators' attention in the way that squeaky wheels get the grease. Look at the families you know: Some children are getting better services and more attention because their parents are persistent. After enough parental squeaks and a growing awareness on the part of the system that the squeaking won't go away until something is done, services, like grease, are usually applied. Negotiation determines how much "grease" is used.

Negotiation is always a serious game which parents must play for high stakes (their children's futures) and at some cost (their energy and time). But it is a serious game for school people too, especially when their jobs or advancement in their careers may be in jeopardy. They may need to prove to someone in a higher position that they were tough-minded, tight-fisted, and fiscally "responsible" in their negotiations with parents, and that in fact they did not just "give everything away."

Although you will find yourself negotiating with school people in a number of ways, such as arranging a time to visit the classroom, setting an appointment to read your child's records, and finding a mutually convenient time to meet with your child's teacher, the most intensive and challenging negotiation will usually happen in the meeting(s) when the IEP is developed. This is the time when all your preparation and rehearsal will pay off.

To be an effective negotiator, you must begin by bringing to the bargaining table those qualities that parents use to achieve successful collaboration: a willingness and determination to share the information you have; a readiness for honest disagreement, discussion, and compromise (as long as it leads to a plan which benefits your child); and a strong belief in your ability to make a valuable contribution to your child's IEP. But for negotiation you must be stronger in these qualities—more informed, more assertive, and more confident. You must be prepared to be more critical in your judgments about the other members of the team, and, on occasion, suspicious of the motives which led to the program proposed by the school people. You must make a case for improved or new services, and be ready to work hard to convince people, some of whom may not be all that interested in what you have to say or may even resent your "interference."

Being a negotiator, however, does not mean that you arrive at the meeting with a list of service demands from which you will not budge even one inch. After all, your plan or list of services may not be the best one for your child. You at least need to hear the ideas, suggestions, and criticisms of the school people before you can make a rational decision to accept or reject their recommendations. Therefore, remain open to suggestion, and even disagreement, as long as the process is an honest one, meaning that everyone is at least trying to understand what the other person is proposing. When a proposal is rejected or accepted, it should be done for educational reasons, not because of the old myths or because the school is holding the line on the budget.

You may find negotiation necessary for only one issue in developing the IEP for your child. In that case, you may reach an agreeable compromise or even win your point and find yourself thinking, "Negotiation isn't so bad after all. I got something good for my child just by speaking up. This negotiation can really pay off." On the other hand, you may find yourself in a situation where the school people are giving nothing away and you must argue every step of the way for the tiniest concessions. You start thinking, "This is exhausting. How will I make it through the meeting? Negotiation is hard work. It would be easier to give in." However, even when negotiation is very difficult, by the end of the meeting you may have convinced the school people of the need for certain services.

Let's look at some examples of parents in negotiation. All the parents have come to the meetings with a prepared list of services their children need, ranked in what they see as the order of importance. They first listen carefully to what the school people have to offer. (By letting the school people present their ideas or plans first, the parents may find that most of the services on their lists are also priorities for the school people.)

"We could try it." Colin Dwyer listens carefully to the school people's presentations. He is pleasantly surprised by the agreement between his list and their plan.

> *Mr. Dwyer:* I'm impressed with the services you have laid out. You seem to really know my daughter and what she needs. Leela has made a lot of progress in school. Through your efforts, she is almost totally mainstreamed. I have only one concern I want to raise: She is two years behind in math.

Principal:	She has made progress in every other area. We don't want to push her too hard.
Mr. Dwyer:	I don't want to push her either. But if Leela had some extra tutoring, she might catch up and be in regular class all the time.
Sp. Ed. Teacher:	I see from the reports that she's in the resource room one hour each day and gets her math instruction there. That should be adequate.
Mr. Dwyer:	I had something else in mind. I would like her to be in a regular class with a special tutor after school.
Principal:	The teacher has a full work schedule and can't be expected to tutor after school.
Mr. Dwyer:	I realize that, but couldn't some other person be hired as a tutor?
Principal:	That means more money, and you know how tight money is.
Mr. Dwyer:	I understand the pressures on you. But in two years Leela goes to junior high school, and it would be nice if she could go as a regular student. Listen, I think what you're offering is great, but I also think this small addition could make a lot of difference. Couldn't you arrange for the tutor?
Teacher:	I'm not convinced that Leela will improve with the tutoring.
Mr. Dwyer:	But you're not sure it won't work either. How about a trial of a few months?
Principal:	We could try it for a few months, I suppose. But in three months we'll review it and . . .

Note that by letting the school people lead off, Colin Dwyer found that he had only one point to negotiate. He was pleasant (congratulating the school people on the plan), assertive (keeping to the issue of the tutor), and willing to compromise (agreeing to a three-month trial).

"It isn't needed." Eileen Martin has to work a little harder in the negotiation process. After listening to the school people present their plans, she realizes that they are talking about last year's program which, to her, is clearly inadequate—there are no special therapies, the class size is too large and physical education meets only once a week. She realizes that the situation requires a strong effort on her part when the school people tell her that the meeting is already half over and that she must sign the IEP today.

Although her first response is panic ("The program is just awful and I have to sign now! Help!"), she takes a long look out the window, relaxes, and reminds herself that time is on her side. The IEP is too important to rush. She then speaks up in an assertive manner and tells the administrators calmly what she feels her child needs, what is wrong with the program, and why. Her composed, assertive manner tells the school people that she too expects to be a reasonable but nevertheless active participant in this process, that for her the task is a very serious one, and that her evaluations and recommendations will become part of the proceedings.

She goes through the proposed program point by point and asks for specifics:

Mrs. Martin:	You say Patrick should have gym, but you didn't say how often, how long, or who his teacher would be.
Principal:	It would be the usual number of times.
Mrs. Martin:	I'm sorry, Mr. Brennan, but I don't know what that is. Could you be more specific so that we could write it into the program?

Principal: Two or three times a week.

Mrs. Martin: Three times would be better. My son, Sean, who is in regular class, has gym three times a week.*

Principal: Yes, Mrs. Martin, three times each week.

Mrs. Martin: Now, I'm not clear on the goals for Patrick's physical education plan.

In this way, Eileen Martin pursues the specifics of the IEP. She asks to see reports; she asks questions of the teachers and specialists. The negotiating process is continuous and Mrs. Martin is working very hard. Finally, both sides are deadlocked over the issue of an increase in speech therapy:

Mrs. Martin: Patrick needs speech therapy every day. His speech is his major drawback in all his activities.

Principal: He already has speech twice each week, which is more than anyone else in his class, and, frankly, he hasn't made much progress.

Mrs. Martin: That is only partially true. He hasn't made more progress because he's not getting enough help to make a further difference. He needs more. Actually, speech therapy has clearly made a difference. Before he got any, he had no speech. With twice-weekly therapy, he is now speaking better and more

---

*Children in special classes are entitled to physical education the same number of times as children in regular classes unless there is some reason the individual child would not benefit from the program. They cannot be excluded or have reduced time because regular classes are using the gym.

	often. It is reasonable to expect that more therapy will produce still more speech.
Principal:	We don't have enough speech therapists to serve all the children who need help. I can't offer you any more. I'm very sorry.
Mrs. Martin:	Yet we all agree that this is Patrick's biggest need!
Principal:	I don't agree that five times a week will help more. And besides, I can't offer it.
Mrs. Martin:	It seems that we have a difference of opinion concerning Patrick's needs and his profiting from speech therapy. Also, you seem to be saying that even if you agreed that he needed more, you could not provide more. How might we solve this? (She looks at the teacher.)
Teacher:	I have a suggestion.* What if the speech therapist continued to come twice each week but spent some of that time working with me to help me set up a language program for Patrick. Would that help?

Eileen Martin expresses her interest by pulling her chair closer to the educational bargaining table, asking for more specifics. The principal breathes a sigh of relief and leans back in his chair (he, too, finds negotiating hard

---

*Many special education teachers complain that they have very little contact with the specialists and would welcome advice about working with their students. They are more than willing to follow the directions of the specialists in order to help their students to greater achievement in the classroom.

work!) while the teacher outlines a cooperative language program between the therapist and herself. The parent agrees but with reservations: She wants weekly contact with the teacher or therapist to measure the effectiveness of this new approach. The teacher says that meeting every week would be difficult for her, so the parent suggests a weekly phone call and monthly meetings. This suggestion is accepted.

In this kind of bargaining, the school people first offered something which was not acceptable. When the parent asked for more, backing up her request with a sound and assertive argument, they offered something else. Through negotiation all parties reached a mutual agreement about the service to be provided. Eileen Martin worked hard, and in the end got a program she believed was good for her child.

The example also shows that the parent, by remaining open to new ideas (in this case, the teacher's), was able to obtain a more beneficial program than the one she originally proposed. Her child now stands to gain through more attention to his language development (from two people) and more time in the classroom to be used for learning other skills, as well as group opportunities for improving language performance.

"It's not our responsibility." Some parents encounter strong resistance to their concerns and requests for services. Sometimes the old myths are the cause of this resistance, and a lot of time and energy must be expended to counteract them. Other times, it can be honest disagreement between the parents and the school people. When this is the case, someone at the negotiating table is likely to ask questions and want to explore your concerns. The most difficult times are those when the school budget alone (though sometimes presented under the guise of the school's lack of responsibility) is determining the process and you find that the conversation seems to be leading nowhere and discussion is being closed off. These are the times when you, the parent, will need to remind the school people of their legal responsibility under the law.

Norman Johnson's request for adapted physical education for his son, Mark, is being turned down. He is not sure whether the school people really believe that Mark is doing well in gym or are trying to avoid the cost of providing a special service:

Principal: I know you'd like Mark to have the program, but we don't believe he really needs more than he's getting right now. Besides, that's a special service.

Mr. Johnson: I'm not sure I understand what you mean by special service.

Principal: It's an extra; it's not part of our regular program. If you want to pursue it on your own by finding some after-school program, that's up to you.

Mr. Johnson: I have my copy of the 94-142 regulations here. It says that adapted physical education is a school service. If Mark needs this service, he's entitled to have it. I observed the gym program: There are so many distractions that Mark is lost in there. He might as well have no gym program.

Principal: Well, if you think he'd benefit from more time in the classroom, we could . . .

Mr. Johnson: I'm sorry if I haven't made myself clear. Mark needs a physical education program designed to meet his needs. I feel that it is one of the most crucial parts of his IEP. To be quite frank about it, I would have a great deal of difficulty signing the IEP if it were not included. However, if you feel you do not have enough information and want to have Mark tested . . .

Principal: Maybe we should take another look at Mark before we make any decisions.

Note that once Norman Johnson suspects resistance, he first makes sure that he understands what the principal is saying, then makes specific reference to the law, ignores the attempt at diversion ("more time in the classroom"), and finally makes it very clear that the IEP will be unacceptable without the crucial service. His suggestion that the school might look into further evaluation is offered from a position of strength because he is fairly sure from his observations of Mark that a qualified evaluator is bound to find that Mark needs special help.

Norman Johnson is going through the worst kind of negotiation, in which money, and not the child, appears to be the prime concern. Because of his knowledge of the law (as well as his determination), Mark's father may bring about the needed change in his son's program. The negotiation process, however, is not completed until the specifics of the agreement are written down in the IEP. The three parents in the examples will finish the process when the IEP is presented to them in full detail, describing the plans which they have worked out with the educators at the meeting(s).

Most parents will use negotiation in dealing with the system and most will achieve a reasonably successful IEP for their children. There will, however, be a few parents who, in spite of good or even extraordinary negotiating skills, will not be able to achieve a beneficial program for their children. These parents have a more demanding job ahead of them.

PRODUCTIVE CONFRONTATION

When parents find themselves in a situation where they are being asked to accept or sign an IEP that is presented to them without their participation in its development, when every request for an improvement in service is rejected ("There's no money" or "Your child is getting too many extras already"), or when, after a cordial meeting with much discussion, parents receive an IEP which does not include their recommendations and does not meet their child's needs, then parents must be prepared to move beyond the negotiation phase by rejecting the educational program. Negotiation fails when both sides say no. The system says, "No, you can't have anything more or any of the important things you have asked for," and the parent says, "No, I cannot accept the program as it is written for my child." Parents must then be ready to confront the system with its failure and to show their commitment to obtaining needed services for their children.

School systems sometimes say no to intimidate parents. Parents must be prepared to deal with that no in a productive way. Accepting the school's refusal is not productive, not from the point of view of your child's future. Therefore, you must let the school people know you do not accept the program. The first step could be a call to the special education director or principal to say that you intend to reject the school's program and that you are prepared to do so in writing, but first you want to check out the possibilities for reconciling differences before appealing to a higher authority. If there is no chance to renegotiate or if you have unusual difficulty reaching the administrator, then you must reject the IEP, stating your reasons for rejecting the program in writing.

Sometimes your verbal or written rejection is enough to bring more cooperation from the school people. They realize that you were not intimidated and you are not bluffing. (Never bluff about your child's future. Say what you'll do and then do it.)

When negotiation fails, you must be prepared to move to productive confrontation, an often long and drawn out, but necessary, process. It is discussed at length in chapter seven, the next-to-last chapter of the book. It is there because it is a last resort to use when other means have been tried and have failed.

Perhaps you are worn out at the thought of doing still more work and planning when you have just finished working so hard in order to do a good job of negotiating. An important consolation is that all the work you've done and information you've gathered will be essential in working through the process of productive confrontation. Your new skills and self-control under fire will help you through the next phase.

In this chapter you have begun to understand how you may been manipulated or pushed into the role of isolated, co-opted, or reactive parents. Most of you didn't get there by yourselves; you had some help from the system. This "help" came in the form of statements which we can label "snow jobs." There is one important difference between snow jobs and myths, which snow jobs sometimes resemble. Myths are things which people actually believe; they are ideas which need to be challenged and changed. Snow jobs, however, are strategies designed and used by some school people to make their jobs easier by excluding certain children from needed services and even from school. Snow jobs are common enough that you should be prepared to deal with them.

SOME POPULAR SNOW JOBS

When people in school systems face parents who are asking for services for the first time, a number of school people may say things that are intended to discourage the parents from making their requests. Some of these statements may be dishonest, insulting (to the child and the parent), and even illegal. Naive and trusting parents may take the statements at face value and creep quietly home, perhaps never to ask again. But informed parent advocates know the standard "snow jobs" and learn how to recognize new variations; they can reply to distasteful and illegal statements by using P.L. 94-142 for support.

We Don't Have the Money

The law makes it clear that *all* children are entitled to a free public education. Even before P.L. 94-142 was passed, lack of money was not a legal excuse for denying education. Most parents didn't know this; they thought they and their children were getting favors if services were available, and if their children were at home or in state institutions not receiving education, they more or less accepted the situation.

If your child is not in an educational program, you have the right and the obligation to insist that your child immediately receive services. The school is in violation of the law until your child is placed in a program, and in flagrant violation if they know your child is without a program and are doing nothing.

If your child is in a program which is not meeting his needs, you should request a new IEP which will include services to meet those needs. If the school people do not agree with you on those service needs, they must argue with you in educational terms, not in financial ones. Do not accept lack of money as an excuse for denying services.

Children like Yours Can't Benefit from Education

This is another snow job designed to put you and your child down, and to keep you from demanding the services to which your child is entitled. Remember, the law provides for all children, not just for those who will learn to read and write or become fully independent adults. No matter how handicapped your child is, she is included under the law.

Whether your school system has the ability at this time to provide your child with a beneficial education which meets her needs is another matter. But the law requires that schools provide it, and this may mean that your system needs to quickly take steps to educate your child.

Note that in this snow job the schools try to put the responsibility for their failure on your child because she doesn't meet their expectations of the kind of child they like to serve. You, as the knowledgeable and committed advocate, place that responsibility right back where it belongs—on the shoulders of the school system—because you know your child can learn and which programs can benefit her.

We Don't Have Any Children like This

This statement (a variation of the one above) is sometimes made with a sign of distaste: The implication is that your child is too handicapped, too different, and even too grotesque to be served by the system. One parent with a partially ambulatory, physically disabled child with high intelligence was told by a school superintendent that "your child is a basket case and doesn't belong in a public school." This child later went to a private school with non-handicapped students and did well. Clearly, he could have succeeded in a public school if some supportive arrangements had been made.

Hearing such statements is a devastating experience for a parent. If you have any reason to expect that unfair and insulting remarks about your child may be made to you, be sure you take someone with you when you go to meetings. It is amazing how much language gets cleaned up when there's a witness present. You may still have to deal with attitudes and excuses, but the personal insults will be reduced.

The Classrooms (or Facilities) Are Not Accessible

Not only does this statement violate P.L. 94-142, but it also stands in violation of Section 504 of P.L. 93-112, which guarantees the civil rights of the handicapped.

One administrator told a parent that her child could not attend school because the second grade was on the second floor, and her child could not get there. He made it sound like the eleventh commandment: The second grade always was, is, and shall be on the second floor. No accommodation was going to be made for her child, although the administrator could have moved the second grade down one floor, or even installed an elevator if he wanted to spend the school system's money.

Accommodations can be made (most classrooms can be moved), renovations can be started (ramps, new doors, lavatories accessible to the handicapped, and, if necessary, elevators), or a combination of accommodations and renovations can be undertaken to meet the needs of physically handicapped children without extraordinary expense (for example, relocating a classroom is cheaper than installing an elevator). If your child could benefit from the programs (regular and/or special classes) in your local school and is being excluded because the facilities are inaccessible, you have the right and the obligation to insist that programs be made accessible. A strong and outspoken parent advocate can bring about the needed changes.

Children Can Be So Cruel

This statement is usually coupled with the recommendation that your child be placed somewhere else, not in his local school. What school people are suggesting here is that they would like to protect your child but they have no control over all the other children in their schools. This is nonsense because school systems have numerous rules to regulate the behavior of their students (such as when to arrive, talk, eat, or move, and what to wear). Furthermore, the purpose of the schools is to educate, not only in academics but in values as well. When school administrations make a strong commitment to handicapped children, the nonhandicapped children will become more accepting and supportive of children with handicaps. School systems (and society in general) have protected and prevented nonhandicapped children from having contact with handicapped children, and, in doing so, have done a disservice to all children.

You can remind the school people of their obligation to educate children and to foster through education an understanding and acceptance of disabilities. You can also say that you will be watching closely to see what efforts they make and how successful those efforts are, that you understand some of the difficulties they may face, and that you will help by finding films and speakers (yourself included if this is something you feel comfortable about) to talk to both teachers and students, but that you cannot accept the "cruelty" of students as an excuse for the system's continued violation of the law.

Your Child Would Benefit More from a Workshop outside the School

Parents of young handicapped adolescents have heard this cop-out. Occupational training may be a very good goal for your child, but it should happen in the schools, which is where it happens for most kids. Sending children outside the system to rehabilitation programs which usually lack the varied programs offered by schools, such as physical education, speech and motor therapy, and academics (even at beginning levels), denies handicapped children the opportunity to work and socialize with other students of their own age. You may tell the school people that you will appreciate their help in finding a workshop placement if it is necessary when your child is older, but right now your child belongs in school.

She's Ready to Graduate

This is good news for a parent unless the adolescent still has educational needs which have not been met. The school may in fact be trying to push your child out for reasons that do not include her well-being. "Graduation" is usually the end of the special therapies and academic assistance which your child may still need. If you know that your child needs more education, do not accept "graduation" on the school's timetable—when she's sixteen years old, or seventeen, or eighteen. In some states the law covers students through age twenty-one, or even older (see Appendix B for age ranges).

If your child is in a regular class and wants to graduate with her classmates, you and your child will have to make the decision together. If your child is in special classes where students do not enter and leave the system at the same time, most of the decision will fall on you. Do not make your decision solely on the school's recommendation for graduation. As always, base your decisions and recommendations on your child's needs.

THE SNOW JOB CHALLENGED

Not all of you will have to deal with school people who make statements like those we've discussed. But if you are subjected to snow jobs, you must speak up. Tell the speaker that the statement is wrong and that it is not an excuse for excluding children from school. If you feel the school person is in error and misguided, show her how to understand the needs of children in another and more valid way. If you find yourself dealing with the occasional school person who intends to put you down or drive you away, let her know you find the comments offensive and a poor excuse for denying service. You may even wish to put your understanding of what was said in writing, making sure that your report of the comments is accurate, and send the letter to the person who made the remarks (the next chapter covers writing letters to school personnel). In most cases, you will get back the "I'm-sure-you-misunderstood-my-comments" letter, which will usually deny the remarks, tell you what the person "really" said, and indicate that the school is aware of the difficulty and already taking steps to correct it. Your letter can do more than correct the school person's offensive or erroneous remarks; it can bring you a written promise of improved service for your child. Whichever way you choose to deal with the school people, you let them know that you will not be put off by such statements because you are serious about getting an education for your child.

In order to effectively combat the people who are putting your child down, you want to strengthen or even develop some basic skills for dealing with school people. The next chapter will help you to apply skills you use in your daily life to the specific task of communicating with the school system.

Four

Basic Skills:
"Hey, I Can Do That!"

"Mrs. Blatt is very busy. I don't know when she can return your call."

"I know that you have been waiting for your child's IEP. But we have many children to serve, and we will get around to it as soon as we can."

"Your child's record contains professional reports which are too technical for you to understand. We would be happy to interpret them to you, but we cannot give you copies."

When parents hear statements like these when they try to get information or services from school people, they feel helpless. They need to know what to do to get the response and action they are looking for. At this point you understand some things you may not have understood or been aware of before. You now know more about the potential problems in getting services from school systems than most people, even those inside the system. You know the common educational myths and the various ways school systems deal with parents. While all this information about possible pitfalls and stumbling blocks will be useful, it may make you feel a little timid or reluctant about setting forth to right what is wrong with your child's educational plan.

Remember that you will probably not have to deal with all the problems detailed in this book. Your child's program may already be a good one or need only a few small changes. As an informed and confident parent, you are in a better position to be a good judge of the quality of the current program, and can thereby feel more secure about your child's educational program. Informed? "Yes," you may be saying, "I may now know more than perhaps I wanted to know or was prepared for. But confident? How can I be confident in dealing with all these experts who always have a fast answer to give me? I don't have the skills to keep up with them."

This chapter will demonstrate that you do in fact have skills which you regularly use in your day-to-day living, but which you, confused by the myths and lacking knowledge about the system, didn't apply in your inter-actions with school people. Furthermore, the book will help you to strengthen and refine those skills in ways that will prepare you to deal effectively with people at every level of the educational system.

Perhaps you do not think of yourself as someone who deals with systems or people who provide services, but you do it often, maybe even every day. If you manage a household (or live in one), are employed or run a business, have friends, make purchases, pay bills, belong to a club, or, in short, interact with other people in routine and sometimes complex ways, you are already using many of the same skills that will help you to obtain your goals when dealing with the educational system.

Check yourself against this list of skills:

1. Verbal Communication Skills: Have you used the phone to accomplish any of the following tasks?
   a. Changing or canceling an appointment
   b. Registering a complaint
   c. Persuading someone to change his opinion or intention
   d. Selling or buying something
2. Written Communication Skills: Have you written a letter doing any of the following things?
   a. Sharing news or information
   b. Requesting information
   c. Saying thank you
   d. Registering a complaint about a product

3. Planning Ability: Have you planned any of the following things?
   a. A menu
   b. A party
   c. A trip or vacation

4. Ability to Keep Long-Term Commitments: Have you ever signed any of the following kinds of contracts or agreements?
   a. Purchasing an appliance on time
   b. Buying a house
   c. Taking dancing or driving lessons

5. Self-Confidence and Assertiveness: Have you ever returned a product in person because it had one of these flaws?
   a. Not as advertised
   b. Defective
   c. Delivered too late
   d. Wrong size

6. Interpersonal Skills: Have you ever had to work with one or more people in any of these situations?
   a. Planning an event or activity
   b. Reaching a decision together
   c. Resolving an argument
   d. Solving a problem

Even if you have not done everything on this list, it is likely that you have done most of the items.

When you did these things, were you successful? Did you get the appointment changed or the right item in the color, size, or working order you wanted? Even if you didn't get what you wanted, you learned something, such as that old receipts and check stubs are necessary, that you should have asked for the store manager, or that taking a friend with you for moral support can be helpful. Learning something or knowing better is a kind of success because you increase your chances for success in the future. This may be a small satisfaction when you feel you have failed, but with more opportunities, thought, and time you can become a "pro" at getting satisfaction.

All this may be fine for buying a bathrobe or for getting an adjustment on a phone bill, you are thinking. There you are dealing with salespeople or service people. But we are supposed to be talking about education, and, after all, educators aren't sales or service people—or are they?

Educators are most definitely service people. Their job is to deliver a service to your child for twelve or more years, a service which should benefit your child and which you can approve of and support. Keep in mind that everyone who works in the school system, from the superintendent to the custodian, was hired to perform a service to the children of your town or community. As for being salespeople, some parents who have had a bad experience can tell you about the "bill of goods" they were sold by school people. So the skills you have used with salespeople may be appropriate to use with some school people on certain occasions.

"How will I know if the service is the right one for my child? It's easy to know when a vacuum cleaner isn't working, but education is more complicated. I'm no educational expert." You begin to know if the educational program or service is working by asking yourself these questions about it:

1. Has the educational program been explained in a way I can understand?

2. Is my child's Individualized Education Program being followed?

3. Is he getting the special help in the amounts promised?

4. Is he making any progress?

5. Is he progressing at a satisfactory rate?

6. Is he making progress outside of school (at home and in the community)?

7. Does the program have drawbacks or limitations (too many stairs, too few school hours)?

You may have some "I don't know" answers to the questions, but that's okay because now you know where to start looking. Your job is to find the answers to the best of your ability. In doing so, you will probably develop your own questions for the school people. You may end up with "yes" answers, in which case you can relax a little and feel good about your child's service. If your answers are "no," however, you should get ready to go over the IEP again, either to be sure it's actually in operation or to change it if it's not meeting your child's needs. (All the time you are doing this you are alert to myths that could hinder your effectiveness. If necessary, you will read chapter two again to give yourself confidence and to remind yourself that you are one kind of expert—an expert in information about your child.)

Yes, it is much easier to judge the effectiveness of your vacuum cleaner than your child's school program. But by observing your child and looking at his performance and school history over the years, you will begin to make judgments, perhaps weak and tenuous at first, but stronger as you gain confidence in your own natural ability to evaluate your child and his progress in school.

"But if I am convinced that my child's program is insufficient, I'm afraid I'll get emotional when I ask for things for him. After all, my child is much more important to me than anything I would buy." Of course you will feel a lot of emotion. Recall what was said in chapter two: Your feelings for your child make you a concerned and committed parent. Without them, you would be a poor advocate and an even poorer parent. When you use and control your feelings, they can be your best asset.

Consider how you react in your everyday experience to a defective product or service: Have you ever found that when you became angry about it you also became determined to get satisfaction? Your controlled emotion may have kept you going through numerous phone calls, letters, and trips to the store. Emotion can be the carefully stoked fire that keeps you going to the finish line. You can control and channel it into successful dealings with the school system.

Unlike your everyday purchases or services, education goes on for a long time. Only when your child reaches the upper age limit for special education do the services end.

At any time during your child's school years you can request a review of his program and, if necessary, a new or revised program. Your skills will be put to good use. For all of you will deal directly and formally with the system at least once a year, during the IEP Annual Review, and you should have a number of informal dealings throughout the year, particularly with the teachers and specialists. For some, you will be working with the system over months as you advocate for the right plan for your child. So let's look at the skills you have and see how to use them to meet your child's needs.

USING THE TELEPHONE

Most people use the phone every day to make personal and professional appointments, call friends and acquaintances, order services or products, or have bills corrected. They call physicians, politicians, radio stations, or garages, expecting a response within a reasonable time. Yet nowhere are people as timid or apologetic as they are apt to be when calling representatives of the school system. They will tolerate being put on hold, waiting for a return call, or even getting no return call at all with a humility that is astonishing. Even on the telephone they exhibit the behavior of the old school pupil who is willing to wait indefinitely without complaint. When they do finally get through or get a return call, they are apt to be more grateful than the situation warrants. And if they make a complaint, they use language so apologetic and weak that their complaint is hardly recognizable as one. For example, a weak complaint to the special education director might sound like this: "Oh, Ms. Danielson, you are really good to return my call. I'm sorry to bother you at school where you are so busy. I hate to trouble you, but Josh's bus isn't coming to pick him up until forty-five minutes after school starts. Can anything be done to get it here a little earlier? I'd be so grateful if you could help."

Parents who talk like this are usually afraid of rocking the boat. Yet if this parent doesn't start being more assertive, Josh may end up spending as much time traveling to and from school as he does in school, especially if he leaves school early so the bus can be available at the regular closing time for the regular students. (Yes, some parents accept the early return, as well as the late pick-up.)

How would you talk to the telephone company if they continued to overcharge you? You would certainly not apologize for their error. You would probably make it quite clear to the company representative that there was an overcharge that you expected to be corrected immediately. In the same way, Josh's parents should make it clear that there is an error—Josh is being deprived of the full school day to which he is entitled—and that an immediate correction by the school system is expected.

If, like other parents, you feel intimidated by school people and act humble and apologetic, you can begin to change by making a firm resolve to be more assertive. (Remember that assertiveness need not mean aggression or rudeness. See Appendix A for books about developing assertiveness.) Of course, resolution alone will not make you assertive. Timid behaviors are habits that have grown strong over time; to undo them you must practice new, assertive behaviors.

The best place to start is in private rehearsal. Imagine the phone call you want to make or recall one you made earlier with the changes you would make:

1. What do you want to get as a result of the call? (I want Josh picked up on time.)

2. What difficulties or roadblocks might you expect in making the call? (The special education director won't be in. They'll put me on hold and forget about me. Or the director will tell me it isn't possible. She might get angry, or maybe I'll get upset or angry.)

3. Anything else? (List other concerns or expectations you can think of.)

4. Now think of things you can say (you can write them down, too): *first*, to yourself (Josh has a right to a full day; I will speak up without hanging back or being timid; I will not be put off; the issue must be dealt with immedi-

ately); *second,* to the person you are calling (identifying yourself again, stating the problem, stressing its urgency, and stating your expectation that she will resolve it); and *third,* to the secretary or receptionist who answers the phone (say who you want to talk to and who you are; if the special education director is not available, state why you are calling and stress the urgency, and say where you can be reached and when).

Now think of what they might say to you and how to deal with problematic responses (it's fair play to imagine the worst possible responses just in case you find them). First consider what to say if you can't reach the person you are calling right away:

Secretary:	The special education director isn't in. May I take a message?
Mrs. Goldman:	Yes. (Provides information: name, phone number, and problem) When can I expect her return call?
Secretary:	I will give her the message as soon as she's out of the meeting.
Mrs. Goldman:	Please tell her I will be waiting for her call.

or

Secretary:	The special education director is out of town today but will be back to-morrow. I'll give her the message first thing in the morning.
Mrs. Goldman:	Okay. Please tell her I will be waiting for her call then at this number . . .

or

Secretary:	The special education director is a very busy person. I don't know when she will have the time to call you.
Mrs. Goldman:	Please tell her I am waiting for her call. If I do not hear from her today, I will call again first thing tomorrow morning.

Then consider the range of possible responses (best to worst) from the school person:

Sp. Ed. Director:	Hello, Mrs. Goldman. This is Ms. Danielson. I didn't know Josh was being picked up late. Of course he should be picked up on time. I'll speak to the person in charge of transportation as soon as we hang up. If there's any problem, I'll get back to you; otherwise, expect him to be picked up on time.

or

Sp. Ed. Director:	We've been having a problem organizing transportation. Can you give me a few days to see what I can do?
Mrs. Goldman:	Yes, but this has already gone on for a few days (weeks). I'll call you at the end of the week if things haven't improved.

or

Sp. Ed. Director:	Look, Mrs. Goldman, we don't have enough buses to get everyone to school on time. We give first priority to the regular kids who can really benefit from school.
Mrs. Goldman:	If you need to stagger the bus schedule, it should be done fairly so everyone has a full school day.
Sp. Ed. Director:	(Growing more irate) We can't change the whole schedule for one kid. Josh's class doesn't do much anyway.
Mrs. Goldman:	(Controlled) Ms. Danielson, when I called I thought we had a transportation problem. Are you telling me the program is poor as well?
Sp. Ed. Director:	No, I'm not. I'm telling you I can't do anything about the bus.

| *Mrs. Goldman:* | Can you tell me who can? Can the school superintendent do anything? |
| *Sp. Ed. Director:* | I don't know. Excuse me, I have another call coming in. |

These examples, plus your own, give you an idea of the range of possible responses, good and bad. Being prepared to deal with difficulties makes it possible to manage them when they arise. As you imagine these and other examples, think them through and act them out: "If she says this, then I'll say that"; or "What if she says. . . . Mmmm! What will I say then? Oh, I know . . ."; and "If things get out of hand, I'll find a way to end the conversation and call later when I'm feeling calmer."

When you rehearse a potential situation, you are developing those new behaviors that you need and will use later on. Practice (alone or with the help of a friend or family member) will strengthen the assertive behaviors you want in your package of advocacy skills. With a little bit of private practice, you may feel you are ready for a live public performance. With any notes you need in front of you, you pick up the phone and perform what you have rehearsed.

The phone is a good place to start being assertive with school people because you only have to be concerned with what you say. You don't have to worry about how you look, where you should sit, or if anyone is noticing that your knees are knocking, you are chain-smoking, or you have bitten your nails to the quick. Your attention is focused only on what you say and they say. Also, you can close the conversation and make a fast exit if you become too nervous: You can invent an excuse, a polite social lie, such as your boss has come into the office or the doorbell is ringing insistently.

In your first performance, you may or may not get what you want. Keep in mind that this is only the first step in your new approach to getting services. If you didn't get what you wanted, you have some material to review and evaluate:

Were you able to get past the secretary? Why not? Did you stress the need as strongly as you should have? What can you say next time that will make a stronger case? Did the other person's statements leave you angry and speechless (or intimidated)? What will you say next time?

You now have some idea of what treatment to expect when you call the school system, so you can decide what you will do in the next call. Back to rehearsal and practice again. You are developing a routine of strengthening your new assertive behaviors in a series of stages:

- expectations
- private practice
- live performance
- examination and evaluation of your performance and the school person's

Repeat this routine every time you deal with the school system, and you will find new ways to improve your performance and increase your effectiveness.

Whenever your child has a school-related problem— her educational needs, including transportation and lunch, are not being met—you should be ready to pick up the phone and call the school people. You also use the phone to make contact for sharing information, scheduling meetings, and, in later calls, reminding people that the problem still remains and that you are waiting for them to take action to solve it.

It is up to you to make certain that your child's needs are not neglected. If you had an elderly, ailing parent living with you when your heating system went off because of a power failure, you would watch the thermometer like a hawk and inform the power company that there was a person in your home who was at risk because of the situation. You would not be likely to wait without complaint for very long. Now, while the periods of reasonable waiting time for the power company to restore service and for the school to develop a beneficial program for your child differ in the critical amounts, time is a real issue. Delays of weeks or months can be crucial for your child's welfare. In a very real way, children with handicaps are at risk if they do not receive the basic educational and special services they need. The telephone is one of your tools to keep school personnel on their toes; use it with them just as you do with others in your round of daily activities.

If you are put on hold and abandoned, do not fade away because the school people are too busy or not interested. Instead, hang up, call back, and tell them you were on hold for ten minutes; ask that they please put you through to the person you called. That is, treat them the same way you treat the department store personnel when you are having a bill adjusted.

If you are getting upset during the phone call, always keep in mind that you can terminate the call at any time. Being aware of this can sometimes help you stay calm long enough to complete the call. But if you feel you are working up to saying something you will regret, get off the phone, but not by banging down the receiver. Instead, use the polite social lie because you may have to see this person again and you don't want him to have any real criticism of you that will interfere with developing a good program for your child. Always save the polite social lie only for extreme cases when you feel you must remove yourself from a situation in which you are about to become either aggressive or intimidated. It is an excuse given to the school system to buy you time to regain your control or confidence. In many cases, the school people will suspect, if not realize, what you are doing and may even welcome an end to a conversation that promises to become unmanageable. You, of course, never lie or distort the information about your child: That is one of your most important contributions to the IEP process and must not be tampered with. But using a social lie to prevent an argument and maintain cordial relations with school people can be wise strategy in some circumstances.

If you are waiting for a return call, you need not hover over the phone all day for several days just on the chance someone will call back. On your first call state the times you can be reached, for example, before noon or after 2:00 p.m. (after all, you may have to leave the office or go out to buy groceries). If in a day or two your call is not returned, you call back, telling them you are still waiting, and ask to be put through or given a reason for the delay and a time when the call will be returned.

If you are not getting through after a reasonable few days, ask the person who is answering the phone whether it is necessary to write a letter to get to speak to the person you have been calling. If the question by itself is not enough to bring the desired person to the phone, sit down and write the letter. That will often bring results because requests you make by letter are stronger and harder to ignore than spoken requests.

The telephone should be your usual means of contact with the schools. In most cases, it will bring the desired results or at least an improvement in the situation, which may be satisfactory. You increase the chances of getting results by sharpening your everyday telephone skills. But when you know that you have made a reasonable effort to contact and share information with the schools, and using the telephone isn't doing the job, you then turn to another basic skill—writing.

WRITING LETTERS

Letters are another basic tool, one that is generally used less frequently than the telephone. Most of you will probably need to write only a few letters in your career as an educational advocate for your child; some of you may never need to pick up the pen; but, for a few of you, the pen (or typewriter) will become a crucial instrument in getting services for your child.

For those of you who write letters as part of your regular job or for social or volunteer activities, writing letters to school people may present little difficulty.

However, many parents seldom have the need to write formal letters except for the letter of complaint to a business or shop. Furthermore, letters to school people may involve more than straightforward complaints, although complaints will generally be the reason you write to them.

"Writing letters to the school system! Who? Me? I'd make a mess of it. I wouldn't know what to say." Your concern is understandable. But is a little of that concern coming from the old school pupil whose writing in English class came back red-penciled, corrected, slashed, commented on, and graded? You didn't worry about being graded on the phone; instead, you were concerned about what you said, and what response you got. And since you are no longer the school pupil, you need not worry about things like penmanship, creativity, fancy language, and form; instead, you are concerned with facts— who, what, when, and where, and with getting the services your child needs. The kind of simple, direct letters you may have written to the gas company or the Better Business Bureau will serve as well for the school personnel.

Let's look at a sample letter:

> 110 Main Street
> Your Town, State 11111
> October 13, 1980

Ms. Betty Danielson
Director of Special Education
Local School
Your Town, State 11111

Dear Ms. Danielson:

Josh's bus is coming to pick him up one hour after school starts. He is missing a lot of school and he should be in school for a full day.

I have called you six times (September 22 and 29, and October 2, 7, 9, and 10) and was not able to reach you. I left messages with your secretary but you have not called me back.

Will you please arrange to have him picked up on time and call me so that I'll know everything has

been taken care of. You can reach me at work
(555-1023) from 8:30 to 3:30.

Sincerely,

[signature]
Julia Goldman

This letter is short and simple, but it does the job. It gives
the information about the problem (transportation), the
parent's past efforts to have the problem corrected (including the number of phone calls and dates), and where
the parent can be reached. It also states what the parent
wants, in this case, the bus to come on time.

Here is another example of a letter to be used when
phone calls have not done the job:

12 Broadway
Your Town, State 22222
January 5, 1981

Mr. Vincent Larsen
Principal
Local School
Your Town, State 22222

Dear Mr. Larsen:

My daughter, Ellen, does not have an Individualized Education Program yet. I spoke to her teacher
in October about setting up a meeting. Then I
spoke to you at the end of November and you said
you would set up a meeting in December, but it
never happened. Now January is starting and Ellen
still has no IEP.

Please set up a meeting right away so that Ellen
can have the program she needs and to which she is
entitled. I will be waiting to hear from you.

Sincerely,

[signature]
Basil Hunter

This letter, also short and simple, reminds the principal of previous conversations in which the parent tried to get the school people to do their job (to set up the meeting to develop the Individualized Education Program), and of the time that has gone by without any action by them. It also requests action from the principal. Mr. Hunter could have included the specific dates on which he talked to the teacher and principal about getting the IEP process started. Doing that might have been a little more impressive and businesslike, but this letter has enough information to do the job.

The next letter could follow phone calls or meetings when a school person has said something which the parent believes to be in violation of the law. This letter is a request for confirmation, meaning that the parent writes what she thinks she heard the educator say, and asks that the educator confirm or deny his statement. The following letter is an example:

3636 Park Street
Apartment 2B
Your Town, State 33333
April 19, 1981

Dr. Gregory Simonn
Superintendent
Local School
Your Town, State 33333

Dear Dr. Simonn:

When we met in your office on April 7 to discuss the location of my son Russell's program in the basement of Greenwood Junior High School and my request to have the program transferred to the main floor of the school, you said some things that bothered me.

I understood you to say that it would be impossible to move the class because all the other classrooms are being used by the regular students and

that the lighting in the basement is adequate because children in that class aren't able to read.

Did I understand correctly? Are you planning to
keep Russell's class in the basement?

Please let me hear from you as soon as possible
since I am very concerned about Russell's program.

Sincerely,

[signature]
Dolly LaVigna

The request for confirmation is a tricky letter to write. It
should be used only to advance your cause and not just to
vent your anger or distress when you suspect that you or
your child has been insulted. (Usually a parent's direct
looks during meetings will put an end to careless comments.) When you write this kind of letter, you are in fact
giving the school person the opportunity to deny, re-
phrase, or qualify his statements, and to reassure you that
efforts are being made to resolve the problem. Since
your letter is a record of statements you think you
heard, the educator is often eager to write his "you-have-
misunderstood-me" letter, also for the record. That return letter usually includes a statement of the school
person's efforts to correct the situation. What may have
been an unpleasant situation for you now can be turned
to your advantage. The administrator's written intention
or promise, signed and dated, can be used by you as a
lever to improve your child's program. You can hold the
administrator accountable for his own statements, which
are now a matter of record: The return letter, carefully
preserved in your file (see p. 117), is that record.

Some parents will need to write a letter rejecting the
IEP. These parents may have done a marvelous job of
advocating, but they were unable to reach agreement with
school people about the IEP because the school people
did not share the parent's views, were not able to write

the program's goals in precise language, or resisted the parents' requests for budgetary reasons. Here is an example of a letter rejecting the IEP:

5 1st Street
Your Town, State 44444
June 17, 1981

Dr. Winona Brown
Chairperson, IEP Team
Local High School
Your Town, State 44444

Dear Dr. Brown:
    I want you to know I am rejecting my son Arnold's IEP which I received in yesterday's mail. The program does not match the items we agreed upon at the meeting. For example, speech therapy is scheduled once per week for fifteen minutes instead of three times per week for half an hour, and the objectives for Arnold's reading program are fuzzy. The plan does not meet Arnold's needs.
    What is the next step? I can meet with you during June or July to see if the program can be corrected and we can come to agreement. I will be waiting to hear from you.

Sincerely,

[signature]
George Watson

cc: Parents' Advocacy Center

Mr. Watson makes it clear that he is rejecting the IEP and backs up his rejection with some specific complaints about the program. He indicates he is willing to work with the school to try to reach an agreement; he wants to negotiate further, rather than move immediately to confrontation. His letter not only informs the school people, but also stands as a record of his quick and interested response to the IEP and of his willingness to pursue the issue to some mutual agreement.

None of the four sample letters is fancy or long; they are short, clear, simply worded, and to the point. The best letter is the shortest one necessary to do the job. Also, short letters are often the first ones to get read. When school people receive letters several pages in length, they sometimes set them aside until they have more time. There are, however, some basic, simple mechanics to writing a businesslike letter to schools.

Your address should always be included on your letter so the school people can contact you easily.

Dates are important, so always put a date on your letter. When you have need to review your file on your child's educational program, you will want to know when you did what, or how long it took the school to do something about the problem. Next year or even later this year you may not remember in which month you wrote the letter.

The school person's full name, title, and location at the top of your letter is not only polite and businesslike, it is information you need for your records and future activities, and which you can share with people you may want to ask to help you deal with the school, such as representatives from parent organizations or legal advocacy organizations. You want to make it easy for them to advocate with you: By sharing your letters, they will not waste time trying to track down school people.

But what if you don't know a person's full name or title? Call the school and ask for it:

> *Mr. Watson:* Would you give me Mrs. Brown's full name, please.
>
> *Secretary:* Do you mean Miss Rachel Brown at Southern Junior High School?
>
> *Mr. Watson:* No, I thought Mrs. Brown was at the high school where my son is a student.
>
> *Secretary:* Then you must mean Dr. Winona Brown.

> *Mr. Watson:*   I think so, but this person is chair-
> person of the committee for my son's
> educational program.
>
> *Secretary:*   That would be Dr. Brown, who chairs
> all high school special education pro-
> grams.
>
> *Mr. Watson:*   Good. What is her official address?

Don't be afraid to ask how the name is spelled; some names have very strange spellings. And don't be timid about taking up people's time to get the information right. Your correctly addressed letter will expedite the process. A letter addressed simply to Mrs. Brown could go to the wrong person or get lost in the school system. Dr. Winona Brown will not only be pleased to see you know her correct name and position, but will also know that you are a businesslike advocate.

The information in the letter is just that—information. It is not opinion, rumor, or hearsay. You deal in facts like dates, people, services poorly given or denied, and what you want from the school system. You write in simple, clear language to prevent misunderstanding, and keep the letter short to encourage the recipient to read it immediately (since you are in suspense while waiting for an answer). If you are not sure that your letter says what you want it to say, read it to a friend or relative in person or over the phone. Discuss it. If it doesn't express what you meant to say, enlist the other person's help to get it right. Just don't fuss excessively or forever; a simple letter will do the job.

The closing of your letter should include your signature and your name (typed or clearly printed underneath your signature). If you want to be called, add your phone number (home or office). In short, make it very easy for the school people to know who you are and where to reach you. Your carefully composed letter provides no excuse for delay in contacting you.

Should your letter be typed or written? After you have reread the rough copy of your letter and made your corrections (perhaps you deleted or revised a sentence which sounded sarcastic, included some important dates, or restated your request more strongly), you may find yourself worrying about legibility and neatness, especially if you don't type. Ideally, good typing is better, since it's prettier, cleaner, and easier to read; but it is not necessary to do the job. If you have a friend or child who types, enlist her help in preparing the letter. But if your collection of available family and friends consists of bad, worse, and awful typists, a carefully handwritten or hand-printed letter is far better than a typed letter full of errors and crossed-out words. As always, you want the school people to immediately understand the problem and act on it.

Your Copy of Your Letter

Whether you type or write your letter, always keep a clear copy for yourself. You can use a carbon, or, even easier, have your letter reproduced on a copy machine. When you are dealing with the school people, you need to know what you have said and when you said it. You should not rely on the school system to provide you with that information. Just as you get and keep a receipt as a record of your purchase when you buy something, you also keep a record of your correspondence. Your copy of the letter is a receipt to keep as a record of your request or complaint. No matter how rushed you are to get the letter out, never mail it without keeping a clear copy for your personal file, one sharp enough to make another clear copy to share with other people who want to assist you in your advocacy efforts. (See the section Using Your Allies in this chapter.) All of your letters, sent and received, will become an important part of your records.

Certified Mail

Certified mail means that the post office makes a special event of your letter and gives you a record, in the form of a post card, of when the letter was delivered and who received and signed for it. Some people use certified mail for every letter they send to school systems and agencies. However, certified mail not only requires more of your time, energy, and money, it also sets a certain tone: It implies that the school personnel will only take action when they are tracked down or pushed. Unless you have strong reason to expect resistance, the first letter can go out by regular mail; it will usually receive a response. But if you do not get one after a reasonable time and a follow-up telephone call reminding them you are waiting, send out your second letter by certified mail. (See the section on Special Records later in this chapter.) In general, the more collaborative your relationship is with the school, the more you will use the phone and regular mail; the more strained, complicated, or adversarial your relationship is, the greater the need for certified mail.

Formal Copies to Others

When the school system is slow to take action, you may want to let the school people know that you are sending copies of your letters to others interested in helping your child get school services. There is a standard form that will indicate on your letter that you are doing this. (See letter of rejection, page 112.) In the bottom left-hand corner of your letter show that you are sending carbon copies (cc's) by writing:

> cc: Parents' Advocacy Center
> Rep. Mark Forsyth
> Mrs. Valerie Perske

Here the parent is sending copies to three places. You may wish to send only one or you may wish to send more, depending on how many people you think should know about the action you are taking.

Carbon copies can often help to move resistant administrators to action. However, if you have a good relationship with the school people, you may want to hold back on using carbon copies. Like certified mail, they imply that the school people need pushing to do their job. You can always make copies of your old correspondence later on and send them to whomever you choose. For your records, you should note who has copies of your letters.

KEEPING RECORDS: YOURS AND THEIRS

"What do I know about keeping records? I'm not a clerk or accountant. As for a file, the few pieces of paper I have could fit in a standard envelope with room enough left over to hold all my household bills!"

In fact, just about all of you keep some records. Don't you save your canceled checks, paid receipts, and tax forms, write appointments on a calendar, have a photo album or baby book, or even save old matchbooks from restaurants and bars you've visited? If so, then you do keep records of events and activities in your life.

"But they're not in a file or a filing system," you say. Are they in a drawer, a shoe box, an album, or an envelope? Can you find them when you want them? Then you already have a filing system which can do the job for you and your child. But you need to know what you should be keeping and collecting for your child's special 94-142 file.

Records You Already Have

Have you over the years collected any of these things:

- notes from *teachers,* either on pieces of paper or in books that go back and forth from school to home?
- notes from *specialists* both inside and outside the school system?
- notes *you* have taken before, during, or after your visit to your child's school or your phone conversations with the school people?
- notes from *anyone else* which describe your child's achievements and failures, progress or lack of progress?
- samples of your *child's* school work or creations from past years?
- reports from *camps* or recreation and community activities which describe his skills and needs?

- reports and evaluations from *doctors* and other medical specialists?
- *school* reports, including report cards, evaluations, and educational plans for your child?
- letters which the *schools* have sent to you—notices of meetings to develop your child's education programs, notices of suspension or exclusion of your child from school, and denials of your requests for better services and placement?
- copies of letters *you* have written to the school system—letters of complaint or request?
- letters (or copies) written in your child's behalf by an *outside professional*, advocacy organization, or lawyer?

Many of you will have some of these records; a few of you who are already active in your planning and advocacy may have practically everything on the list; but some of you have nothing except for a few of your child's schoolwork papers. That's okay: You can now begin to save and to collect the various papers, evaluations, and documents you need. Make a list of what you have, and prepare to add to it. Some of the basic items for your file are letters (or copies of letters) which you have received or written, copies of special education laws and regulations, and materials on your own and your child's rights from advocacy, parent, or legal organizations.

How useful will all this information be to you? If you are lucky, you may use very little of it. However, even lucky parents can't predict which information they will need. If you have to work hard to get the school system to comply with the law in providing services to your child, you will need every paper you can get, so save everything. When the time comes, you will be glad that you have created a record file which is as comprehensive as you can make it. After all, in managing your bills, you don't save some of your canceled checks and throw the rest away because you know that if the department store makes a mistake in billing you, your canceled checks are the information and evidence you need to prove you have paid your bill. Information is help and power. Here's how to get more.

School and Agency Records

Schools and other agencies (hospitals, clinics, camps, and special services) have stacks of records. Sharing records between agencies is a common practice. Parents are generally asked to sign a release for a "mysterious" document—an evaluation, test result, or report—to allow one agency to send a record to another. The document is "mysterious" when the parents are not given an opportunity to read and review the information they are being requested to release to some other agency or to the school. When parents cooperate by signing releases without seeing the documents, they are acting out of ignorance, allowing the professionals to share and reproduce information that may be harmful or insulting to the child and also to the family. In order to be a responsible parent and advocate, you must know what information is being given out on your child, and that means reading the records.

In the past, a number of assumptions and prejudicial statements were entered into students' school records, such as "antisocial child," "hostile parent," "father may have a drinking problem," or "student lacks skills and should be tracked for lower level vocational program." Statements like these were based on educators' impressions, often with very little (if any) evidence to back them up.* However, the statements stayed in the students' files,

---

*Professional educators aren't the only ones guilty of occasional inaccurate records. Physicians and other specialists also prepare records with inaccuracies. Carefully read all records for mistakes. One parent reported that her child's last medical evaluation report stated that he had had multiple hospital evaluations when, in fact, he had had one (this was an informational error) and that the child could do only the most rudimentary arithmetic when, in fact, the child had unusual math skills (this was misinformation resulting from the difficulties of a stranger assessing the child in a strange environment). Parents need to correct such inaccuracies by writing out the corrections and formally requesting they be inserted into the child's file.

and often teachers, looking at the files, decided that a student or parent was a troublemaker and treated the person accordingly. This type of treatment had an effect on the students' programs and progress. Parents never saw these statements so they were unable to fight back.

Now, however, P.L. 94-142 gives parents the right to read reports, to correct the record by having the school amend it or by placing a statement prepared by the parents into it, to limit the access of other people to their child's records, and to have copies of the records (for which the parents may have to pay). Students over the age of eighteen are also entitled to read their school records. Not only do these rights guarantee that parents can have the information they need to be good advocates, they have also caused those educators who used to write biased and occasionally libelous statements into records to be careful about what they write down. With the coming of P.L. 94-142, a lot of records were cleaned up. Chances are you will not see judgments about "cold, disinterested parents" in your child's file nowadays. If you do, you must have that file corrected so it will be factual and accurate.

Some schools may resist your efforts to read and copy your child's records. You must keep repeating to yourself and to them, "I have a right to these records." If you are timid, rehearse what you will do and say before you go to the school. If the school people resist, go back with a copy of the regulations or a statement from your state Department of Education notifying you of your legal right to read the records. If they continue to resist, write your simple but effective letter to the superintendent, describing your efforts and asking her to make the records available to you.

Eventually you will be sitting in the school office with the complete (cumulative) record in front of you. (Make sure you have the complete school record for your child and not a summary record, which is a partial record.) You have brought your list of what you already have in your own file, and are about to review the school file to see what is in there and what you will want for your file. You will take notes on some documents; you will see others which you want in your file or which are too long for you to read and understand in the time you will be in the school office. In reading the file you may realize that some of the documents are missing, such as an old speech evaluation, the teacher's reports from 1975, or a letter from you which you asked to be included in your child's file. Make a note of the missing item(s) and inform the school people that the file is incomplete. You make your list of the school file. Now you have two lists:

Home File	*School File*
IEP 1978	Teacher Reports 1974, 1976, 1977
IEP 1980	
Penmanship Papers 1975	IEP 1978, 1979, 1980
Camp Summertime Report 1979	Intelligence Test Results 1978
Telephone Notes 1980	Speech Therapist's Evaluation 1979
My letter on transportation problems, 1980	Psychologist's Report 1980
Note on missing items	

When you have finished, decide what you want, perhaps the 1979 IEP (you should have had a copy anyway), the results of the intelligence testing, and the evaluations of the speech therapist and psychologist. You might also want a teacher's report from 1976 to show your spouse because you think it contains some statements which should be removed.

When you approach the principal or her assistant to ask for copies, you may encounter some resistance:

" I'm afraid the person who does the copying is tied up now. Perhaps another time."

"Now, Mrs. Carroll, what do you want these reports for? They are full of professional language which you can't really understand. I'll tell you what you want to know about your child."

"We can't be spending the taxpayers' money to reproduce all this stuff for dissatisfied parents." (Remind the principal that you are also a taxpayer, and that in the recent past many parents were paying taxes to support regular education while their own handicapped children were denied educational services by the school system.)

"This teacher's (or psychologist's) note is a personal communication. It can't be copied or even removed from the file."

First respond with reasonableness to these attempts to limit your access to your child's records:

"I can wait a reasonable time for the copies and will be happy to return tomorrow or the next day when the copies are made."

"I will pay a reasonable cost for the copies."

"I would like to make a reasonable effort to read the reports and prepare a list of questions on what I don't understand."

"The professionals' notes in my child's file are part of her record, and, therefore, I am entitled to copies."

By presenting yourself as the informed, committed, and businesslike advocate, you will get the copies of the records you want. You may have to resort to your telephone and writing skills to get them (adding phone notes and copies of your letters to your growing file), but your persistence will pay off.

Medical records from hospitals and clinics may be hard to get. In some states (but not all) patients have the right to information. But your physician or other health professional may resist giving you access to the full medical record. You can, however, request and expect a summary report on your child's condition relevant to her educational program. Some medical professionals are comfortable only when they are sending information to other professionals* (from the clinic to the school, for example) because of their own "mere parents" myths. This practice is a put-down, but remember that *once the information or report is in the school file*, you have the right to see it and have a copy.

When you have begun to collect the various records we have discussed, the shoe box you had in mind for the job may be looking smaller and smaller. How will you organize all these papers into a manageable file?

Organizing Your Records—The Best Method

Any container (large manila envelope, shoe box, small carton, drawer, or file box) that will hold the papers you have collected with room for more is fine for the job. But if setting up a fancy system helps you to feel businesslike and confident, then do it. The key to a well-organized file is access—your records are in one place and you can put your hands on just the paper you want in a few minutes. Then what is the best way to organize your file for this kind of access and efficiency?

The best filing method is the one that works for you. Remember, it's your file and you are the one who will be using it. You can set it up alphabetically, by year, or by category (schools, specialists, camps, and other). If you are good at remembering names, you can file from A to Z; if you remember times and events better, you can file by years. There is no one system for filing.

A *log* (a bound or loose-leaf notebook) is essential to your system; it will help you remember whom you con-

---

*So firm is this professional-to-professional communication that one parent who asked for a letter explaining why his son was being rejected by a special hospital school program was told by the social worker that she could not send out such a letter without a release from the parent. The social worker realized she was asking the father to release a letter to himself. Her solution was to get the release and send the letter to the public school special education director with a copy to the parent!

tacted, when you contacted them, and what you and they said. Any time you deal with the school system or other agencies, make an entry in your log. Your entry should include these items:

- date
- name of person you contacted (by telephone, letter, or visit)
- person's agency and position or title
- topics discussed, promises made, and deadlines for action

It will also help to keep the names, titles, and phone numbers of people you are and will be dealing with on the inside cover or the first page of your log. These should include the following:

- your school superintendent
- your special education director
- specialists who are working or have worked with your child
- resources for information and support

You may not have all of these when you start; you will be adding as you continue your work in your child's behalf.

You may not need or even use all the information you collect for your files. But you are prepared to deal with almost any issue that may arise. The prepared and informed parent is the effective advocate.

Special Records

If in your advocacy efforts you are constantly meeting resistance or indifference, you may want to resort to *certified letters* (see p. 115). Since the post card which serves as your record that the letter was delivered can be easily lost, staple or pin it to your log or folder as soon as you receive it.

Pictures are a special kind of record. Very few of you will ever need to take pictures, but there are a few cases in which they are necessary, and they are very powerful records. If your child has been physically abused (bruised, bitten, or otherwise injured), if your child is on medication and beginning to look downright sickly, or if your child is rollerskating despite the school's insistence that his motor skills are poor, you should seriously consider taking a photograph of your child's condition.

This is a hard thing for parents to do in cases of abuse. They naturally prefer to take happy and attractive pictures of their children, and they want to forget how their children looked when they were abused. Usually, however, parents can't forget: They keep their mental pictures, but they can't use their memories as hard facts. Pictures are especially necessary when the children involved cannot communicate, and, therefore, cannot provide testimony in their own behalf. If you ever find your child in such a situation, take pictures, as heartbreaking as that may be, and you will have strong evidence to prevent a reoccurence for your child and other children.

One parent regretted the fact that she took no pictures of her disturbed and brain-injured son when she had to remove him from camp. He had "acted out," and, in being restrained by a staff person, suffered multiple bruises about the head and face. She was concerned that an unqualified staff person who had injured her son was allowed to continue to work with handicapped people, but she had collected no evidence to back up her complaint.

Another parent of a child in a state institution was able to bring about a review and change of her child's medication simply by showing pictures of him in his deteriorated state and before the medication to a physician outside the institution, who took action to get the child off medication. The child's appearance and health immediately improved.

Pictures, home movies, and audiotapes of happy events and activities can be important evidence in making a case for your child's skills. For example, if the school people insist that your child's motor skills are poor, pull out your snapshots (or have the meeting set up for your home movies) of your child roller skating or cross-country skiing. If they minimize your child's language skills, play audiotapes you have made at home which demonstrate your child's competence. When you have clear evidence of your child's capabilities, use that evidence.

Releasing Records and Signing Forms

You have been concerned so far with gathering documents, but you also need to be concerned about *how your child's records are used and to whom they are released.* In the past, parents were denied access to their children's records when practically everybody else—credit bureaus, police departments, mental health clinics, and even professionals doing research—could request and get confidential information about the child. P.L. 94-142 has put an end to that. Not only do you have the right to read or copy your child's records, you also must give your written consent for other people (except for school employees) to have access to your child's file. Even in the case of school employees, there is protection for you and your child: The school must keep a list of personnel who have access to your child's file. Make sure you see this list. Ask why individuals are on it. You may find out for the first time that a particular specialist is seeing your child. You might want to ask why the psychologist is counseling your learning disabled child when the school has been reluctant to provide a learning disabilities specialist to help your child with her academic needs; you may find that your school has assumed your child's "emotional" needs are a priority while you feel her academic needs should come first. The information may be new, startling, and occasionally disagreeable. But the informed advocate is in a position to be a better advocate.

When you are asked to sign a release for your child, you should know several things before you sign:

- who wants the records
- for what purpose(s)
- what the content is of the specific record, report, or evaluation being released

Before you sign any release, you should know what you are signing away. The only way to know is to read the record. You may even want to ask for a copy of the specific record for your files.

Remember, you do not have to sign the release if you feel that releasing the information will not benefit your child. When you are careful, even stingy, about confidential information about your child, you are merely protecting your child's rights. If you have in the past signed what is called a blanket release, giving permission to the schools to release any or all information to a number of people or agencies, don't be alarmed. You can fix that by writing a note to the school system withdrawing your permission to release records and explaining that you feel you did not understand the seriousness of the release form. A letter, rather than a telephone call, is needed here because the school has a written record of your earlier permission; you want them to have a written record of the withdrawal of your consent. Because of P.L. 94-142, very few school people will ask you to sign a blanket release because they know that it is a very weak piece of paper and that they would have a hard time defending their actions if the parents chose to complain. Should you be offered such a blanket release form to sign, politely refuse and inform the school person that the law requires *informed consent* before records are released, which means that you need to know the specifics before you agree or refuse to sign.

Never sign anything unless you feel you fully understand the agreement. A written release is one form of agreement; the Individualized Education Program is another. When you are asked to sign the IEP, check to make sure that all the information you have agreed upon is entered into the form. Do not accept the "trust me and we'll fill the blanks in later" approach. Signing a half empty IEP is like giving a blank check signed by you to the school people who will later write in the amount, which is almost guaranteed to be fewer or less adequate services for your child. You should insist that the contract/

agreement be complete and that you understand it before you sign it.

When the IEP is complete and you approve, sign where it says "I accept the plan." You don't like the plan? Then sign where it says "I do not accept the plan." If you are not sure about the IEP, tell the planning team you want to take home a copy of the plan to think about it. Like car salesmen, the school people want to close the deal, and most will try to get you to sign on the spot. Don't do it! This is an important decision and you are wise to take your time. The law is on your side.

These concerns about releasing and signing documents are serious ones. Your responsibility to your child is to do your homework, speak your piece, and take the time you need to make the right decisions. This section on records is an important one because records are the rock on which you build your case for better and more beneficial services for your child.

Making the case for your child is hard work, demanding that you bring both emotional and physical energy to the task. You shouldn't have to do it alone. In fact, don't do it alone! There are allies and resources you already know, and more that you will seek out in the course of your advocacy career.

USING YOUR ALLIES

In your everyday life you use allies regularly. When you had to take your child to the hospital emergency room and were shaking so badly you couldn't drive, you called a friend or neighbor who drove you. Or, when you impulsively signed the contract with the door-to-door salesman, you called the Better Business Bureau or a consumer protection agency for information and advice on what to do because you were unsure about whether you were being cheated. Another time, your trash still wasn't being picked up after many calls to the town hall, so you called your town representative, who took care of it. And when you were having trouble assembling the Christmas toys for your children, you called a friend who came over, read the directions with you (or for you), and together you managed to do the job.

In much the same way, you can call on individuals and organizations who will give you the help and support you need to be a strong and effective parent advocate. Use their information, skills, talents, interests, and power to get the right program for your child. But who are these people and what can they do for you?

The Advocate's Advocate

Perhaps the single most important ally you have is the person you choose to be your personal advocate, your special 94-142 buddy. Ideally, the person you choose to be your personal advocate should have these qualities:

- cares about you and your child
- agrees that your child has the right to an education which benefits him
- is willing to commit some time and energy to you and your child
- can work in a cooperative way with you
- is willing to learn something about your child's needs and P.L. 94-142
- can speak up when necessary
- knows her personal strengths and weaknesses

Having all these qualities may be a tall order for most of the people you know who come to mind: "My neighbor seems really sympathetic but I think she feels special education is just baby-sitting and a favor," "My brother would be terrific, but every time we try to do somethin together, it ends up in an argument," or "If only my friend, Martha, were here instead of in another state, she'd help me." Three strikes? Not really; perhaps that neighbor can be converted to a strong belief in special education through your convincing arguments.

Keep going. Who else is there? Other neighbors or friends? Your clergyman (himself or a recommended member of his flock)? Professionals outside of the school system who have worked with your child? Ask yourself if they would have enough time available to help you. Mentally explore all possibilities: You are looking for someone whom you can trust and who cares about your child. Okay, now you've done the review and you think you've come up with the right person(s), or you've come to the conclusion that there's no one to help you.

No one? Well, you wouldn't be the first parent to walk a lonely road. But before you give up, ask yourself if you are being too critical. If you are convinced that you are not demanding absolute perfection, then you must begin to look for help outside the circle of people you know.

There are organizations (perhaps you are already a member) that may be able to help you find an advocate. These are generally parent or citizen groups organized around a specific handicap or across a range of disabilities (Appendix A contains a list of organizations). You may already have some material about these organizations in your house. If not, look in the yellow pages of the phone book under social services; call any organization that looks promising. The first one may not be the right one; tell the person at the other end a little about your problem and ask him to refer you to an organization which can help you. When you do reach the right group, explain your problem and tell them that you need help in getting a suitable education for your child. They should respond in one or more of these ways:

- taking your name and other information
- transferring you to a person who will take your case
- setting up an appointment for you to meet an advocate
- recommending a person in a nearby town who can help you
- giving or sending information in everyday language to help you understand your rights and your child's

"But these are strangers and you said it was important that the parent's personal advocate should care about the parent and the child. How can strangers care?" These strangers can be the friends you haven't met. Most of the people who work (volunteer or paid) as advocates for handicapped children have a strong emotional, professional, and moral commitment to getting good educational services for all children with handicaps. They will care about your child because he is a member of a class of children who have been deprived or forgotten. You can rely on them to help you.

Your organizational advocate will want to meet with you to discuss your child and your school system and to review the records you already have. She may bring you information about the law, a copy of the law, the regulations, or how-to handouts. She may also plan to be with you at the IEP team meeting and other important meetings after that.

In some cases, where parents live in sparsely populated areas or where the organization is overloaded and understaffed, you may have to do most of the work on your own. That need not mean you are completely alone. You can work out an arrangement where you keep in touch with the organizational advocate or advisor by phone. Ask to call before meetings to get advice, and after meetings to report and ask for more advice; offer to send documents (IEPs, evaluations, and correspondence) to your long-distance advocate for review and comments. Even with problems of distance and understaffing, if the school system is acting in flagrant violation of the law, the long-distance advocate may put in an appearance at a later meeting. Just when all hope seems lost, the cavalry arrives.

The day of the first IEP meeting arrives. You have an arrangement worked out with your long-distance advocate over the phone, but you still have to go to the meeting alone. Enter the "warm body." This is the person who lacks most of the qualities you look for in an advocate. She is a well-meaning friend or relative you have begged or pressured into going with you. You have made it clear that your "warm body" only has to be there, look alert, and nod once in a while when you are talking, and that she doesn't have to say anything except possibly, "I'm Fran Henderson, here to help Gerry Bronsen." To the school people your friend is seen as a witness to what goes on in the meeting. Your friend in fact may be a very poor witness, but the school people don't know that, and past statements like "That kid belongs in an institution, not in a public school" become, "Well now, fitting your child into the program presents some difficulties. It may take a little time." For the parent who has ever been on the receiving end of cruel statements, this kind of improvement makes it possible for the parent to at least function at the meeting.

Occasionally, even the "warm body" comes through. Your friend may tell you after the meeting that the principal wasn't listening to anything you said, that the physical education teacher seemed interested in everything you said about the things Linc does around the house, or even, halfway through the meeting, burst out with, "How can you say Linc is only good for ten to fifteen minutes of work when I watched him yesterday rake and bag leaves for two hours?" Just having a friend at a meeting is a source of support, but if that "warm body" turns into an observer, a source of information, and a champion for your child, you may find that you have created an advocate.

Your personal advocate can do the following things:

- *listen* to you talk about your concerns, fears, strengths, and weaknesses, what you want for your child, and what you think your child needs
- help you *sort out* all these things into the important and not so important (set priorities), into the realistic and the not yet manageable, and into solid data and areas that need more information
- serve as a *spokesperson* and a *source of information* about your child, either through direct personal knowledge or indirectly through reading your records

- be a *coplanner* with you as you develop a plan of action
- be your *witness* and *source of personal support* as you go through the process of getting a good school program for your child

We will be talking more specifically about the role of your personal advocate when we get into the IEP process in chapter six. What you need to know right now is that you don't have to do the job alone. Help is out there. Getting help may mean that you have to reach out aggressively to other people, perhaps setting aside your pride or your timidity. When you find your 94-142 buddy or personal advocate, you will feel the load lighten and the job begin to look manageable.

"What if my buddy is like me? It could be like two of us going over Niagara Falls in a barrel, instead of one. We wouldn't have enough information or power to change things." Fortunately, you have available still other allies whom you haven't considered yet and who are a powerful source of information and pressure.

Organizations

There are both private and public agencies out there which are set up to help you: They include parent and citizen organizations like ACLD (the Association for Children with Learning Disabilities), ARC (the Association for Retarded Citizens), SAC (Society for Autistic Children), and others which operate on national, state, and local levels. They can be sources of information and pressure. If you do not have a local organization, contact your state or national organization by letter or by phone (Addresses of some national organizations are listed in Appendix A) and say you need help with P.L. 94-142. Tell them what you know, ask them what you should know, and explain to them what you think your child needs. They will send you information about the law, about the nearest chapter of the organization, and perhaps about other organizations in your vicinity which can offer you information and assistance, such as developmental disabilities protection and advocacy agencies, public interest law firms, and other special projects or advocacy agencies. When you have received and read the information sent to you by various organizations, you will begin to feel a little more assured about the job ahead of you. But other questions may start coming to mind, and your personal advocate may be raising questions too. Write them all down; don't be afraid they will sound dumb. You'll learn that the only "dumb" questions are those that aren't asked.

When you have collected a stack of information pamphlets, brochures, and laws, start by reading the easiest materials (shortest, simplest language and largest print), then read the ones that are a little harder. By the time you get to the most difficult ones (with the fine print), you will already have learned quite a bit from your reading about your rights and your child's. Read all the materials; underline and mark them up. Later it will be easier for you to find just the line or phrase you want. Share the informational materials with your personal advocate. You want him to be as well-informed as you are becoming. Perhaps he is better at reading and understanding the information than you and can help you to understand more. That's a bonus. Maybe he needs the material explained and you have to try to make those explanations. That's a bonus too. Every time you have to explain the law, you get better at understanding it and at talking about your child's rights.

Are there other ways that private organizations can help you?

Newsletters. Get on their mailing list to receive their regular publication, which may contain up-to-date information on the law, notices of meetings where you can meet other parents who share your problems (and may have solved theirs), and notices of workshops and conferences which deal with special education.

Workshops and conferences. These are opportunities for you to hear about special education problems and solutions. They give you a chance to have some of your questions answered and to make contact with people who can be a source of help, like a parent who has a child just like yours or an agency which is monitoring special education in your town, county, or state, and wants to hear from parents.

Advocates. The organization may help you find a personal advocate to work with you from the beginning of your advocacy efforts, or may offer to troubleshoot for you should the going get rough.

Pressure. Organizations can serve as pressure groups to bear down on local or state departments of education when school people are in violation of the law. Your case could be the one they have been waiting for to swing into action. Or your letter to them describing your experiences with the school can bring forth the formal letter to you (or the school people) stating that the school system is in violation of the law and your child is entitled to the service you are asking for. (Send a copy to the school system, keeping the original for your file. Since school systems don't like to see their sins in print, they may finally come through with the desired service.) The organization may even send a representative to go with you to the IEP meeting or the mediation session ("I am Mrs. Kerr, representing the Statewide Parent Coalition and here to assist the parents in this case"). Because organizations represent numbers of people (as opposed to your one or two), they can often put effective pressure on school systems.

There are also public agencies like your state Department of Education which are supposed to serve you. State agencies are funded with public money to provide service to the public, but unfortunately they seldom put pressure on local school systems unless some outside group leans heavily on them. There are exceptions, of course, but they are rare. State agencies, like the school systems in chapter three, tend toward business as usual and do little to help the parent advocate get the appropriate educational services. Do not rely on your state agency to pressure your school system.*

What you need from your state Department of Education, and what you are entitled to get, is information. You can ask for and get copies of the state and federal laws, regulations, and departmental policy statements which go out to school systems. Call or write asking for specific information. This can be difficult when you are asking for agency policy statements because you may need to know the title, number, and/or date of the statement. If you are lucky, you will reach one of those dedicated public servants who works to improve service; this kind of person can be enormously helpful to you in tracking down the information and sending it out to you. Be appreciative. On the other hand, you may reach someone who doesn't care or whose hands are tied. You will have to use your skills or allies to get the information, such as a formal letter of request (stating your willingness to pay a reasonable cost, if necessary) or a letter or call from a private organization or your political representative.

Your state education agency may have already prepared some pamphlets on 94-142, which they are usually happy to send out. Get them; they have useful information in them. However, when you compare them with the advocacy pamphlets, you may find the state material has left out a few important (to parents) items of information, such as the parent's right to take a personal advocate to IEP meetings or the right of the child to have a second independent evaluation when the parents believe the first evaluation to be inadequate.

---

*One parent who was excellent at writing letters and keeping files used to send copies of letters she wrote to the local school department to the state education agency. When nothing happened, she wondered why the state agency was not bringing pressure to bear on the local school system. When it was pointed out to her that her letters were going to members of the same "club," that is, public agencies, she amended her approach to include sending a copy of each letter to a citizen advocacy organization.

Know your agencies and what they can do for you. Don't hesitate to call on them when you need their help or information; public agencies are funded by your tax dollars, and private agencies are supported by citizens like you. You should consider joining organizations which try to help parents with children like yours. You can support them by membership contributions, by being active (a little or a lot), and ultimately by offering yourself (the successful parent advocate) to serve as personal advocate to a parent who reminds you of yourself when you didn't know what to do or where to go.

Elected Officials

Politicians are another resource available to you. "But what does my representative (or councilman or assemblyman) know about special education? And why should he be interested in what happens to my child?" Your representative probably knows very little about special education; she may even know nothing about it. A few will be knowledgeable, but chances are they were educated by other parents like yourself who called for help and support. The point is that elected officials don't have to know anything about special education to help you: They can provide the needed push, the pressure, that gets you what you want. Their political power is your resource. When you are having trouble getting a copy of the special education regulations from the state education agency, you call your state representative's office and explain, "I have called and written the state Department of Education for regulations and received nothing." You will be asked for specifics: what regulations and who you talked or wrote to. You will also be asked your name and where you live to find out if you are a voter or potential voter from the representative's district. The office will usually call the state agency for you. You may even get a follow-up call that day from the official or an aide telling you that the state agency has been contacted and a copy of the regulations is in the mail, and that if you do not receive it in a few days, call back. You, of course, warmly express your appreciation for the official's or aide's help.

But why did the state agency respond to your elected representative and not to you? They were quick to respond to your representative because she belongs to the group (legislature or assembly) that every year approves the budget which the agency needs to operate. The agency wants to keep happy the people with the power to make appropriations decisions.

But why did the representative respond to you? After all, you are just one person. To the representative, however, you can be a very important one person: You are a member of her community who is a voter, a potential supporter, and a person who can tell other people in the community what a great person she is. Some of your elected officials may have a natural concern and sympathy for your problems, but all are concerned with votes.

If an official is unable to help you, it may be necessary to contact one in a more influential position. Perhaps your child needs a residential school placement but the school people refuse to write it into the IEP because there is no money in the budget. You have called a member of your school board and your state representative, but they weren't able to help. Why not call your congressman? He is working to get federal dollars into the communities in his district, including yours. It may be that your town is depending on the congressman to obtain a federal grant for a revitalization program. A call from his office to local officials who want to please him may set the wheels in motion and get your child the program he needs.

When you are encountering roadblocks in special education and you feel that a little push will clear the way, use political people to help you get the appropriate services. When you call their offices, identify yourself as a constituent of the district they serve. Give them the information they need to help you—the law, the section of the regulations you are dealing with, the names and positions of the school people, and a clear explanation of what you want. By the time you reach the point of calling your elected officials, you will probably know quite a bit about your rights and your child's; share this information freely.

By all means, talk to the official's aide; she may be the most knowledgeable person in the office. If you insist on talking to the official, you may find yourself in a three-way conversation where the official keeps calling on the aide's help before he can answer any questions. Deal with the most knowledgeable person in the office. Let your official do what he knows and does best—make phone calls to public administrators and agency heads to get things moving. Don't expect your official to go or send someone to meetings with you or help you develop an IEP. Use your official to give the system a shake when a little shake will put the gears in motion.

Use your power over the official carefully. Don't threaten. The official knows that if you're dissatisfied, you aren't going to beat the drum for him at the next election. Maybe the official made a real effort to help you but it failed, and maybe you will want to come back to use his services another time on another issue, so keep the door open. Thank him for the time spent with you.

Whether or not you got what you were after, you did help to educate your official about the problems in special education. He will be more knowledgeable when you call next time. Some people call their officials regularly: They tell them how they want them to vote, ask them to have street lights fixed and vacant lots cleaned up, and complain about tax bills, high-rise buildings, and police protection. These people expect action, or at least an explanation, and they almost always get one or the other. If you and your child can be helped by your elected officials, don't be afraid to call them, and remember that it can be hard for an elected official to turn his back on a concerned and caring parent, especially when he wants to look good to the voters.

Special People

There are other people who can serve as sources of help, information, or power. They are the professionals who have worked with your child outside the system, the "good guys" in the school system, and the lawyers you may have to hire if you and the school people cannot reach agreement on your child's IEP.

The professionals outside the system who know you and your child are most certainly a source of information. Before you decide to use the outside professional, make sure she can find the time to attend the IEP meeting and that you and she are in reasonable agreement. Everyone has small differences, but you should both agree on the basic and priority items that you want in the IEP. Call or make an appointment with your outside professional to discuss these issues. When you feel comfortable with the statements the outside professional intends to make (you understand the jargon-free explanations and you feel the reasons are good), talk over your concerns about the upcoming IEP meeting. Sharing these concerns with your professional gives her a chance to plan in advance how to support you at the IEP meeting.

Your outside professional can also bring a little power to the meeting. As a professional, she has the status that comes with specialized training and expertise, which impresses the school professionals. If she is well-known in the field, her name and presence add more weight to your side. If she works out of a prestigious institution— a university or medical school, for instance—there is more pressure on the school people to acknowledge the expert's recommendations and make some attempt to meet them. Your outside professional's appearance at the meeting tells the school people that she thinks your child's case is so important that she is willing to take time from and rearrange a busy schedule to be there. Her presence stamps your child's case "IMPORTANT." Since you may be (or may end up) paying for the professional's time, her presence also indicates the seriousness of your commitment: Not only are you willing to invest your time, energy, and emotion, you are also prepared to spend some hard cash to see that your child's interests are protected. (You are paying only for the specialist's time at the meeting, and not for the educational services to which your child is entitled by law. With your efforts, these will be included in the IEP.)

Your outside professional is one of the special resources you use. In most cases, it would be impossible to use her as your personal advocate because of the time required for planning and meetings. However, the information, the support for you, and the status she brings to even one IEP meeting can strengthen your case.

The "good guys" in the school system who are trying to help you get the services your child needs are a hidden resource. They can offer you information and behind-the-scenes support. They can tell you what problems to expect at the meeting and what they feel your child's priority needs are. Teachers and specialists can be an invaluable source of information about the system, as well as about your child. Think what a help it would be to you at the IEP meeting if you knew that the reason for holding back special services was because of the budget. And you thought it was because your child could only handle so much intensive therapy! Properly informed, you will now insist on and hold out for more.

"But my child's teachers and specialists don't give me inside information like that. I get the party line." While there are some teachers who will only preach the gospel according to the school budget, there are some who do regularly share information with parents, and there are more who would like to but fear the wrath of other school people if they are discovered helping parents ask for more services.

How do you find, develop, and support the school personnel who give you inside information or make individual recommendations? First, you find them by sharing one to one on a personal level your information and concerns. When they realize that you are being open in asking their advice, they may directly voice their own limits and concerns, or perhaps, momentarily caught up in their own emotional concern for your child, they may let slip information such as that there is a ceiling on special services. The good advocate considers these personal statements from inside professionals as privileged communications, not to be publicly expressed; you reassure the insiders that you respect their confidence and that you are grateful for their demonstration of trust and concern. The good advocate supports his inside resources by protecting them.

When you get inside information, how can you use it without identifying its source? You ask yourself where else the information could have come from. Do you have any old reports, evaluations, or educational plans that contain or support the information recently given to you? Have you previously discussed with an outside professional the needs which are surfacing again? Another constant and reliable source is your own past and present observations of your child. Your confidential discussion with your inside professional may have triggered an old memory: "A few years back, our family doctor said we should consider special visual testing for Ned sometime in the future; even though he tested 20/20, the doctor thought he might have some focusing problems"; "Maybe Josie does have some memory problems; I just thought her poor recall was lack of attention"; or "That sounds like the article I read last month in *Downhome Family* magazine." If you think about it for a while, there is usually some recent or past experience to which you can attach your new information, so you can use it and at the same time protect your inside resource.

Not everything said in a one-to-one conversation needs to be confidential; in fact, very little will be. But whenever a school person says to you, "I shouldn't be saying this" or "This is in confidence," you should realize that you are probably dealing with a "good guy" trying to share inside information with you. "This is beginning to sound like cloak and dagger stuff," you are thinking. "Why can't it all be up front?" In many systems all will be up front, including the problems. In some systems, however, you may be the only person without inside information, and to be an effective advocate you need it. Consider your "spies" to be Special People Inside Educational Systems, special because they are willing to risk a little trouble to help you and your child.

Lawyers are another resource, usually an expensive one. They should be your last resort when your other resources have failed. Do not think they are necessarily a short cut to the services you want.

Educators are not at their best trying to think, discusss, and plan educational services in the presence of lawyers. They are likely to become careful of what they say for fear they will offend someone or violate someone's rights or some school policy; they are afraid of saying the wrong thing at the wrong time to the wrong person.

If you appear at your planning meeting with legal representation, the school people are going to feel intimidated and call out their lawyer. Immediately the situation will become very structured, formal, and legalistic. Lawyer talks to lawyer and points of law and procedure may predominate. You may find that your educational concerns may get less attention than you expected.

Because each side has its own lawyer to represent its interests, collaboration and informal negotiation become next to impossible. What might have been a working group (you and the school people) becomes an adversarial situation ("It's either them or us"), and any new options or creative alternatives which might have developed in the group process can be lost in a legalistic format.

This does not mean that you can't privately consult your lawyer at any time. If you have reason to believe that the school people are misinterpreting the law or denying your rights or your child's, check it out with your attorney. He may tell you to finish up the IEP and forward a copy immediately, offer to call or write the special education director and explicitly lay out the provisions of the law, or suggest he attend the next school meeting "because these people need to know that you can't be put off by their misinterpretations of the law."

Give the educators a chance to do their thing before you call out the legal troops. Besides, you know your child best; you certainly know better than your lawyer which services will benefit your child most. When you and the school people have completed the process, agreed on some services and disagreed on others, you will have clarified the issues. Then the lawyers can come in to argue about those specific services you want and can't get, using their legal expertise and special knowledge of P.L. 94-142. The time for lawyers is when collaboration and negotiation break down, and it's clear that you and the school people have irreconcilable differences.

Using lawyers will be discussed in chapter seven. For now, you need to know that many parents have been involved in developing good IEPs without legal advocates, but that some parents have found it necessary to bring a lawyer into the process to get the desired and appropriate services. You should say to yourself:

> I will do the best job I can, and I will use all the resources I can find; but if my best efforts fail, I am prepared to go the whole route and engage a lawyer to help me.

This kind of self-statement will give you confidence when you are dealing with the system: You remind yourself that you have something to fall back on. Your confidence in yourself delivers a message to the system that you are involved down to the line.

USING SPECIAL PROPS

There are things you can bring, wear, or do at meetings with school people to impress them with your business-like approach to achieving a beneficial education for your child. They are little things, but since every little bit helps, they are worthy of your consideration.

Your Well-Used Copy of the Regulations Can Look Impressive

Before you go to any meetings to plan a program for your child, you have already obtained a copy of the regulations. As you read them, you mark or underline parts you will want to use to make your case. Reading the regulations (alone or with help) is part of your basic preparation. But when you arrive at the school with a well-worn copy, it is a signal to the school people that this parent has done his homework and is not likely to be put off with vague answers or promises. You may feel you don't know enough, but they don't know what or how much you know; they will become very careful in what they say for fear you will flip to Section "QRS" and explain their legal obligations to them. This may seem like a bit of games-manship, and sometimes it is. Remember all the times you may have been confused or put off by jargon or faulty information, and enjoy the feeling of power and the bene-fits that can come from using your special props.

How You Carry Your Papers Can Be Important

Another prop you may find helpful in impressing school people is the way in which you carry your papers. One personal advocate who assists a number of parents relates that her briefcase alone impresses a number of school people, who often assume she is a psychologist, a lawyer, or a social worker and treat her (and the parent) with more respect. If you work or have worked in a field where people carry briefcases, by all means use yours or consider buying one. On the other hand, if you are a construction worker or waitress, it might seem a little phony to arrive at the meeting with a briefcase. You can still impress them with a clipboard, large manila envelope, or loose-leaf notebook in which all the papers you will need at the meeting are filed. This is appropriate for everyone. You demonstrate your businesslike approach in the way you prepare and handle your materials. Remember, you are trying to impress, not deceive. You don't have to tell everything, but your behavior and statements should be honest.

What You Wear Can Make a Difference

When you go to meetings, it can be helpful to dress con-servatively, that is, in a businesslike fashion. This doesn't mean you should rush out and buy a three-piece suit or a dull dress you will never wear anyplace else. It does mean you should plan on leaving the sneakers and jeans, the loud sportshirt, or the flaming pink, ruffled dress at home. If you don't feel at ease wearing a tie, don't wear one. If the brown skirt is too short or tight, wear something else. You'll have enough concerns at the meeting without squirming in your clothes. If you are still in doubt about what to wear, look around at people in the bank or at church until you see someone who dresses quietly and in a way in which you could be comfortable when meeting with school people (or you can read one of the books on how to dress listed in Appendix A). The clothes in which you present yourself can deliver the message to the school that you are a serious parent advocate.

"What does it matter? I'm still the same person without a briefcase and not dressed up. These aren't the issues. My child's education is what counts." You are right; these are not the issues. But it is amazing what can impress people. School people, like others, are impressed by appearances. And while none of these special props by themselves will do the job of getting the services you want for your child, they can help to establish you as a businesslike person. You will need and use all the support you can get to do the job, with grace when possible, with props and pressure when necessary.

You have ahead of you just one more task to complete in which you will practice your newly refined skills and prepare yourself for the IEP process. You are about to take a critical look at your child's program in action.

Five

Program Evaluation: On the Other Side of the Classroom Door

"I don't have to go to school to find out how my child is doing. I get the reports."

"The principal won't even answer my phone calls; and you expect him to let me visit the classroom!"

"What do I know about evaluating a classroom or a teacher?"

If you find yourself raising objections like these, you must first understand that in order to be a good parent advocate, you have to know what kind of program your child is in now. Your child probably has an Individualized Education Program (IEP) which the law requires; various reports or report cards may have been sent home to you; and you may be having regular talks with the school social workers, psychologists, specialists, or teachers.* But have you seen the program in action, or is

---

*If your child is not in an educational program, chapter six will tell you how to "help" the school system find your handicapped child.

If your child is in school but does not have an IEP, you will learn how to start the IEP process for him. What looks like a problem—no IEP—can be an advantage. Since you will be starting from scratch, you, as an informed advocate, can make sure that the first IEP is a good one.

If your child has a poor or inadequate IEP, you will learn how to obtain a better one.

147

your knowledge just secondhand, transmitted by various school people? While the information you receive from school people is useful and important, the only way to have firsthand information is to visit the classroom so that you can judge for yourself whether or not the program is appropriate for your child, and what changes or additions to the program might benefit him and increase his rate of progress. Remember, that's what P.L. 94-142 is all about: an education that is appropriate and beneficial for your child.

But who are you, a mere parent, an outsider, an intruder, to attempt to evaluate what goes on in your child's school? How can you, a lay person, presume to assess the effectiveness of the teacher in your child's classroom? Remember our discussion of myths in chapter two: Teachers do have special training and skills which must be acknowledged; however, the range of special educational needs, disabilities, and teaching methods to correct or improve a child's performance is so broad that an individual teacher cannot be expected to have all the answers, or even to have asked all the right questions about a given child. You can assist the teacher by at least asking some of the right questions about your child. Indeed, many teachers have been helped by parents' questions and reports. You are the overall expert in the area of information about your child. In addition, you are often the pipeline through which information flows to the school in making its evaluations of your child (and your family). It is your right to request that information about the classroom and your child flow back to you.

THE RIGHT TO VISIT:
GETTING INTO THE CLASSROOM

Visiting your child's classroom (regular or special education) is your right in most states, and not a privilege or special favor granted by the school system. In twenty-six states and the District of Columbia, you have the explicit right as a parent to visit your child's classroom at *any* time during the school day if you first notify the school office.* A general rule of thumb is that your visit can be arranged at reasonable times upon reasonable notice.

Many parents have never asked to visit their children's classrooms; if they have visited, it was on a school Open House Day when all parents are invited. Open House Day does not give you a realistic picture of what your child's school day is like because the teacher talks to many parents, many people are coming and going, and the day may be arranged to show children doing their best work.

Parents may be reluctant to ask to visit the school for fear of intruding. Some school personnel may strengthen this idea ("We would like to have you visit, but it would disrupt the class, you know"). You need to recognize that some of the fear of intrusion is another response stemming from your own school days ("Where is your class?" "Are you supposed to be in the hall now?"), and one you should now overcome. A well-prepared, businesslike parent who has come to quietly observe and who will talk with the teacher after school (in person or by phone) is hardly being intrusive. The children will notice you when you enter the classroom, but will soon return their attention to their work and their teacher.

Remind yourself of why you are not an intruder:

1. You have the implicit right to visit and observe your child's program (explicit in most states).

2. You are a mature adult whose presence in the classroom will not interfere with the educational process.

3. You have the responsibility as the natural and long-

---

*The National Committee for Citizens in Education has a wallet-sized Parents' Rights Card which describes the rights of parents of all children in public schools, including the right to visit your child's classroom, the right to read records, and the right to conferences with your child's teacher. Since parents' rights may differ from state to state, this handy little card tells you which states grant which rights. For the address and phone number of this organization, see Appendix A.

term advocate for your child to see and evaluate what kinds of teaching and services your child is actually getting in his daily program.

You are now ready to approach the school system with your reasonable request to visit your child's classroom.

You can begin with an informal request. If you are meeting with the teacher for a parent-teacher conference, if you will see the teacher or principal at a PTA meeting, or if you are dropping by school to leave boots on a stormy day, a cake for the sale, etc., your on-the-spot request is casual and friendly. The happiest and most promising response you can get is "Yes. Let's arrange a convenient time. We like to know that our parents are interested in their children's education." When you receive this type of response, you can arrange a mutually convenient time with the teacher when you can see the activities in which you are most interested (perhaps reading, speech therapy, or gym).

However, you should be ready for a range of responses when you ask to visit. These responses can range from simple surprise to suspicion ("Why do you want to visit?"), reluctance ("It might disrupt the class"), or downright resistance ("Parents are only allowed to visit during Open House which is scheduled in six months" or even "Parents are not allowed to visit").

Surprise may not be a problem. You may in fact be the first person to ask to visit the class at a time other than the annual Open House visiting day. Your expressions of parental interest in your child's education may be enough to result in arranging a time to visit.

This is not the time to express concerns (if you have them) about the shortcomings of the program. Remember, you are at the evaluation stage; you want to look to see what is happening. After you have seen the class in action, you may then have some criticisms, recommendations, or praise, which will be grounded in actual onsite observations by you.

Suspicion may or may not be resolved by your expression of interest in the school program and an obligation to follow your child's educational career through regular observations. If you feel the school's suspicion is merely the visible tip of their deeper reluctance, then you may need to say that it is your understanding that visiting is a right that parents have, and ask if the school has that same understanding. Usually, this is enough to lead to an arrangement for visiting.

Reluctance may be demonstrated by statements such as "We don't encourage parents to visit," "Parents tend to disrupt the work of the students and teachers," or "I'm sure a talk with the teacher would give you all the information you need and allay any fears you might have."

Such statements are usually intended to intimidate or at least convince you to stay away from the classroom. You must respond by restating your interest, your right, and your ability to observe in a classroom without it being a disruption. When your statements do not lead to the desired arrangements (however reluctantly the school makes them) and you are beginning to feel you are up against a stone wall, you are probably right.

Resistance is the name for that stone wall and it is apparent in such statements as "Parents are not allowed to visit classrooms" or "There is one day a year set aside for all parents to visit. That is the only day we can allow visitors." These are put-downs, designed to keep you away and in your place. It is amazing how many parents accept these "rules" without question. But you know better: You know that an advocate without information is a weak advocate, and that important information is on the other side of the classroom door. No wall is insurmountable; with the proper tools (appropriate assertiveness, script, partner), you can get to the other side of the wall.

If you are one of the unlucky parents who, in this first informal encounter, finds the school people's surprise or suspicion becoming reluctance and resistance, and feels increasingly uncomfortable, insecure, and distressed, know that you can stop this "exchange" at any stage by simply saying, "Today I am pressed for time, and I will call you back in a day or two to finish this discussion." If you are pressed to stay because the school person wants to settle the discussion in his way, embellish your excuse with a polite social lie, such as "I am already late for my dental appointment." Leave right away and go home or out for a cup of coffee or an ice cream sundae (you deserve a reward, both for hanging in during a difficult session and for knowing when it's time to get out of a situation because your effectiveness is being undermined). It's very important that over your cup of coffee you write down all you can remember about the interview:

- what you said (including when you will call)
- what he said
- how you felt (intimidated, nervous, insulted, overwhelmed)
- what the issues were
- what additional information you need
- which people you may need to help you (see section on the Advocate's Advocate in chapter four)

Date this account for your files which you are now keeping faithfully.

Go over your information on the interview: Were either you or the principal fuzzy in your statements? Practice privately—next time at least you will be more clear. Were you nervous or too easily intimidated? Private practice or rehearsal will help here too.

Did you need more information about your rights? If so, there are sources you can consult. Contact the local school board and the state Department of Education for information. Ask for the name and number of the law which allows you to visit your child's classroom, ask to be sent a copy of the policy which defines your right (you will, of course, be happy to pay a reasonable cost for the copying of the policy/law), or ask the officials for their response affirming your right in writing if you feel you need it. If the answers you receive are vague or non-committal, then ask if there is a policy or law that prohibits your visiting, and request a copy of it if it exists.

Is this becoming a situation where you need an advocate? Can your friend who was the PTA president help you? Is there an advocacy or parents' group which can give you information? Would a call to your state representative, assemblyman, or city councilor hasten receipt of the information you need from the school board or Department of Education? Your politicians can be powerful and valuable resources. You may, however, wish to save them for the times when other resources seem to be failing.

Remember, you said to the school people you would call back in a day or two. It is a cardinal rule that you follow up on your promises to call; this will convince the schools that you mean business. Does the collection agency stop with one request? After all, you are collecting on your rights and your child's future.

Before calling back, you need a little more planning, including some rehearsal. When you rehearse, try to think of a range of possible outcomes or responses, and think of several which are best for you. Here are some examples of what can happen when you return the call:

Mrs. Lawrence:	This is Mrs. Lawrence. I promised the principal, Mr. Smith, I would call today.
Secretary:	I'll see if he's available.
Mr. Smith:	Yes, Mrs. Lawrence. You caught me at a bad time the other day. I don't see why we can't arrange a time for you to visit. Ms. Thompson, your child's teacher, will call you and set something up.
Mrs. Lawrence:	Thank you, Mr. Smith. I appreciate your helping to set up my visit.

You may be thinking, "Why didn't you say so the other

day and spare me the grief?" but now you can afford to be generous and polite—you are going into the classroom.

Another example you rehearse may be a less satisfying outcome of your effort:

Mrs. Lawrence:	This is Mrs. Lawrence. I promised Mr. Smith I would call today.
Secretary:	Sorry, Mr. Smith is in conference now and can't be disturbed.
Mrs. Lawrence:	What is a good time to reach him?
Secretary:	I really can't say. He's a very busy man.
Mrs. Lawrence:	I see. Would it be better if I put my request in writing?
Secretary:	That may not be necessary. Let me give him your message and I'm sure he will return your call if he can.
Mrs. Lawrence:	Thanks. I'll be home (or at this number) from 1:00 to 4:00 p.m.

You wait until almost 4:00, but there is no call. You can use the polite social lie as a way of showing that you will not give up, while sparing people the accusations about not calling:

Mrs. Lawrence:	Hello. I'm sorry, I was out of the office (house) for a few minutes and wonder if Mr. Smith is available to talk with me now.
Secretary:	Sorry, he's out of the office again. Perhaps you could call again tomorrow.
Mrs. Lawrence:	Uh huh. Any special time?
Secretary:	I can't really say. Try in the early afternoon.

You have been writing in your records the dates and numbers of your calls. Repeat the calls one more day, but if you are still unsuccessful, you should begin to compose your letter (discussed later).

But suppose you finally get the principal on the phone.

(He has realized, after four to six calls, that you are really not going to go away; your message is being received.) You may be told the following:

Mr. Smith: Sorry I did not get back to you, Mrs. Lawrence. What can I do for you? (As if he's forgotten!)

Mrs. Lawrence: I would like to know when I can visit Mimi's classroom.

Mr. Smith: Oh, yes. Well, I suppose we could arrange something . . .

or

Mr. Smith: This is against our usual policy and I would like to check with the school board . . .

or

Mr. Smith: I told you the other day that we do not allow parents to visit.

You can imagine even more conversations than are presented here and be prepared to continue to make your request until the issue is resolved. At some point, with a resistant principal, you should consider putting your request in writing. Here's a sample:

12 Park Street
Your Town, State 55555
October 28, 1980

Mr. Alfred Hart
Principal
Local School
Your Town, State 55555

Dear Mr. Hart:

On October 5, I asked you to set up a time for me to visit Gilda's classroom, and you told me parents are not allowed to visit.

On October 7, I called your office twice. You did not return my call. On October 8, 9, and 10, I called again, without success. When you did return my

call, you said you would check with the school
board. That was two weeks ago.

In the meantime, I have checked with the state
Department of Education about visiting rights, and
they sent me a copy of Public Law XYZ which says
that parents do have visiting rights.

Please write me to set up a time to visit my
daughter's classroom.

Sincerely,

[signature]

John R. Fontanez

You will probably send this letter to the principal alone
unless you feel he is practically immovable. You may
then want to send copies of this letter to others (see
chapter four, Formal Copies to Others). You have, of
course, kept a clear copy of this letter for your files.
Usually, this kind of a letter does the job and you can
begin to plan for your visit.

Should there be a school policy which actually prohibits your visiting, then you must look for other ways to
find out what goes on behind the classroom doors. Could
your child's instruction be videotaped (videotape equipment is almost as standard school equipment as are pen-
cils and paper) and shown to you? Is there a trusted
professional outside of the school system who has worked
with your child in the past and who would be interested
in visiting the classroom? It would be hard for a school
to refuse admittance to a professional person who has
worked with your child. If such a person agrees to visit
in your place, do sit down beforehand and share your
questions and concerns with your professional friend.
Perhaps you could read this chapter together.

One way or another, you, someone, or something will
be on the other side of the classroom door at a time
agreed upon by the teacher, and during which you will
get the information you want.

THE CLASSROOM ASSESSMENT:
AN APPLE FOR THE TEACHER?

You begin to gather information about the teacher when you arrange with her to set a time for your visit. Although this might seem like a great deal of arranging, it will be easier now because the front office has stamped approval on your right to visit. Be prepared for the same range of responses (acceptance, surprise, suspicion, reluctance, or resistance) as you were with the principal. You will, in almost every case, be able to work through the problem exchanges through negotiation and compromise, and by being flexible and expressing consideration for the teacher's scheduling difficulties.

Explain to the teacher (by phone or after school) when you can come, how long you want to observe, which activities you would like to observe (perhaps for this first visit you don't really care; you just want to see the classroom in action), and what questions you have about the educational program.

Present the teacher with a list of times you are available. If you can come any time, then say so. If you have other responsibilities which limit your availability, your needs and activities should be respected by the teacher. If you must take time off from work to come to the class, make it clear that you may have to make arrangements that are difficult for you, but that you are willing to do this because you are very serious about your responsibilities to your child.

Try to pick a day when you will see a representative sample of the program. Some days are better than others for visiting. Avoid Mondays, especially after vacations, days after a holiday, and Halloween, Valentine's Day, etc. On these days you may not see a representative sample of the children's or teacher's performance.

Within your schedule, ask the teacher which days or times she thinks would be best, that is, more informative or most relevant to your concerns. The teacher may state her own preferences. If you can make it and if you feel the preferred times will give you the information you want, then accommodate the teacher (demonstrating your flexibility). In doing this, you can present yourself not as a threat, but as a cordial person and a possible future ally.

Compromise may be necessary. For example, if you would like to see the class for two hours, and the teacher would like you to visit for only half an hour, you may be willing to accept the half hour if you can arrange to visit at other times as well. Or you may have trouble taking time off from work, and, considering the difficulties, a minimum of an hour makes more sense. On the other hand, seeing the activity you want to see may be more important than the length of time you are there. You and the teacher should work out a mutually agreeable length of time.

The accepting teacher will ask you *what* you want to see; the suspicious or reluctant teacher will ask *why* you want to observe and may probe for your complaints. You should try to reassure the suspicious teacher by saying again that you are interested in your child's program and that you may have some questions the teacher will be able to answer later. The suspicious/reluctant teacher may merely be a nervous teacher who is uncomfortable being observed, or she may have received a message from the reluctant principal that this parent is trouble. The way you present yourself can do much to allay the teacher's concerns and even fears. The more comfortable the teacher, the more representative her performance on the day you visit, and the better the information for you.

If you find that your talk with the teacher is deteriorating and you are losing control or not making your best case, remember the polite social lie and remove yourself from the situation. If necessary, you can call back at another time to make the final arrangements. Keep notes on all conversations for your file.

Preparation for Your Visit

The time is set. Perhaps arranging your visit was easy or perhaps you feel like you've been through the Battle of the Bulge. Either way, you now need to prepare for your visit and ready your props.

First reread the IEP. You do have a copy, don't you? If not, get one fast; you are entitled to a copy and you need it. On the IEP mark the areas of your greatest concern; then make a list of the things you want to observe (for example, reading program, teaching materials, or how the teacher uses her attention). Review any notes you have in your records, such as the teacher's openness or reluctance to your visit, previous teachers' comments on your child's behaviors, abilities, and performance in school, and your child's past progress or lack of it in certain areas.

Have your notebook ready for the observations you will make during your visit. Your notebook is important for two reasons: It will be difficult for you to remember all your important impressions and questions if you don't write most of them down, and your notebook also gives you something to do and another place to look in the classroom if you are feeling nervous or tense (you probably will be).

Plan and practice your behavior before the visit: how you will enter the classroom (quietly, cordially, and on time), how you will take signals from the teacher (where you sit or stand, whether or how you should respond to the students' questions, when to ask your questions), and what you will do if you become tense (do relaxation exercises, read your notes, or draw a map of the classroom).

When you and your materials are ready, then read some fiction, take a walk, or do whatever it takes to relax you. Remember, this is just your first assessment visit; you may not understand everything you see and you may not have all your questions answered. If you need more visits, you know how to arrange them now. Reward yourself for good planning.

Your Entrance

You arrive on time with your notebook under your arm, and you enter the classroom quietly with a pleasant expression on your face. If you feel tense or even angry, think about something pleasant, however remote, if that's what it takes to put a small smile on your face. Your entering behavior should suggest the careful and cooperative observer, not the avenging angel arriving at last, and not the nervous and emotional parent. The way you move into the room and your glances to the teacher tell the teacher that you want to take direction from her on what you should do in the classroom.

You note the teacher's response to your entrance:

1. You get a cordial glance and a nod to a chair set up for you at the side or back of the room, and the teacher continues the lesson.

2. You are invited to the front of the class and the teacher introduces you to the students. (If you are offered a chair at the front of the room, let the teacher know you feel you would be less of a disruption sitting in the back.)

3. You are ignored and left to decide where you will sit, stand, or lean.

These are your first observations. You are not making judgments now; you will make them later when you have all your notes and observations to consider and evaluate.

Classroom Setting

Begin your observations by noting the physical arrangements in the room; draw a simple map. If you are a bit tense or uncomfortable, this is an easy way to begin. It may help to relax you and possibly the teacher too as she sees that you are interested in the total environment and not there just to criticize or pounce on her style or performance.

Your attention to the setting is not just busy work, however; you will gain important educational information from your map. You note several types of things:

1. First, the location of the classroom:
   a. Isolated (Is it in the basement or a separate wing distant from general school activities?)

or

    b. Integrated (Is it alongside or mixed in with the regular classrooms, or close to general use rooms, such as the cafeteria, gym, music room, etc?)

2. Then, the room's general characteristics:
    a. Large or small
    b. Sunny (or well-lighted) or gloomy
    c. Warm or cold
    d. Well-kept-up or deteriorating
    e. Quiet or noisy (Perhaps it's too close to the cafeteria or gym, and no one else wants the room.)
    f. Anything else that seems important to you

3. Finally, the teacher's organization of the room (how the teacher makes the best use of what she has):
    a. Location of the teacher's desk (Is it in the center in front of the room between the students and the blackboard, or is it located in a front corner where the teacher can easily move to the blackboard and to the students without being constantly in the students' line of vision?)
    b. Location of the students' desks (Are they in the traditional arrangement of students in rows facing front, small groupings of desks, a circle of desks reminiscent of kindergarten, or individual desk arrangements?)
    c. Any special areas of the room set aside for individual instruction, quiet reading and learning tasks, free play, or crafts?
    d. Location of equipment and materials (Are things located where they are used and accessible so that there is a minimum of wasted and possibly disruptive movement; for example, if the free play area is at the back of the room, are the games there too, or must the student walk through or around other working students to find a game? Are the materials and equipment easily available to the teacher: Can she pull out what's next and needed fast?)
    e. Anything else that seems important to you

Any single characteristic of the classroom may not be all

that important, but the total picture is. Is the room generally pleasant and well-organized? Have you noted many good things and perhaps a few minor deficiencies? Is the teacher making the best use of what she has?

Perhaps you are just a bit nervous about evaluating the setting (falling into the "mere parent" trap). How can you, the nonprofessional, assess a classroom planned by the professionals? The answer is that you do it the same way you assess any setting for people. A classroom is a place where people live and work; the people are children and the work is learning. And you know about people and work: Do you run a household? Do you manage or work in an office or shop? Then you know that a dark room can be depressing and hard to read in, that you can't do a good job if you can't find your tools, and that it's hard to concentrate on reading or writing in a noisy room or office. Use what you know and apply it to the classroom.

You will begin to notice other things based on your own everyday experience. You may see a classroom that looks neat—everything is stacked in orderly piles—but the teacher can't seem to locate the materials readily. Neatness and organization are not always the same thing. Your teacher's classroom may look a little disorderly but you see that she knows exactly where everything is, and her lessons flow smoothly. Use your judgment.

Look at the way students are seated as well as the arrangement of the room. You may notice a child at the back of the room who is squinting at the board, and wonder why that child is not seated near the front of the room. Or you may see a child in the middle of a group who can't seem to attend to the paperwork, and you think that child might do his work better if his desk were put at the edge of the group. If your own child has a hearing problem, you may be happy to see your child seated near the front of the room, or distressed that he is far from the teacher and probably hearing very little. (Make a note to discuss this with the teacher.) Trust yourself to make good observations and to ask important questions. Your judgments, based on what you know, can be very sound.

General Activity

Now that you have some good notes on the physical setting, use some of your valuable, everyday experience and your good ideas to assess the way the teacher works and interacts with the students. This is harder, but in a short time you will be making observations that you will feel are reliable. Here are some important questions:

1. Is the teacher generally supportive and friendly to the students? (The behavior of both students and teacher will give you the answer here.)
   a. Note the teacher's tone of voice, frequency of smiles, and how and when she gives attention and touches the students. (Touching depends on the students' ages: Younger children appreciate and generally respond to being touched by a friendly, caring teacher, but older students may not like being touched at all.)
   b. Do the students seek out the teacher's attention?
   c. Do they like to do things to please the teacher?

You know your own child, your other children, and their young friends, so you have a basis for evaluating the teacher and students' interactions!

A word of caution is needed here about individuals' teaching styles. Every teacher is different from every other teacher; each has her own style. Some are outgoing and effusive; others may seem serious or even a little stern. Some will seem very loose or casual in the way they run their classrooms; others will run a tight ship, and you may even feel they are a bit rigid. If you have questions or concerns about the teacher's fairness or caring, watching how the students respond to the teacher will give you some of the answers.

2. Is the teacher in control of the classroom?
   a. Does she have a schedule that she can stick to

and in which the students can finish the assigned work without teacher pressure or nagging?
b. How does the teacher deal with disruptions? (Are the disruptive children getting most of the attention, or does the teacher help the students to improve their classroom behavior by giving them attention when they are engaging in productive behaviors like cooperation and diligence?)
c. Has the teacher established classroom rules, such as how the students are expected to enter the room, the proper way to get the teacher's attention, and when they will be allowed to have free time?

3. Is the teacher generally skillful in teaching the students?
a. Does she know how to break down learning tasks into steps, however small, to help a student learn a task?
b. Are the teacher's directions clear enough so that the students know what is expected of them?
c. Does she prepare work that the students can do with a good chance of doing it well?
d. Does the teacher go to a child who is beginning to look like he needs help and offer it before the child falls behind or gets lost in the lesson?
e. Does the teacher circulate among the working students to give a word of praise, a pat on the back, a helpful new direction, or a correction?
f. Does the teacher prepare students by telling them the lesson will be over in a few minutes, and, when time is up, end the lesson on a good note?
g. Does the teacher offer or plan to give extra help later to the student(s) who needs more time and help from the teacher?

4. In individual work, is the teacher able to be organized, consistent, and yet flexible?
a. Are the individual sessions obviously planned,

with the teacher giving clear signals and the help the child needs?

b. Is the teacher able to present the child with different directions when the child is having difficulty understanding the first ones, and to offer physical help ("I'll guide your hand in writing this letter") to one child while offering verbal help to another ("This should look like a circle we didn't finish. That's a nice letter C")?

c. Can the teacher end a session that isn't going too well with some feeling of competence or success for the student ("These letters are really hard. Just make me a nice letter A and we will be all done")?

d. Can the teacher plan to correct, modify, and improve the session for the next time?

What a lot of questions to be asking yourself while you are trying to observe the class in action! How can you possibly watch everything and remember all these points? You need to know that you can't watch everything, and even if you could, you couldn't see everything during one visit. But you will see enough—enough to realize that the teacher is a caring person and a skillful teacher, enough to be concerned about the teacher's competence or motives, enough to raise your own questions to the teacher when you and she sit down to talk about your visit, or enough to know you want a return visit to satisfy unanswered questions.

The questions presented here are your practical guide to getting the information you need to make good decisions about your child's program and educational future. As you use them to help you to observe, you will begin to develop your own questions and your own valid comments. The questions become easier when you draw on your own daily living experience to understand the classroom. For example, the last time you made something only to be told what was wrong with it is like the experience a student has when the teacher says, "This problem is wrong" and doesn't praise the nine problems done correctly. You know the feeling that comes when efforts go unrewarded, and you know that there's a better way. The more you draw on your own experience to understand the experiences in the classroom, the better observer and critic you will become. It may take more than one visit, but on each visit you will see more and you will see more clearly.

Materials and Curriculum

Up to this point, we have discussed observations you can make about the teacher's style and ability in working with all the students. Now we want to look at what is taught (the curriculum) and how (the materials and methods). It will be difficult for you to make good observations in this area except as it affects the one student you know really well—your own child. For example, you know that your child remembers everything he sees but very little of what he hears; that he can tell you a terrific story but can't write it down because he can't hold a pencil well, can't spell, etc.; or that he does things well with his hands but can't do simple arithmetic. This is the kind of information you have circled on the IEP and in your notebook. Use your notes to help you remember all these points as you watch the teacher work with your child, and as you watch your child working alone with the materials.

1. Are the materials presented to your child at his level of skill:
   a. Is the material at the right age level? (For example, if your twelve-year-old retarded child is starting to read, are the books he is given about things older children are interested in or are they baby books?)
   b. Does the teacher use materials that take into account your child's learning style and strengths? (For example, your child is good with his hands but poor at math, so he uses blocks or some other objects to help solve simple arithmetic problems.)

2. Does the teacher adapt the prepared or purchased materials to your child's skills and interests?
   a. Is the material presented in the amounts and the form your child can use? (For example, the arithmetic problems are at the right level but the print is so small or there are so many problems to the page that your child is making errors that would not be made were the print larger or were there fewer problems to the page.)
   b. Does the teacher involve your child by using special topics your child cares about? (For example, the teacher uses writing and reading assignments about your child's own experiences, arithmetic problems that are about planes or baseball, and books about teenagers or celebrities.)
   c. If your child falters, can the teacher reframe the question to help him answer successfully?

3. In tutoring sessions with your child, is the teacher prepared with alternative materials and ways to teach?
   a. Can the teacher provide on-the-spot prompts, cues, and assistance which your child needs (a letter to trace, a physically guiding hand, or a new verbal instruction)?
   b. Does the teacher let your child drop back to an earlier skill level to end the session pleasantly?
   c. In an individual session, can the teacher take the responsibility for a difficult lesson and say, "This is too hard" or "This is too much work" and add, "You've worked very hard. Let's stop now"? Or is the teacher determined that your child will do all of it, no matter what? Even the best materials will not work if the lesson is too long or the child is under too much pressure.
   d. Does the teacher provide short practice sessions for your child's special difficulties, either in a tutoring session or for independent desk work?
   e. When your child is doing work that is difficult on his own, is the teacher aware, close by, and

regularly monitoring to see that he is doing the work correctly and not making mistakes that will have to be unlearned and that will interfere even more with his progress?

4. Is the teacher helping your child to develop feelings of competence and independence:
   a. Can your child answer most of the questions the teacher asks?
   b. In group sessions, does the teacher make sure to call on your child when there is a strong chance he knows the answer, or are the children called on randomly?
   c. Can your child do most of the independent desk work without a lot of help from the teacher?
   d. Is the independent desk work an opportunity for learning or is it busy work? (For example, your child, who has poor writing skills, spends most of the time laboriously copying from the board.)

By looking at the materials and by watching the teacher and your child work, you will know if your child's special needs are being met, and new and active learning is taking place.

5. If, during your visit, a specialist (speech, reading, physical therapy) enters the room to work with the class, to take a child from the classroom, or to return a child, watch the interaction between the teacher and specialist.
   a. Is the specialist welcomed?
   b. Do the teacher and specialist exchange questions and information?
   c. If the specialist works in the classroom, do the teacher and specialist work together or does the specialist work alone with a single student?
   d. Do the teacher and specialist arrange a time to talk to each other?

How specialists and teachers work together affects the progress of their students. This is something you may want to discuss with the teacher when you meet after your classroom visit.

During your classroom visit, be prepared for a few surprises. It may be that your child, who seems so dependent on help at home, behaves quite independently in the classroom and even initiates activities on his own. Sometimes you will see new strengths (and weaknesses) your child has when you see him outside the home.

THE FOLLOW-UP INTERVIEW: USING YOUR PERSONAL SKILLS

After your first visit, you will have some good notes, a lot of information, and a lot of questions to ask the teacher. You will also have some idea of the kind of reception you can expect from the teacher when you sit down to talk. Did your entrance into the classroom bring you a friendly nod and a place to sit, or were you ignored? During your observation, did the teacher occasionally include you with a smile or a comment, or did you never make contact? Did the teacher seem relaxed, nervous, indifferent, or even hostile? Use your experience with people in general (and your past experiences with the particular teacher) to guide you in your approach to the teacher.

You will be presenting concerns, questions, and information to the teacher. Since you want the teacher to accept your comments as valid and to openly share with you her concerns and knowledge, you might begin by trying to put her at ease. Teachers do get nervous too. You may be the first parent to make an independent visit; your motives may not be clear to the teacher; or the last parent to visit the classroom may have found fault with everything, even the teacher's taste in clothes.

During your personal interview, you will be able to tell if the teacher accepts or rejects you and also if the teacher is friendly, bored, or suspicious; you will begin to know whether the teacher is confident, overconfident, or insecure, and whether the teacher is competent, inexperienced, or inept.

The friendly, accepting, confident, and competent teacher is the ideal. If you have found such a teacher, your work will be easy (at least at this level of the system). Some of you will have to deal with the other extreme— the rejecting, suspicious, self-satisfied, or inept teacher. (Keep in mind that even this teacher, reluctantly or indirectly, does provide you with important information about your child's program and future.) Most of you will deal with teachers who have some good skills and some faults. If you work carefully and thoughtfully with your child's teacher, you can make that teacher your ally in getting good educational services for your child.

Making the Teacher an Ally

Begin your interview by telling the teacher you enjoyed visiting her class, and talk generally about the good things you saw in the classroom. Sometimes this will be easy ("That was a terrific math lesson. It looked like all the students were interested and working hard," "You certainly manage to get my child to do a lot of work. I'm impressed," or "You are so well-organized that everything seems to just flow in this classroom"). Other times you will have to reach to say something positive ("What a nice room you have here," "You certainly have your hands full," or "I'm very interested in what you were doing during the writing lesson"). This is not the time for you to deliver the total and absolute truth, or for you to tell the teacher how you think the class should be run. Nor is it yet the time for you to present your most serious concerns and criticisms. At this moment, you want to establish a good relationship so that you can obtain some solid information from the teacher and *begin* to share some of your own.

Be sympathetic in what the teacher has to say. If excuses are offered, they may be valid ("My aide is out sick today," "The speech therapist didn't take one student today, and, on the spot, I had to prepare extra work for him," "I don't know why the kitchen next door is so noisy today. It was impossible to teach the reading lesson, and I had to change the schedule from reading to crafts"). Be understanding and use the excuses as an opportunity to set up a second visit when conditions may be better.

Next, begin to ask your questions. It is a good idea to present your concerns and observations in the form of questions such as "What was Phil doing with the blocks during the math lesson?" The teacher may tell you that Phil can do his math better when he can use the blocks as an aid to solving the problems. This may be a good answer, but perhaps it looked to you like more play than work was going on. You may think that the teacher needs to do a better job of monitoring and providing individual help more often. You think about how to phrase your concern before you speak:

> *Mr. Ouelette:* Knowing Phil's difficulties, your approach makes a lot of sense. He did well at first, but did you notice that he seemed to slow down a little bit toward the end of the lesson?
>
> *Teacher:* Phil is not a good worker.

or

> *Teacher:* I meant to get back to him halfway through the lesson to give him the help he needs.

The first statement tells you that you may have trouble working with this teacher; the second statement tells you that the teacher understands your child's needs. You should express your support for the good teacher's intentions and performance ("It must be hard to be in so many places at once, but I'm glad you understand Phil's short attention span").

Ask for explanations about materials and methods: "How will this picture book series help Stanley learn to read?" "I notice that you have Thelma sitting at the front of the room. Is that to help her pay attention better?" or "Why does Horace do his reading in that little box (carrel)?" Since you are a parent and not a professional, you can ask all the "dumb" questions you want.

So don't hesitate to ask for further explanations, and, if necessary, ask your question another way. Does the teacher answer you in jargon? A good teacher can explain to you in terms you can understand. Is the answer better or clearer the second time around? If so, the teacher is trying to communicate with you but probably needs more practice dealing with parents, and you, of course, are a willing subject.

Present your concerns as questions: "Brian is so active. Is it possible to give him more opportunities to move around?" "At home, Sheryl's speech is hard to understand. Do you think she needs more speech therapy?" or "Do you think Jeremiah has a visual problem? Should he be tested?" Questions are generally less threatening to a teacher than statements (which may seem critical) or demands. You are not presenting yourself as Mr. or Mrs. Know-It-All Parent; your questions imply that you value the teacher's responses and the special information she can give you. If you are presenting yourself as a sympathetic, interested, and concerned parent who is not there to accuse and who can be trusted, you may get some good and useful answers, such as "Yes, I do think Sheryl needs more speech therapy" or "Jeremiah definitely needs visual testing, but, when I have asked, my requests have been turned down." You can then let the teacher know that you appreciate her honesty and that you will ask the administrators for the service, but that your request will not put an extra burden on the teacher: Your request will be, "My child has a serious handicap and needs more . . ." not "Ms. Newsome said that . . . ."

As you establish yourself as a supportive person to be trusted, you may find the teacher asking you questions, such as "Do you think Lionel would do better if he sat near the board?" "What are Dorca's special interests that I can use to make her reading more rewarding?" "Does Nick need a lot of help in getting dressed at home?" or "Is Desmond as shy and quiet with the neighborhood children as he is in school?" Now the teacher is looking to you as a source of information about your child. Show your pleasure and appreciation by giving the best answers you can without appearing to criticize the teacher. If you don't have the answers ready, tell the teacher you will watch your child more closely at home and get back with the information later by note, or, better yet, by phone. This could be start of productive and frequent communication between you and the teacher.

A good teacher wants and needs the information you have about your child. Your information, suggestions, and questions may stimulate the teacher to new ideas about how to teach your child, just as the teacher's (or specialist's) ideas and reports may lead you to find new ways to help or deal with your child at home. A good teacher and a good parent can make a formidable team.*

If you and the teacher have a good relationship and good communication, you are likely to have a greater impact on your child's educational program. You will have opportunities to shape the teacher's behaviors, not only with you but also in the classroom with your child. By telling the teacher what you saw that you liked, there is a good chance that the teacher will do more of what you liked (teachers enjoy praise too, as long as it's genuine). When you praise, you can offer little suggestions or questions which will further shape the teacher in the direction you want; for example, "I see Daryl's written work is getting much better. Is that because you are giving him extra help? It's working great and Daryl seems a lot happier." The teacher feels good, and you will get more of what you want.

---

*Ten years ago the writer worked with an extraordinary teacher to develop school and home programs for her son. Although at that time the writer had no special education training or experience, the teacher treated the parent as a collaborator, with weekly calls to the home to share ideas, discuss areas of progress (or lack of it), brainstorm, and jointly develop new techniques or treatments. Given the state of special education at that time, it was an exhilarating and astonishing experience for the parent, which led to great benefits for the child.

There are several ways you can become a more and more important resource and ally to the teacher. For example, you might ask the administration to get the occupational therapist (or the visual testing) both you and the teacher want for your child. Because the teacher wants to work more closely with the speech therapist (and you agree on the importance of that teaming), you have written into your child's IEP that the speech therapist will meet regularly with your child's teacher and provide a plan for language activities to be done in the classroom by the teacher. Or you speak up to the administration about giving more gym time to your child's class. You use the teacher as your private resource, and you become the teacher's special resource.

The effective collaboration of parent and teacher can happen when mutual respect and trust are established. Sometimes this can happen quickly, but it usually takes several productive and pleasant meetings. An inexperienced or insecure teacher may need a lot of your support; an established and competent teacher may need to see that your observations and suggestions are carefully considered, relevant, and valid. You need to know that the teacher is sensitive to your ideas and your child's needs. You and the teacher can become educational allies in the service of your child.

But what do you do when you have presented yourself as a concerned and interested parent who wants to support the teacher, and find that you are dealing with a rejecting or disinterested teacher?

Dealing with the Reluctant Teacher

The "reluctant" teacher is probably the one who made it difficult to make arrangements for visiting the classroom; she probably ignored your entrance to the classroom or introduced you in such a way that you were made to feel like an intruder who was being granted a special favor; and she did not look at you during your visit, or, if you did receive glances, they were not warm ones. You may feel that you have been on the receiving end of indifference at best, and, at the worst, anger, or hostility. (Note that a nervous teacher also may not welcome or look at you. But you know how to recognize nervous people: For example, they may lose their place in thought, speech, or action, or drop things. Some pleasant and supportive glances from you may help to put this teacher at ease.)

Occasionally you will meet a reluctant teacher who, on the surface, seems to do all the rights things—greets you, indicates where you should sit, and smiles at you. But you feel the smiles are cold and the teacher is the original iron hand in the velvet glove. You mentally note these feelings and plan to check them out during your personal interview with the teacher. Your feelings are important: They are your antennae that signal you that something is going on. Respect your feelings, but do not act on them until you have more information. When you sit down with the reluctant teacher to discuss your concerns and observations (in the form of questions, of course), there are some things to watch for which will tell you that you are in fact dealing with a reluctant teacher and which will help you assess the potential difficulty in working with this teacher.

First, you are likely to hear that your child's lack of progress is due to his faults and disabilities ("He's lazy," "He's incapable of doing the work," or "His paperwork is always messy") or your inadequacies as a parent ("You must talk to your child about his behavior in school," "Do you ever do things with your child?" or "I wish you would not try to teach your child at home. It only makes my job more difficult"). You may have expected as much from this teacher whose only previous contacts with you have been to inform you by note or phone that your child had a fight during recess or ruined a schoolbook. But even when anticipated, this kind of cold and insulting reception is very hard on parents. You must remain cool, take notes, and continue to ask your questions.

Second, you are likely to hear jargon from this teacher in response to your questions. Attempts on your part to get answers you can understand will lead to still more jargon, and continued efforts to gain clearer communication bring forth statements like "It's very complicated, Mrs. Richards" or "Why not leave the teaching in the hands of the professionals?"

Why, you may ask, are you even talking to this creature who seems bent on putting you down and insulting you and your child? What can possibly be gained by going through this process? Information! However unpleasant, you are still gaining valuable information about the teacher, the classroom, and your child's educational future. You are making worthwhile observations about the teacher's style, personality, inability to deal with parents and students or inability to communicate what she does. Your direct questions haven't been answered, but you intend that they will be, if not by this teacher, then during the development of the IEP, by the special education director or someone else who has the capacity to speak plainly.

When you feel you have as much information from the reluctant teacher as you need or feel you can handle, you can end the interview with a brief "thank you for your time" (you need not wait to be dismissed). Go home and finish up your notes, which should include some direct quotes. For now, congratulate yourself for having done a good job of collecting information which you will put to good use when you approach the administration to plan for your child's educational future.

Dealing with the Incompetent Teacher

Some of you at some time may encounter a teacher who is a nice person and who is devoted to the students, but who is simply not a competent teacher. You learn to recognize this teacher by your child's lack of progress, and, during your visit, by the absence of beneficial educational activities in the classroom. This teacher may smile a lot and run a beehive of activity, but the activity is basically busy work. You realize that your child is doing the same work he was doing last year, or even the year before. You see the students start tasks which they never get to finish; the teacher works without a well-organized plan; the educational goals set for the children are too low or vague; or there are too many free activities. The teacher may be kind and the children seem happy. What more could you want for your child? You want an education, and you want one which will benefit your child.

When your observations and discussion show that you are dealing with an incompetent teacher, you are really in a difficult position: Who wants to complain about a fond, well-meaning teacher and happy children? It will help you to remember that public education for handicapped children is time-limited. Your child has only so many years left in school, and those years should be used to maximum advantage.

In your personal interview with the teacher, carry on your discussion in terms of your child's needs. Never personalize the discussion by commenting on the teacher's inadequacies. In some future discussion with the special education administrator, your theme will be only that your child is not making progress in his present classroom and needs to be considered for another placement. Even then, you should not make statements about the teacher's lack of competence, but focus on the program's inadequacies. Your observations and assessment of the teacher's competencies will probably be both valid and useful, but be careful about how you share this information. You are on more solid ground when you are talking about your child's needs.

Most of you will deal rarely, if at all, with the extreme types of teachers we have just discussed; many of you will deal with teachers who are sometimes overworked, overwhelmed, inexperienced (on the job or with parents), or involved in a temporary personal crisis. You can bring along these teachers by your interest, support, information, and concern.

Learning about classrooms and teachers was the last step in your basic preparation for the big event—participating in the process of developing an appropriate IEP for your child. Everything you have read in this book has been leading up to the moment when you, the knowledgeable and practiced parent, sit down at the working table with the professionals to plan your child's educational services. The IEP process is the heart of P.L. 94-142. The next chapter will take you step by step through that process, helping you to identify potential problems and to use your information and skills to your child's advantage.

Six

Close Encounters:
Working Out the Educational Plan

Mrs. Russell was mailed a copy of her son's IEP with instructions to sign and return it immediately to the school principal. When she called the teacher to ask what she should do, the teacher told her to sign it because it would save time, since the IEP was based on some informal discussions they had had a few months ago. When Mrs. Russell expressed her concern that there was no written objective for physical education, she was told, "We'll work that out when the school year starts."

Janetta Fox, in a similar situation, refused to sign the IEP and insisted on a meeting. She dreaded the meeting, but at the last minute, she found an advocate to go with her. The first meeting was not enough, so they are preparing for the second meeting.

As soon as Nick Fraser was diagnosed as learning disabled, his father requested an IEP meeting. Although he had to take time off from work, he was able to arrange a day when his workload was light. When he received a copy of the IEP agreed on at the meeting, he found that the extra math tutoring he requested had been omitted. He requested another meeting but the special education director told him the omission was an error and a corrected copy would be put in the mail. Mr. Fraser will wait a few more days before calling again.

Now it is your turn to initiate and actively participate in the process of developing an Individualized Education Program (IEP) to meet your child's needs. Perhaps you have already been through an IEP process which was

179

arranged, orchestrated, and completed by the school system and in which you put yourself and your child's future totally in the hands of the school people. It was all quite friendly, and the IEP was wrapped up in less than an hour; but you may have accepted an IEP which did not meet your child's needs. You may want to take another look at your child's completed IEP as you read this chapter and consider whether you have justification for requesting a new IEP.

Maybe you have just received the IEP in the mail and haven't signed it yet. Make sure you read this chapter before you sign. Or possibly you have received a notice informing you that the meeting is being held this week (or next), and you are in a panic because there isn't enough time to prepare yourself. Relax: There's time. That notice is not a court summons requiring you to appear at the appointed time. P.L. 94-142 gives you the right to negotiate a meeting time which is convenient for both you and the school people. Don't be afraid to ask for another week or two if you feel you need it to prepare to be the well-informed advocate. If you haven't yet visited the classroom, this might be a good time to ask the school people to arrange a visiting time for you. If there are reports and documents you want, you can ask for them, adding that you don't wish to create a need for a second meeting just because you are uninformed.

As you become involved in the IEP process, you may be feeling nervous. In times past, you were content to sit on the bench while the others played out the game; but your benchwarming days are over. Now that you know something about how the system works, and about your skills, knowledge, and rights, you realize that dealing with the system this time is a whole new ball game and you will be an active participant. Your nervousness is okay when you are knowledgeable and prepared for your part: It is the same with a good athlete or performer before the big event. However, if you are paralyzed by fear, you will need more relaxation and some more rehearsal.

A moderate amount of skepticism is okay too. By now you know that you should ask questions, and that you are entitled to answers that make sense to you. Your former total trust of and reliance on the school people have been replaced by an unwillingness to accept everything on faith. You want to know why particular recommendations are appropriate and how they will meet your child's needs. This does not mean that you substitute total suspicion for your former blind faith, or that you are looking at every school person's statements as potential traps leading to an inferior educational plan. It does mean that before you agree to the IEP (or any of its components), you expect to be convinced, by explanations you can understand, that your child will benefit. When you are not convinced that a recommendation is a good one, your skepticism impels you to get further justification for the recommendation or to develop another, more beneficial, recommendation.

Pessimism, however, is not okay. Some parents will say, "They didn't pay much attention to me last time. Why should they want to include me this time?" They will if this time you are more knowledgeable and more assertive than you were before. If you go to the meeting expecting to be ignored or put down, that's what will happen; it is hard to be assertive when you are expecting to fail. Your pessimism can contribute to an inferior IEP. By the end of the meeting you will prove to yourself that you were right, "They didn't pay attention to me this time either," but being right is small satisfaction to parents who want better services for their children and don't get them. Set your pessimism aside and go to the IEP meetings with some confidence in your abilities and with some realistic expectations of success. You will achieve at least some of your goals for your child and maybe a better plan than you thought possible.

Many parents, at the point of entering the IEP process, still hang back, saying, "Do I have to? Can't the school people develop an educational plan without me?

After all, it's their job." Of course, they can develop a plan without you; some school people would even prefer to do it without you. But it won't be the best plan or even the right plan for your child. The school people (and your child, above all) need you as an active participant to help develop the plan best suited to meet your child's needs. If you have more than a little stage fright, go back and reread or skim the earlier chapters to remind and reassure yourself of your importance in this process. Commit yourself to working through the IEP: No more hanging back. Set your pessimism and extreme nervousness aside, and get ready for the meeting.

ARRANGING THE IEP MEETING

Chances are your school system has already held or is calling an IEP meeting for your child since it is the school's responsibility under P.L. 94-142 to identify handicapped school-age children. In fact, every state has been mandated to perform a search (Child Find) for handicapped children in need of educational services. However, some children may still be "undiscovered." As your child's agent, it is up to you, the parent, to see that he is "discovered" as soon as possible.

Here are some examples of unidentified children and some suggestions for bringing them to the attention of the responsible school systems:

1. Your child is approaching school age. It is increasingly obvious to you that she will require special services, but you were not aware of the Child Find, so your child was not discovered. You can now call up your local school system to tell them that your child is almost old enough to begin school and you know or suspect that she has a handicap. Your phone call may be enough to set the wheels in motion. If anything in the phone conversation leaves you with the feeling that the school is not likely to swing into action, then sit down and write a letter informing them that you "have a child (give her

name) who will be _____ years old* in (give the month), and who is expected to enter school this September," that you suspect your child has a handicap, and that your child needs to be evaluated and to have an IEP drawn up. Record in your log the date you contacted the school system, the method of contact, and the content of the conversation or a copy of your letter.

2. Possibly your child has been a regular class student in school but is doing poorly and you suspect that he has an undiscovered handicap. If this will be the first contact you have made with the school system, you might start with a phone call. But if you have repeatedly mentioned your situation to the teacher and the principal and have not gotten any response, you should send a letter by certified mail. Explain in your letter that you have reason to suspect your child has a handicap and that you understand it is the responsibility of the school system to evaluate such children and plan an appropriate education program.

3. Perhaps your child was in a special education program before P.L. 94-142 took effect, and because she was already being served, you think or were told that she doesn't really need an IEP. This is not true! Your child is entitled to the full treatment under P.L. 94-142, and that means she should have an IEP which can include new evaluations, some of which you may have wanted for years.

Here, your school system is at fault. Forget the phone

---

*States differ in age of entry into special education services. The majority of states begin to provide services at age five; a large number serve three-year-olds; and some even serve children in their first year of life. To determine if your child is now age-eligible for services, contact your state Department of Education or the Council for Exceptional Children (see Appendix A for address and phone number). A chart of ages of eligibility as of May 1, 1980 appears in Appendix B.

and start with the letter. The letter should simply state that your child has never had an IEP, that you understand that under P.L. 94-142 she is entitled to an IEP, and that you are requesting one as soon as possible. If you believe that your school system has made an oversight or been careless, then send your letter by regular mail. But if you suspect real reluctance on the part of the school system, you should begin your active advocacy with certified mail.

4. You believe that since your child is in a private school, he is beyond the responsibility of the public school system. This too is wrong. If you have a handicapped child, it is the responsibility of your school system to develop an IEP and monitor its implementation. If the school system is paying for the private placement, it is accountable for ensuring that your child has an appropriate educational placement. Even if you have elected and are paying for a private school placement which has not been approved by your school system, you still have the right to request an IEP meeting for your child. The IEP assessments could uncover new and valuable information about your child. This new information may give you reason to consider placing your child in public school (or it may further convince you that your decision to place your child in private school was the right one). In communities where school systems provide services to private schools such as parochial schools, you may find that your child is entitled to some publicly supported special educational or related services. Send your request for an IEP meeting to the public schools, stating your child's present placement and your understanding that he is entitled to an Individualized Education Program, including evaluations.

5. Because your child is living in a state institution, you believe that she is outside the responsibility of the public school system, and that she is receiving services already. You may be wrong on both counts. The school system is still responsible for your child's educational program and must identify, evaluate, and plan for your

child. It may be that the institution provides basic custodial services and few or no educational services for your child. If so, to whom do you turn for the IEP? The school system. Prepare your letter to the director of special education in your town, informing her that your child is a resident of a state institution and that you are asking the school system to initiate the IEP process.

If there are other reasons the schools did not find you and your child (perhaps you recently moved into the community), help them out. Although the legal responsibility for identifying your child is the schools', you are perfectly willing to help them find him. Again, send your director of special education a letter of introduction and ask that the IEP process be put in motion for your child.

Perhaps some of you were found, but the services are still wanting because the IEP process may not have been satisfactory or in compliance with the law. For example, your participation in the process was minimal or even zero because of one or more of these practices:

- The IEP meeting was held upon short notice.
- The meeting was held at a time when you couldn't be there.
- The meeting was conducted in jargon and there was little opportunity for you to ask questions.
- English is not your primary language and there was no one at the meeting to help you understand the discussion.
- You were not given the opportunity to read your child's records before the meeting.

For these and other reasons, if you believe your rights to participate in developing your child's first IEP were violated, you should notify the school system in writing that you were not actively involved in the original IEP because of (state your reasons) and that you are requesting that the IEP meeting be reconvened so that you may rightfully participate, as defined by P.L. 94-142.

When you are notified of a date for the IEP meeting, you are entitled to negotiate the date. A cooperative school system will call in advance of the notice to discuss times which are mutually convenient, and then send you a notice stating the agreed-upon time. A school system which is resistant or tends to manage parents by control or intimidation will send an unexpected notice. In this case, if the time is impossible, or even difficult, you should respond in writing, stating the problem and requesting a more convenient time.

If you experience serious difficulty in arranging the IEP meeting, you must aggressively pursue the school system through letters and calls by you and people willing to help you in your advocacy efforts. Reread chapter four, especially the sections on writing letters and using your allies. A certified letter from you with a formal copy to an agency or political representative, or a phone call from a citizen organization may be necessary to bring about the desired meeting.

Whatever was required of you in calling or setting a time for the IEP is entered in your log. Later on your records will support you if there is undue delay or difficulty and you need to complain. They also provide a check on your memory: When you review your log, you may find that you talked to the secretary and not, as you thought, to the principal (time to get on the phone again and make sure this time you reach the principal in person), or a convenient meeting time in fact was arranged three weeks after your request, not months later, as you in your impatience imagined. Once you have the meeting conveniently arranged so that you have one to two weeks lead time, you begin your final stage of preparation.

PREPARING FOR THE IEP MEETING

In the week or two before the scheduled meeting you have some important work to finish so that you can present yourself as an informed and active parent participant in the IEP process. If you have already been collecting information, visiting the classroom, and readying records, you can use this time to prepare yourself:

- Organize your records and your thoughts.

- Get copies of items not in your files, such as missing evaluations or more information on the law.

- Make your list of concerns, questions, and recommendations which you want considered in the development of the IEP.

- Talk to your personal advocate about what the meeting will be like and plan what her role will be.

- Write down statements you want to make to the IEP group and to yourself for personal support.

- Rehearse your role in the IEP process, including management of any difficulties which could arise.

If you discover, while preparing yourself for the meeting, that you have good reason for delaying or changing the meeting (you are missing some evaluations in your file or waiting for recent evaluations to be completed, or your personal advocate cannot make the scheduled meeting), do not hesitate to negotiate another meeting time. You are not trying to make life difficult for the school people. You may in fact simplify their jobs by coming fully prepared.

In these weeks before the meeting give yourself sufficient time to do the work but also allow yourself some time off for relaxation. All work and no play can make an uptight advocate. If you are overworked, you will be a less effective participant. Besides, you deserve some reward for the time and effort you have been putting in.

Reviewing the Records

This is the time to make sure you have collected all the information you need. One way to do a thorough review of your records is to make a complete list of everything you have in your log or notebook. List materials by year, by topic, or by whatever grouping is going to work best for you (see Keeping Records section in chapter four). Make note in your list of what you consider the most important information for developing a good IEP and determine if there are any missing documents. Plan to have the missing documents in your hands by the time of the meeting. If your file is too large to carry to the meeting, pull out the documents you expect you might want to use at the meeting. If your file is small, you can take it all with you. (If your papers are only one-quarter inch deep and you are the parent of an older child, the file itself can make a statement about the lack of services, plans, and evaluations for your child: "Maryann has been in special classes for six years now, and these are all the reports I have collected. Surely we need to do more for her.")

Not only might you pull out and mark the important documents, you can also underline the sections which appear significant to you and make comments in the margins, such as "I don't know what this means" or "Charlie could do this several years ago." These are the records which you collected to help you work for your child; mark them up in any way that helps you to remember the issues and to communicate them to others—your advocate, the school people, or agency people.

As you go through your files, also jot down issues and concerns to raise at the meeting. For example:

Teachers' Reports, 1979 and 1980;	Reports do not agree. The 1979 teacher report has Randy more capable than 1980 report. Speech report also better for Randy, and is similar to camp report.
Report from Camp Tall Trees, 1979; Speech Evaluation, 1980	Raise speech and independent skills as areas of concern. Stress speech evaluation and camp report at meeting.

Listing items in this way helps you to sort out your concerns and questions, and enables you to use the information you have as support for getting services you want.

Some parents on their first try will find that they are listing everything as important. And they are right:

Everything is important. But some things are more important than others. If you find yourself with an unwieldy list, don't think the job is unmanageable and give up in despair. Go through your "unwieldy" list and star the most important priorities for this year. Look for groupings of items that will support your priorities, as in the following case:

> This year I think speech therapy should have the highest priority. Now, let's see. The evaluation from the Children's Medical Center will help, and so will the report from last year's teacher. Here's something else. With these reports I can make a strong case for the service I want my child to have.

As you go over your records in this manner, you will begin to see how useful they will be. You don't have to do the review in one sitting unless your records are very slim. This is not a test of your endurance. It can be helpful to set the records aside, and come back later when you are fresh for the task.

When you have culled your records for priorities and for back-up information to support those priorities, and when you have organized your thoughts and the list of services which you believe your child needs, you will have prepared the basics of a plan for the IEP meeting. Now share that plan with your personal advocate.

Getting Your Advocate Ready*

By now, based on the information you received in chapter four on the Advocate's Advocate, you have sought and found a personal ally who will accompany you to the IEP meeting(s). Whether you have a strong or weak advocate, a long-distance advocate or one at your side,

---

*It may help you to have your advocate read this section as part of your team preparation for the IEP meeting. It will also help your advocate to read this chapter to understand what the IEP process is, if she does not already know.

your advocate must be fully informed about and involved in the planning for the IEP. All of your preparation in reviewing the records should now be shared with your personal advocate. (**Note:** If, in spite of your efforts, you find yourself without an advocate, you should not ignore this section. You will find some special comments throughout on how to use this advice when you are the lone advocate.)

Begin preparing your personal advocate by sitting down with her and going over:

- your list of priority issues for the IEP

- selected documents which you have deemed important (if your advocate has the time, ability, and interest, you can invite her to read everything you have)

- the people who will be at the meeting and your past impressions of them

- any correspondence you have had with the school people (which may indicate that smooth or rough sailing is ahead)

- information about P.L. 94-142 and the state laws (if your advocate needs this)

- the role (specific statements and behaviors) you hope the advocate can play to support your efforts

- your concerns, questions, hopes, and fears about the upcoming meeting

You must be ready to share all the information you have with your advocate. A sophisticated advocate may want only your list of priorities, a few selected documents, and your verbal report of your contacts with the school system. Your long-distance advocate may, after talking to you on the phone, request that you send copies of one or two documents which he will review before advising you in a follow-up call. Your well-meaning but naive advocate may be overwhelmed by the information. Here, the rule is give your advocate all the information she can handle, and no more. When your advocate protests, back off, suggesting that maybe the two of you should just go over your priorities. Later, perhaps, you can do more preparation; for now, you should respect your advocate's anxieties and concerns.

Any advocate should be informed about what you are hoping to get out of the IEP meeting. Therefore, review your list of desired services, noting which are the most important and which are the least. Let your advocate know that, while you would like all the services, you don't expect to win all your points; you do expect, however, to get your child's most important needs met in the IEP. Explain why these services are necessary, talking about your own experiences with your child, including your observations and your attempts to help him. In this way, you show your advocate how the service is important.

The lone parent advocate may not have someone to listen to his explanation of priorities. In this case, the parent can help himself by playing out the situation, trying to put in words what he wants in the IEP. For example, "I want more physical therapy for Kathy." (Why?) "Because she needs it." (Not strong enough!) "This report indicates that she should be having it daily." (Specific reference, good!) "She has a more pronounced limp now than she had last year." (You're using your own observations to make a stronger case.) By rehearsing your requests and explanations to a fantasy helper, you can learn to criticize your own performance, improve your statements, and strengthen your arguments. Write down your good statements and arguments to use at the meeting or they may be lost.

Documents (selected ones or all of them) are shared with your helpers in the way they can get the most out of them: mailing copies to your organizational advocate, letting your sophisticated advocate read them with or without you, or describing some of the most significant reports in your own words to your naive advocate. They will give you back useful comments and questions which will help you build your case. Don't underestimate the value of naive questions from an inexperienced advocate. Naive questions sometimes cut right to the heart of the matter: "If all the reports you've been describing say that Chuck needs daily therapy, then why isn't he getting it?" You may decide that that question is the one to put to the school system. Give your advocates all the information and papers they want and can handle, but don't overload them. Respect their comments, opinions, and ideas about the information you have shared with them.

At this point, it might be helpful to introduce your advocate to the cast of characters who will be participating in the IEP meeting. Perhaps your naive advocate is visualizing a meeting of Godzilla, King Kong, and Attila the Hun. It may be reassuring to her to hear your impressions of the school people you expect to be at the meeting:

> I found the special education teacher, Ms. Atkins, to be a little stiff and formal with me. But Laura likes her and is finally starting to read for pleasure. Ms. Atkins may not be very good with parents; at least I feel a little uncomfortable with her. Still, she impresses me as a competent teacher. Then there's the regular class teacher, Mr. Hale; he was as friendly as can be and told me what a great student Laura was. But Laura says he doesn't pay any attention to her when she's in his classroom. The special education director, Mr. Green, seems like a nice guy, but he doesn't push for new services. I think he's more worried about the budget than anything else. Then there's the school psychologist . . .

When you describe the school people to your advocate, they may begin to appear less intimidating to her. Your advocate may recognize their similarities to people she has successfully dealt with before. Perhaps she says, "You know, that Ms. Atkins sounds like Ms. Haag, the town's head librarian. She glares at you if you make the least noise in the library. But she knows that library inside out, and if I want to find a book, I go right to her and she finds it pronto. She may be tough but she knows her business. If Ms. Atkins is as smart as you say, maybe she's the one we want to watch at the meeting to see if we are on the right track."

As you and your advocate continue through the cast of characters, you both might begin to think of strategies. For example, you agree with your advocate that it might be helpful to watch Ms. Atkins to see if she agrees or disagrees with your recommendations. If she's the tough old bird you think she is, she may also intimidate Mr. Green, which could be used to your advantage. In your discussion, note which participants, in your opinion, will have the knowledge, the competence, or the power you need behind you at the meeting, when to call on each participant for information, and where hidden sources of support might be. The lone parent advocate will also find it helpful to reflect on the school's cast of characters, and where the expertise or power lies. As you go through your list, you make notes for yourself—expect some support from this person, resistance from that one, nothing from one or two others.

Both the school people and the task of developing a good IEP are now beginning to look a little more manageable. You should remind your advocate and yourself that you are discussing your impressions based on your own experiences and information from your child. Any one of the participants may present himself differently at the meeting and prove you wrong. This is not always an unpleasant experience. The regular class teacher, whom you may have expected to be a mere benchwarmer, might tell the group that he has great difficulty understanding Laura's speech; for that reason, he feels he isn't giving her the help she needs, and may ask about getting more speech therapy for Laura. You may be pleasantly surprised and immediately add your support to his recommendation. Thus, you and your advocate should be prepared to shift gears and strategies when the occasion calls for it.

Your advocate will also need to know how easy or difficult it was for you to arrange this IEP meeting. This is the time to bring out your correspondence with the school system and tell your advocate what problems, if any, you met in arranging the meeting. Hearing about an accommodating school system could help your advocate relax a little; learning about the resistance you encountered might bring forth the response, "Sounds like it could be a tough fight, but we can be tough too." Your review of your correspondence and experience can help your advocate to understand and be ready for what may lie ahead.

If your advocate is naive about special education, provide information about P.L. 94-142. Don't hand her copies of the law and regulations (unless requested) because reading legal language can be difficult and confusing. Instead, give her a few pamphlets which explain in simple language what P.L. 94-142 is all about. Your advocate will want to ask you questions about the law, and you should be prepared to answer them. When you can explain your rights and your child's so that they are understood by someone who doesn't know the law, you will be well prepared to state those rights at the IEP meeting, if that becomes necessary. (This is a good exercise for the lone parent advocate too. Even if you don't have a personal advocate, you should be able to find someone who will listen for five minutes while you explain the law, and then tell you how much he understands.) If your advocate asks you questions you can't answer, go through your materials and find the answers. If you can't find them, then call an organization that can help you. You and your advocate, to the degree you understand the basics of P.L. 94-142, will be better advocates for your child.

Everything discussed above has been in the nature of information sharing. Now is the time for you and your advocate to do some concrete planning. Since you and your advocate will work as a team, you should plan your performance. First look at the strengths and weaknesses of each of you:

- Is one of you more forceful (or less timid) than the other?

- Which of you is more knowledgeable? About which area? (You, of course, know your child best, but a sophisticated advocate may know the law better.)

- Which of you is better at speaking up?
  at reminding everyone of what was said or lost?
  at carrying on an argument?
  at sizing up a group?

- Which of you can be calmer and cooler?

- Which of you (if either) has a face whose expressions are worth a thousand words or the face of a good poker player? (Each can be used to your advantage.)

- Which of you can engineer a graceful shift or exit when the discussion is going nowhere or getting rough?

For the lone parent advocate, a review of your strengths and weaknesses is essential. List them on paper: Look at your weaknesses and think of ways you can manage them. If you are nervous in a group, write down what you want to say beforehand, and plan to take notes during the meeting on what is said. If you are afraid of being pressured into something you don't want, write on a card or in your notebook things you can say, like "I think we need more information about Joanie's performance in this area. I don't want us to get bogged down here." At the meeting you can add, "Could we talk about the daily living skills program, which is very important to me." If you can engineer a shift in this way, you can temporarily reduce the pressure on yourself. You must compensate for the lack of an advocate by careful preparation.

The parent with an advocate must also plan strategies for the meeting. When you and your advocate discuss your individual qualities, you will start to get some idea of how active each of you will be. One of you may play the leading role; the other, the supporting role. You want to balance your styles, strengths, and weaknesses. For example, your advocate may not be at her best with strangers (she seldom speaks up), but she has a memory that would stagger an elephant, and has a good sense of whether groups are working well or doing poorly. Together you can decide that your advocate will play the supporting role. For instance, at the meeting your advocate plans to sit at your elbow with the desired list of services in hand, poking you and making comments to you when things are going well or when you are getting a snow job.

Or perhaps your advocate is a salesperson by nature or profession: Nothing and no one fazes her. This type of advocate will do better playing an active role at the meeting. You might sit across the table from one another so that she can watch your expressions to make sure that she is saying the right thing, that you are not getting too anxious, and that between the two of you, you are able to see everyone's expressions and reactions.

In this way, each of you gets to use personal skills in the style with which you are most comfortable. Your combined assets can make you a more effective advocacy team. You know that it is impossible to predict everything that will happen at the meeting. But if you carefully plan your roles, statements, and signals (to each other), you both will grow in your confidence that at the upcoming meeting something good is going to happen for your child.

As you and your advocate wrap up your planning session, you may want to say something more about your hopes and fears for the upcoming meeting. You might also tell your advocate that your fears are a little less and your hopes a little more because you will have someone who is on your side with you, and because you won't have to walk in alone.*

You and your advocate should plan to meet before the scheduled IEP meeting, perhaps for a quiet cup of coffee and definitely for some last-minute tips or coaching. You won't be reviewing material (unless you just got a copy of a long-awaited report) or making lists of items because you have already done that in your planning sessions. This is the time for you to reassure each other and relax as much as you can. When you leave for the meeting, you and your advocate go together and arrive together.

WORKING THROUGH THE IEP

Let's walk through a sample meeting with you and your prepared advocate. We'll look at everything from greetings and seating arrangements through issues, responses, and dealing with jargon to the conclusion of a carefully written IEP which you accept, modify, or reject. And we will see how and when to cooperate, negotiate, and confront during the IEP process.

Setting the Stage

You and your advocate should arrive on time and greet everyone in a friendly and assertive way—"I'm glad we could arrange this meeting because Harry has needed some changes and more services in his school program

---

*The author once found herself at a meeting without an advocate. She thought she was going to a regular parent-teacher meeting which turned out to be an educational review (an update of the IEP) with six people in attendance. Initially, she was so overwhelmed by the surprise that she didn't think to have the meeting rescheduled. As the meeting continued, this parent grew angry at the violation of her rights and in fact became more insistent on including specific items in the plan. She was successful in getting the plan she wanted (partly because of her angry determination), but left the meeting shaking. It's much better to have a partner, but, even as a lone parent advocate, it can be done.

for some time now. I brought Mrs. Tate, my neighbor.*
She is interested in Harry's progress and has been helping me work on the IEP. I am fortunate that she could
make the time to be here with me today." This kind of
statement helps to put your advocate at ease and defines
her position in the group.

It is not a good idea to say things like "I'm so grateful
to you for arranging this meeting, and I hope it's okay
for Mrs. Tate to come with me." This kind of timid,
hat-in-hand entrance sets you up as a weak parent and
puts Mrs. Tate in the position of being an intruder.
Approached in this way, the school system has already
done you two favors: They "gave" you a meeting and
they let an "outsider" sit in. Your participation in this
meeting and the presence of your advocate are not gifts
but rights.

The physical setting can provide you with advance
information about what's coming. When you sit down to
the meeting, note the physical arrangements. Are you all
sitting at a table like a team trying to solve a problem, or
is the administrator sitting behind a desk which is a
reminder of her authority? Are you going to have to
balance all your important papers in your lap? If so, this
could distract you from the important work at hand.
Ask if there is another room available with a table where
you can all work with the documents in front of you. If
the administrator insists that this is the only room that
can be used for the meeting, then ask for an end table or
another chair to use for your records. A responsive administrator who is honestly limited to that room will
clear her desk as the working table. If you are forced to

---

*You may instead bring your clergyman, a former therapist, or an
advocacy agency representative. Note that this is not the time to
bring a lawyer, who may not only be an unnecessary expense at this
point, but whose presence may so threaten the school people that
they cannot move until they call in their own lawyer. The lawyers,
if needed, are for later.

balance things on your lap during the meeting, then do not apologize when it takes you time to find the report you want. You might say, "If we had a better setup, I could find the document more quickly. Unfortunately, I'm afraid you'll just have to bear with me while I look through my file."

Are you meeting in a place free of distractions, or in an office where you are interrupted by various people and calls not of an emergency nature? Sometimes there will be interruptions at the beginning of the meeting. It is up to the administrator to make it clear to staff that she is not to be interrupted during this meeting, and most administrators will do that. However, if you find yourself at a meeting with constant disruptions which are seriously undermining the development of the plan, you may want to raise the issue of setting a better time: "Ms. Thomas, in the half hour we've been here, you have taken four calls and left the meeting twice." (Who's counting? You! and in your log or notebook as soon as you suspect that the interruptions are becoming unreasonable.) "Although it was difficult for Mrs. Tate and I to arrange time for the meeting, we are willing to reschedule at a better time for you. You obviously have other commitments today, and we need your full participation at this meeting." If things do not quiet down, insist on rescheduling.

In your notebook list who is at the meeting. Were you informed about who would or would not be at the meeting, and are all the participants there, especially the individuals you requested? If not, are the excuses valid? "The gym teacher broke his arm in a freak accident in school today" may be; "The speech therapist is attending an all-day workshop" is not. You are justified in feeling that your child's future is more important than any workshop, and that at the very least, since the speech therapist knew in advance he would be absent, the meeting should have been scheduled for another time when he could be present. You say to the others that it may be necessary for him to be here, but, for the time being, you'd like to see his report. You will then react appropriately to the situation:

No report! Well, without the report we may not be able to finish the program today. Let's see how much we can do.

or

Ah, you have the report. Is this my copy? Give Mrs. Tate and myself a few moments to read it.

Leading Off

The meeting now begins in earnest. If the speech report is presented and you find that it is written in simple language with definitions of complicated terms, don't hesitate to compliment the school people on the clarity of the report—"This is nice. I think I really understand the goals of the speech therapy now." School people need and deserve praise for a good job, too.

If the report is full of jargon and you can't understand it, then say so, and request that it be rewritten so that you can understand it, since this is an area of great concern to you. You are not being difficult: You want and have a right to know. Besides, the group is making decisions which will seriously affect your child, and you will want to carefully review and understand all recommendations and plans before you sign the IEP. Would you sign a contract without reading and understanding it?

If the report is long, you need more time to read it and think about it. Tell the school people you are taking it home and will get back to them later about your child's speech needs.

Being Specific

If you have had time to read the report which was written in language you understand, you may be ready to work through the speech goals of your child's IEP. Ask the school people what they think your child needs and what they have to offer in the way of service. They are the experts; let them go first. They may have developed a speech program which is everything you want. On the other hand, they may be vague. If so, push for specifics:

Not—"Speech therapy"

But—"Speech therapy three times a week with Mr. Hadley, the speech therapist. Each session is thirty minutes. The therapist works with the regular teacher, Ms. Ames, one and a half hours each week, and Ms. Ames provides a language training program (based on therapist's evaluation and plan) for at least thirty minutes each day."

Everything you want that is agreed upon by the group *must be written down in clear and specific terms* so that later on there will be no difference of opinion about the type and quantity of services your child will be receiving. When you have this kind of specificity, you and everyone else understands the kind of service your child will get. You may want to include in the IEP regular meetings for you and the therapist and/or teacher. Again, be specific—meetings once a month, every two months, or perhaps weekly phone contact. Do you also want exercises to do at home with your child? Then say so, and get the specifics.

Remember, talk is cheap (verbal agreements are very weak), and when you go back after a few months to check on the implementation of the IEP, you will be able to advocate for only what is written in the program. With the verbal agreements you may find yourself up against honest misunderstandings, vague recollections, or even loss of memory. And without written agreements you will probably hear about the tight budget and shortage of personnel which does not allow for more service for your child.

The business of getting adequate and accurate information presented, discussed, and recorded at the IEP meeting is hard work. You need a guide.

Asking Your Twenty Questions

In each program or service area, such as fine motor or vocational skills, you should make sure that you have answers to the following questions:

Assessment

1. Is information on your child's present *level of performance* (what he can do and what he can't do) accurately presented, discussed, and agreed upon?

2. Is the information on your child's *learning style* part of the assessment? For example, does your child learn most and best by listening (auditory learner) or by seeing (visual learner)?

Evaluations

3. What *evaluations* has your your child had or does he need? (These evaluations can be done only with your consent. If the school people want your child to have a psychiatric evaluation and you don't agree, you can withhold your consent.)

4. Are the evaluations *comprehensive* and *multidisciplinary*; that is, do they look at the whole child or just a piece of the child? For example, your child is labeled emotionally disturbed and has been seen by a psychologist, but has he been seen by a learning disabilities specialist, an occupational therapist, or a neurologist who may uncover some other specific learning problems?

5. Are the evaluations *nondiscriminatory?* For example, if your child's native Spanish is better than his English, is he tested in Spanish? Or, if your child is visually handicapped, is he given a visual or an auditory test of intelligence? If your child can't make visual discriminations, he will score more poorly on the visual test.

IEP Goals

6. Are the goals written down in the order of *priority* (the most important is first, the next most important is second, etc.), and in the specific descriptive terms that you requested ("one-to-one ratio," not "adequate ratio")?

Implementation of Goals

7. *What service* is to be provided?

8. *Who* will provide the service? The specialist? The teacher? The aide? Any combination of these people? What are their qualifications, training, or preparation?

9. *How* will the service be provided? Which methods or teaching approaches will be used?

10. *Where* will the service be provided? What school or building? What setting—class (regular or special); small group; one-to-one?

11. *How often* will the service be provided? One day per week? Three days per week?

12. *How much* will be provided? Fifteen-minute sessions? Hour sessions?

13. *When* will the service *start?* As soon as the plan is agreed upon and signed? Thirty days later (to allow for hiring special personnel)?*

Meeting Procedures

14. Are the comments and recommendations about the *report* being *recorded?*

15. Do you have your *copy (copies)?*

16. Do you *understand* what you have been given to read?

17. Are you and your advocate being given enough *time and opportunity* to discuss and understand the items presented, to ask your own questions, and to present your own recommendations?

18. If you are *not in agreement*, are your sound and specific reasons for disagreeing being recorded?

---

*If you are expecting a summer program (full or partial) to be part of your child's educational program, make sure it is written into the IEP with specific dates and times. Maybe you're in the IEP process in September and next summer seems far away; but if you forget to write the summer program into the IEP, next summer the schools may forget to provide the program your child needs.

19. If you *are in agreement* about the service, has its implementation been written into the plan in the specific language you requested?

20. Have *all your questions* been answered?

Now, let's apply these questions to another area of concern, such as your child's reading program. The following is a hypothetical transcript of a portion of an IEP meeting using the Twenty Questions as your guide:

Question #1: (Performance)	The teacher discusses her *assessment* of your child's reading level. Your copy was sent to you before the meeting or you and your advocate are allowed sufficient time to read the assessment at the meeting. The teacher reviews:
	Carol is presently reading at a fourth grade level. However, her comprehension is at a second grade level.
	You know that Carol can read more than she can understand because you have done some reading with her at home. You add your general agreement.
Question #2: (Learning Style)	The teacher continues by showing some samples of things Carol has read, and notes that some types of reading materials are better for her:
	Carol seems to do better in comprehending materials that deal in facts and especially with facts that she can relate to her own experiences. While her overall comprehension is at a second grade level, she does a little better with this series. (The teacher shows you and the group one of the readers.)
	At this point, the psychologist speaks up:
	Carol's reading problems may have

something to do with her immaturity and her emotional problems. Her inability to read more abstract material could be a result of her difficulties in dealing with her feelings.

You realize there is a shift here from reading skills to emotional problems, and you intervene:

Before we lose sight of Ms. Payne's assessments, I want to say that my observations of Carol agree with hers. Carol learns and remembers what she can see and do. Emphasizing the concrete can help her read better. She has to understand what she's reading; otherwise, she's only parroting.

Question #3: (Evaluations)

The psychologist refers to his earlier *evaluations:*

Two years ago when I gave Carol some tests, including an intelligence test, she did poorly. From my other observations in the classroom, I thought Carol was a good deal brighter than the test results would indicate. During the testing, however, she became anxious and distracted, which I attributed to her immaturity. Perhaps we need to test her again to see if she has made progress in her emotional development.

You interrupt:

I understand and appreciate what you are saying, but I don't want to move away from Carol's reading yet.

Note that you resist the psychologist's assumptions and the shift away from reading problems.

Question #4:   You ask, "What other evaluations has
(Comprehen-   Carol had?" and are told several others
siveness)   done by school staff. You note that
since Carol has been in school she has
not been seen by a neurologist. Given
that her original diagnosis was "brain
damage," you would like *more comprehensive evaluations*, specifically a review
by the neurologist as well as an evaluation by a learning disabilities specialist.
You feel more information is needed
than one kind of testing—psychological
evaluation—will give. (Throughout the
process you may continue to press for
multidisciplinary evaluations.)

Question #5:   You ask for a description of the past
(Fairness)   psychological evaluations.* As they are
described to you, you realize that they
are basically verbal tests, and you know
that Carol's strengths are visual. You
ask, "Aren't there visual tests of intelligence?" and are told, "Yes, but we use
the most widely used tests, which happen to be verbal." "That doesn't seem
fair," you respond. "It doesn't give Carol
her best shot, does it?" You turn to the
school psychologist and ask, "Can you
give her some other tests that won't put
her at a disadvantage?" The psychologist
is not all that familiar or experienced
with other tests; he feels that it would
be unfair to Carol to do tests he is not
familiar with and suggests that it is best

---

*If there is not time to explain or demonstrate the tests to your
satisfaction, ask the psychologist to set up an appointment for you
to go over the tests.

to leave well enough alone and stick with the verbal tests. You disagree; it is not "well enough" if Carol's true abilities and disabilities are not being measured.

Question #6:
(Priorities)

The teacher wants to discuss her recommendations for reading. "After all," she asks, "isn't reading one of the highest priorities for Carol?" To you, reading and language are part of the same need for your child, and you say so. If you have to separate them for the IEP, then your priorities will be (1) language therapy and (2) reading. Both are very important goals. You want to know how the goal for reading will be implemented.

Question #7:
(What)

The teacher replies that *reading instruction* will be given with the goal being to increase Carol's comprehension from a second grade level to a low fourth grade level in the coming school year. You ask if that is possible. The teacher tells you that she can't promise that the goal will be attained, but she feels that it is a worthy and realistic goal.

Question #8:
(Who)

The teacher indicates that she will provide the basic reading instruction. She will work closely with the *speech and language therapist* to assure that the materials used will be appropriate to Carol's language and reading needs. In addition, the *aide* will work with Carol on an individual basis.

Question #9:
(How)

The emphasis, says the teacher, will be on *concrete basic reading materials*, using the series of readers which Carol is now using with success. The aide will specifically work with Carol on preparing *experience stories* based on Carol's own words and experiences.

Question #10:   The services will be provided in the spe-
(Where)   cial education *classroom* in *small group* and in *one-to-one* instruction.

Question #11:   Small group reading and one-to-one in-
(How Often)   struction will occur *every day*.

Question #12:   The teacher will provide instruction
(How Much)   daily for small group reading and one-to-one instruction, each for one half-hour. In addition, the aide will provide your child with one-to-one instruction for half an hour at least three times each week. This sounds appropriate to you, but you have one question: "What is a small group?" The teacher responds that with her knowledge of the programs of the students she will be teaching, it could range from two to four students, but she expects that for most days three will be the maximum, and that, for one or two days each week, the group size will be two. You ask that the size of the small group be designated in the program as three students.

Note that you required that terms be defined and written down. In this way you can help to prevent that "small group" from growing to six or eight and still appearing to be consistent with the IEP. Because of your request for specificity, you have increased the likelihood of the group remaining small.

Question #13:   The program is beginning to sound good
(When)   to you. There is twice as much overall instruction as last year with a substantial increase in individual instruction. "*When,*" you want to know, will the

reading program *start?*" The teacher explains that she will have a new classroom aide at the beginning of the year and will need a few weeks to train the aide. She anticipates that *within a few weeks the aide,* under her supervision, will begin the additional instruction. *The teacher,* if the IEP is agreed upon, will begin her daily instruction *on the first day* of the school year.

Question #14: (Recording)
The best way to know that all comments and recommendations are being recorded is to ask that they be read back to you. As you listen, check your notes to be sure that the specifics you wanted have been duly noted. If there are omissions or changes, speak up:

> That piece about the teacher and the speech and language therapist was left out. I think that's very important. Please include it in the implementation statements about the goal.

Question #15: (Copies)
Look at your papers. Do you have copies of all reports? The teacher's recommendations? The psychologist's evaluation? If not, speak up:

> I thought Ms. Brousseau's comments on my child were excellent, but I don't seem to have her recommendations. They were not in the report sent to my home. May I have a copy before we finish this discussion on reading?

Since most schools have copy machines, the school people can usually produce the material in a few minutes.

Question #16: (Clear Understanding)
When you get the material, read it to see if you understand it. If not, ask for more explanation. You cannot give your full

agreement until you read and understand everything.

Question #17:
(Time and
Opportunity)

Make sure you take enough time and make the opportunity to present your own questions, concerns, and recommendations. Even the best-intentioned school people may leave you out of the discussion if you never speak up. Someone may not notice you shaking your head in disagreement. You must help to make your own time and opportunity. Whether you agree or disagree, say so and explain why.

Question #18:
(Disagreement)

If you disagree with the reading program being developed, this is the time, when discussion on reading is being wrapped up, for you to say so while the reasons you disagree are fresh in your mind. The school people may not like your criticisms now, but they will like them even less when they think the program is almost done and you unexpectedly pipe up with, "I don't like the reading plan!" Voice any objections you have when the items are under discussion.

For example, if the teacher, when defining a small group, had told you ten children instead of two to four, you would want to object because that was the actual class size and not a small group within the class. You would then want recorded not only your objection but your specific request for instruction in a small group of two to four. Your specific objection is based on your understanding of your child's need, and may in fact make better educational sense than the larger group. It ought to be recorded. (You also recorded your objections in your own notes.)

Question #19:
(Agreement)

But you are in agreement! The reading plan looks appropriate and promises some real benefit for your child. Tell the school people, especially the teacher, that you like the recommendations. Ask that the person chairing the committee read back the specifics—the what, who, where, when, and how(s) of the plan. If any item is vague or has been left out, have that item clarified or recovered and entered into the plan. Work on those additions or corrections until they represent the reading program you are willing to accept. Then, state your agreement and satisfaction.

Question #20:
(Any Questions)

Surely, by now, all your questions about the reading program have been fully answered. Or have they? Review the notes you have been making during the meeting. Remember the discussions with the psychologist about evaluations. That was left up in the air. You may want to seek some closure now or postpone agreement. (If you suspect that the evaluations will be discussed with other components of the IEP, you may prefer to save the discussion of evaluations until the end of the meeting. Write it on your list of things to be accomplished before you sign the plan.) You begin:

Before we go to the next service item, I would like to remind you that we did not finish discussing evaluations. We didn't reach any conclusions that I can remember. I would prefer . . .

Then you may want to say one of the following:

. . . that no further testing be done at

this time. I would like to see the program we have just outlined given a chance to work. Later on we may all feel that further testing will be necessary. When a stronger case can be made, I will be happy to give my consent for further tests.

or

. . . that a neurological evaluation be done along with the psychological testing. I will consent to both evaluations if you can arrange a predominantly visual test of intelligence for Carol.

or

. . . that we settle the matter of evaluations after we have discussed some more of the IEP's components. Since I suspect that Carol has some motor problems, it may be necessary to have more comprehensive evaluations. We may be in a better position to decide later in the meeting which evaluations will be necessary.

In general, as you move from one area of concern to the next (math, adaptive physical education, self-help skills), you are asking yourself and the group the same valid twenty questions until the school people have presented all their recommendations for the education program. During this time, you and your advocate are taking notes on concerns, agreements, and disagreements, as well as making comments, recommendations, and points.

Adding One or Two More Things . . .

The school people have made their recommendations; now it is your turn to present your additional requests for discussion. You quickly review your list of concerns and requests for services to see if any have been left out. From your notes you see that no one has mentioned art or physical education. You want one or both of these items considered in the IEP, and you say so.

The reason you present your recommendations now, rather than at the beginning of the meeting, is that by waiting until the end you may be asking for only one or two things. The school people will have already dealt with some or most of your requests. If you had taken the initiative at the start of the meeting, you would have been asking for everything; now you are asking for "so little."

Hearing the school people first is an important strategy. As professionals, they feel obligated to present as good a plan (based on their professional skills) as they can within the system's constraints. If you have been cool, controlled, and prepared, the chances are that you have engaged already in some give and take during the discussion of at least some, if not all, issues. In this way, you have established yourself as a reasonable person who is both knowledgeable and assertive, as well as concerned and committed.

The wise parent always goes into negotiations with a longer list of services than he is prepared to receive. Your list is made up only of services your child needs (none are frivolous or luxurious), but some services are more important than others, You can star the most important ones—the ones you will insist be met. You are willing to negotiate ones that are less important.

As you review the developing plan, you may see that most of your requests have been included, and you note to yourself, "Speech program looks good. Reading is a little weak, but the gym program is a disaster, and we haven't even discussed the art program."

Presenting Your Case

Given your evaluation, you now present your case. Compliment the parts of the program you like, and express the reservations you still have about other parts—"Harry's motor problems are a serious concern. He needs a carefully planned physical education program with more individualized instruction from the physical education teacher. But he also needs some art therapy to help him develop fine coordination." You hope for both but you are prepared to accept one. The special education director tells you that the physical education teacher is swamped with work and the art therapist gets to Harry's school once a week and doesn't even get to all the grades in the school. Here are some examples of how you can respond in this discussion, depending on how you see your child's needs:

> You say that you appreciate the physical education teacher's problems, but wouldn't it be possible for him to assess Harry and develop a plan which could be used by the classroom aide or student teacher for the first ten minutes of every gym period? This would at least be a start.

> or

> You express your concern and say that you would like both art and physical education because your child's needs are great, but, for this year, you are willing to accept one if both are not possible.

> or

> You request that an evaluation by a physical or occupational therapist be done and that the therapist make recommendations for the classroom, art therapy, and gym to meet Harry's needs.(Perhaps you have talked privately to your child's teacher who agreed with your concerns and who is desperate for help and direction from a specialist.)

Whichever response you make, the message you have given is that your child's motor needs are important and you want something done to help him. Even your weakest response (you will accept either art or physical education) is said with the understanding that next year you will be back for the service you didn't get this year.

When you review your list of services, you may find yourself thinking, "Hey, I've got the most important services, the speech and reading, and that's good. I'd like services to meet all his needs, but I may have to give a little here." If you are keeping score (and you are), your list of proposed services might look like this example (stars denote priority items):

Speech*—satisfactory

Reading*—good but needs more individual attention; make sure time is specified

Math—satisfactory

Music—acceptable

Gym—unsatisfactory (but could be satisfactory if gym teacher and aide work together)

Art—unsatisfactory (but could be satisfactory if teacher gets help and evaluation from the therapist)

Overall, there are more new and specific recommendations in your child's IEP than there were last year, and you feel his needs are being met. You have accomplished what you set out to do. Give yourself a pat on the back or a night on the town: You deserve it.

WRAPPING UP THE IEP

When you have participated in an open and responsive process that leads to an IEP which is appropriate and beneficial for your child, and when that plan has been achieved in an atmosphere of cooperation, collaboration, or friendly negotiation, you are ready to sign the IEP, right? Not quite. No plan will be harmed by a few days' delay. You are pleased with the plan, but you still want to sleep on it just a bit longer.

"Just Sign Right Here"

As the meeting comes to a close, you may be presented with a form to sign. Sometimes you may even be asked to sign an incomplete form with the promise that it will be filled in later (the "we're all friends" approach). You never sign a blank form. It's like a blank check: You don't know what will get written in. Usually, the form will be presented with the information filled in and all is aboveboard, but you still do not sign on the spot. Ask to take it home to read it carefully or to show it to your spouse. After a careful reading, you will sign and return it, or if you have any questions, you will call the special education director to have them answered and the IEP changed and corrected.

Sometimes the schools will mail you copies at a later date for your review and signature.* When you receive the IEP, you and your advocate sit down with your notes to read and discuss it; be sure the plan is what you expected before you sign it. Corrections are made before, not after. When you are satisfied with the IEP— you agree with the services and all your questions have been answered—you return a copy with your signature on the line where it says you accept the plan. If your experiences at the meeting have been positive, you may wish to call the principal or special education director to tell them that the signed IEP is on the way, that you felt the meeting was both pleasant and productive, and that you have great hopes for the coming year for your child. In this way, you compliment the school people on their efforts in the development of the plan and, at the same time, drop a hint that the implementation of the plan will be of great interest to you.

For the time being your work is done. Congratulations! Go back to whatever pleasant things you were doing before you learned about P.L. 94-142 and parent advocacy, while the school people begin the business of implementing the program. Later on you will want to check out the implementation.

---

*If you are handed or mailed only the copy of the proposed IEP that you must return to the school, you should ask for your own legible copy. Most school systems have copy machines available. Because the school people want your signature, it is always easier to get your copy of the IEP before you sign it.

"But I Can't Sign This!"

However, some of you may find yourselves looking at a plan that is poor, even shabby. Not only does the plan not meet your child's needs, it may even appear to be indifferent to your child's needs. If this happens to you, your response will probably be:

> How could this happen after all that hard work and friendly discussion at the meeting? What happened to all those mutually agreed-upon goals? I did everything you told me, and now this—this is not what we talked about. I feel like I've been taken for a ride.

Maybe you did have a wonderful meeting with all kinds of open and friendly discussion and agreements. But when they handed or mailed you the program, you saw immediately that it was full of holes or that your top priorities were lost. When you asked about the omissions, you got excuses for answers. For example:

Mr. Klebanoff: There's nothing here about the implementation of the speech and language goal—the number of times each week, how long, and all the specifics we discussed.

Sp. Ed. Director: We all know what Vicki needs and we are all in agreement. It isn't necessary to write everything down.

Mr. Klebanoff: Oh, but it is. That information is important and should be written down.

Sp. Ed. Director: What if we can't find or even hire another therapist? It's possible with this year's budget that we may have to make do with the staff we've got. There's no point in writing things into the IEP that we may not be able to deliver.

Mr. Klebanoff:	The plan isn't made on the basis of what you can deliver. It's supposed to be an individualized program based on what's appropriate to Vicki's educational needs. I thought it was all set. Why are you backing down now?
Sp. Ed. Director:	Because it may not be possible to give Vicki therapy in the amounts you want for her.
Mr. Klebanoff:	But it's not just me! We agreed on that goal at the meeting.
Sp. Ed. Director:	I'm sorry you're disappointed, but it's the best we can do. You can accept or reject the IEP. It's up to you.

Or maybe you had to work even harder at the meeting, where everyone was given a mimeographed copy of an "IEP." Since your participation in the development of an IEP is an entitlement you have under P.L. 94-142, the preplanned, mimeographed IEP is not an acceptable product. So you started from scratch, item by item, with your twenty questions to develop a program *individualized* according to your child's needs. It was uphill work, but you thought you were succeeding. However, this thing that they mailed you is practically the same as the mimeographed "IEP" which they handed out at the start of the meeting. You feel like you've run the marathon without leaving the starting line. When you complained, you were told: "You can reject the IEP if you don't like it. We think it's satisfactory and we can defend it." Most parents won't meet this kind of stone wall, but that's little comfort to those parents who do.

DEALING WITH YOUR FRUSTRATIONS

Whether you meet your "stone wall" at the beginning of the meeting or face it at the end, it is an extremely frustrating experience for a hard-working and committed parent advocate. You may respond in several ways:

"Where Did I Go Wrong?"

This is often the first response parents make when something bad happens to their child. Parents will search for the flaw in their characters or performance. Of course, it is always possible to look back and find something you could have done differently: For example, "Maybe I should have spoken up more and been more assertive" or "Was I too pushy?" But if you were prepared and your requests were, in your opinion, reasonable and appropriate, you could give a five-star performance and still not get the important services you asked for. When the system is unresponsive, even rigid, and the process breaks down, don't blame yourself. Your job is tough enough without carrying any useless and undeserved guilt. When the process isn't working, you are actually working harder than the parent who is working with school people interested in the child's needs, and you deserve even more rewards for surviving the process (take two nights on the town!). Success isn't only an easy win; success can be hanging in when the going gets rough and the game is going into extra innings.

"You Can't Beat the System"

"The process is a sham. Why did I even try?" Parents who make this response are blaming the system (and that may be putting the blame squarely where it belongs), but they are also giving up. Maybe the meeting was a sham; but it doesn't have to end there. There are still steps, described in the next chapter, that parents can take. If you give up now, the next time you ask for something for your child the school people may find it easy to ignore you. You may have participated in the process, but, after all, when the system took a firm stand against you and your child, you gave up, went home, and didn't bother them any more.

"Yes," you may say, "but I showed them. I didn't sign their IEP." That IEP has since been filed away and there is no one but you to question it. Your child is probably being served under that program you found unacceptable, or perhaps getting even less service because there is no one like you questioning your child's present "IEP." If you did not sign the plan, you can reopen the case by writing a letter to the school (copies to the state Department of Education and others who can help you), stating that you have never accepted the IEP and you are requesting another meeting to develop an appropriate and adequate IEP for your child (see chapter seven).

"I've Put Too Much into This to Give Up Now"

This is the most productive response parents can make. They may feel anger ("Nobody is going to short-change my kid"), desperation ("Daniel needs so much! I can't let him down now"), or even cold determination ("I started this business and I'll see it through to the end"). This response is the starting point for the next phase. All that you have done before is not lost; it is a large part of your preparation for confronting the system. You may add to that preparation, but you are basically relying on the skills and information you have been building.

Actually, most parents will make all of these responses and work through them to gain understanding of the particular process and individuals they have dealt with and to reaffirm their commitment to their children's educational future.

The IEP process is a new and often frightening experience for parents. As they go through it for the sake of their handicapped children, they begin to recognize their own strengths and skills and become more secure in their ability to advocate, negotiate, and develop the services their children need. Most parents will find a satisfactory and appropriate program at the end of the meeting. When they sign IEPs that benefit their children, they will feel good about themselves because they participated in a process which demanded much from them in the way of skills, energy, commitment, and endurance to achieve success. For those parents who find themselves up against resistance, rigidity, and on occasion even hostility, they must temporarily find comfort in their strength and commitment as they continue to work for their goals—the satisfactory conclusion of appropriate individualized education programs for their handicapped children. The next chapter is devoted to those parents who find themselves facing "failure" and frustration. They need to learn how to effectively say no to the system. It is time to look at confrontation.

Seven

Confrontation:
When Nice Guys Finish Last

Harriet Wendell claims she was too nice. Although she brought a list of services she wanted for Charlie to the meeting, she gave in on everything but the speech therapy. The school people finally wrote the speech therapy into her son's IEP. Six months later, Charlie does not have a speech therapist. What more can she do?

Leonard Lawson met with the school people just once and contributed very little "because they never intended to serve Sonia anyway." When he received the IEP, he rejected it immediately and requested an appeal. Now that he is engaged in the appeal process he is worried because he needs to know more about Sonia's school program in order to criticize it.

Although Karen Flynn was prepared and performed well at the IEP meeting, she did not get the services she thought her son, Tim, deserves. She just received a notice from the state Department of Education to come to a mediation hearing and she doesn't want to go because "these professionals always support each other."

These parents need to know more about the productive uses of confrontation. Perhaps you have cooperated, collaborated, and negotiated. You've rehearsed for meetings until you were even saying your lines and making self-statements in your sleep. You may have a file of records, laboriously collected, which is the length of your arm. You have exhausted yourself in your efforts to help develop an appropriate and beneficial plan for your child, yet your child does not have one. Perhaps you feel that you have "failed." But is the failure yours or the school system's? Did the school people fail to recognize your child's special needs? Did they fail to meet your child's special needs? Did they listen carefully to your concerns for your child and your reasons for requesting specific services? Did they explain to your satisfaction and in words you understood why they chose to select certain services and reject others?

As you review your frustrating experience, you may begin to realize that the school people did not take you seriously. They may have been friendly or intimidating; they may have been up front about their refusal to give your child what you believe he needs or they may have feigned acceptance only to present you with a plan that ignored your requests. However they did it, they said no to your requests and your active involvement in developing the IEP, with the expectation (or at least the hope) that now you would go away and leave them to return to business as usual, that you would be a nice guy and not a troublesome parent. But nice guys can finish last and, what is worse, the children of nice guys can end up with poor education programs.

LEARNING TO SAY NO

You may want to go away when the school people reject your recommendations, just as you once were willing to leave your child's education solely in the hands of the professionals. But that was before you read chapter two and learned about the educational myths that have kept parents in their place. Rejecting the IEP is an option which you have the right to choose. Rejecting the IEP may in fact be the biggest contribution you make to your child's educational future.

"But it's hard to say no to the experts." Just as you learned to speak up to the experts, you can learn to say no to them. Be wary of the "old school pupil" who may still survive in your relationships with school people, and who may interfere with your ability to say no to people in authority. You can learn to say no in the same way you learned to speak up at meetings as the controlled, rational, and contributing parent. You do this by planning what you will say, sharing with others your concerns and reasons for rejecting the IEP, backing up your objections with data, and rehearsing in advance of the time when you will say no and say it effectively. Let's look at some examples.

Elsa King went to meetings with school people who were friendly and pleasant. She was devastated when she was mailed the IEP for her daughter, Elaine: The program was the same as last year's and included none of the services Elsa requested so carefully at the meetings. Both she and her husband David agreed that the plan was unacceptable and that they had no choice but to reject it. David wanted to make one last call to the special education director to see if the IEP could be rewritten to reflect the parents' concerns without entering a lengthy process of appeals.

Mr. King:	My wife and I have carefully reviewed Elaine's IEP that you mailed us, and we are in agreement that we cannot accept it.
Sp. Ed. Director:	I'm sorry to hear that. Just what is wrong?
Mr. King:	Well, specifically. . . (He outlines his objections and backs them up with references to his file of evaluations and reports.) Is there any possibility of rewriting the plan to include these important components?
Sp. Ed. Director:	I don't know, Mr. King. The committee worked very hard to develop Elaine's IEP.
Mr. King:	As the IEP is now written, we must reject it.
Sp. Ed. Director:	Give me a few days to see what I can do.
Mr. King:	I appreciate your interest, and I will

call on Thursday to see if you can change the program. Then we can arrange another meeting to rewrite it. But if that's not possible, Elsa and I will be forced to return this IEP with our rejection.

Sp. Ed. Call me on Thursday. I'll see what I
Director: can do.

Note that David King was calm, firm, and specific. His message was clear: The IEP will be rewritten or rejected. And he gave a deadline (Thursday) for action to be taken. If the special education director comes up with a new program that meets with the parents' approval, David and Elsa King will have spared themselves a possibly lengthy appeals procedure by engaging in productive confrontation that is informal and minimal. If on Thursday the special education director says that he can do nothing, then the parents will have lost but a few days.

Delia Norton, on the other hand, had to deal with school people who were constantly patronizing and who rejected her suggestions by using jargon continually. When she received her son Sal's IEP, she was not surprised that it was inadequate. After fuming a bit, she called her personal advocate, Evelyn, to bring her up to date on the situation.

Delia: Evelyn, I just got Sal's IEP and there's no way I can sign it.

Evelyn: Well, we expected that. Give me the specifics, can you?

Delia: That's the problem: There are no specifics. It's so vague that they can do whatever they want and still meet the IEP as written. For example, they have as an objective "regular gym as the schedule allows." Now I ask you, what kind of objective is that? The rest of it is the same way.

Evelyn: Well, Delia, I think you have no choice but to reject the program in writing. The only way to move these people is to show that you mean business. Will you send me a copy? Maybe together we can work up a list of reasons for rejecting it.

Delia: No easy way, is there, Evelyn?

Evelyn: Sending that rejected program back might make them sit up and take notice. It's time someone took them to task.

In this case, the parent's dealings with the system have been difficult from the first day. Since a phone call would seem to be of little value, the parent should formally reject in writing the proposed IEP, noting its faults, such as overall ambiguity or lack of specifics, inadequacy of plans for integration into particular classrooms and activities, or insufficient amounts of specific therapies needed by the child.

Learning to say no to school systems requires the same skills you learned to use in working to develop the IEP process: knowing your rights, using the phone, writing letters, keeping records, and gathering allies. It is harder to say no, however, because disagreement and confrontation are generally unpleasant. If you are the kind of person who always strives to get along and keep everyone happy, you may have to practice a lot to prepare yourself for saying no to the school people. Get out the list of those self-statements you used during the IEP process to shore yourself up when you engage in confrontation.

Earlier you made a commitment to see the process through. Now, as the going gets rough, you must reaffirm that commitment. It may seem paradoxical that the fully committed parent seldom needs to go through a long appeals process to get what he wants for his child, and yet it is true. School people know how to recognize the parents who are determined to see that their children's educational rights are served, and they frequently will provide the requested service(s) when confronted by a committed parent in order to avoid a lengthy, personnel-consuming, and costly process for the school system.

"Are you telling me that I can get what I want just by telling the special education director that I won't accept my child's IEP? That sounds too easy." Surprisingly, it does work that way for some parents; others will need to go farther. There are, in fact, a number of ways and times you can confront the school system. Let's look at them now.

RECOGNIZING LEVELS OF CONFRONTATION

Since confrontation involves face-to-face disagreement with people who are responsible for your child's education and well-being, you, like many other parents, may approach confrontation with feelings ranging from discomfort to panic. You may be worried about possible repercussions to your child—loss of present services and the possible development of unfriendly attitudes toward your child—or about looking foolish or failing. Confrontation is hard on parents.

Set your anxieties aside. By your actions (written and verbal), you are in effect focusing a large spotlight on your child. Everything that happens to your child while you are involved in the educational process will be highly visible. Since school people will be making efforts to look good and to prove that their recommendations for the IEP are better than yours, they are not likely to reduce or stop services, or in any way punish you through your child. School people want to look competent and reasonable, especially when they are faced with rejection of an IEP.

School people don't like confrontation either. Like you, they would prefer agreement, but, like you, they may feel that on some services there is no compromise. Since both parties would like to avoid confrontation, it should be treated like strong medicine—used only in the amount needed. And, of course, neither side should engage in name-calling, tears, or other dramatics which will make confrontation more painful and less productive for all involved.

"Why should I care," you ask, "if I hurt them? Look what they've done to me and my child!" You care because your performance is best when you are controlled and rational, rather than emotional. You also care because when the confrontation is resolved you will have to go back to working with school people on your child's education. The maintenance of good relationships will be helpful when that time comes.

Rejecting the IEP—The First Step

When you receive an IEP for your child which you find unacceptable, you must reject it. If, like Elsa and David King, you have reason to hope that you can solve the problem informally, then you should try that approach first. After you have carefully read the plan, discussed it with your advocate, and noted your specific objections for your personal reference, then call your special education director or principal to state your intention to reject the plan, and your concerns, one of which is finding a way to reach agreement without going through a complicated process involving outsiders. This type of phone call gives the school people an opportunity to reassess the seriousness of your commitment, to take further steps to resolve the disagreement, and to present a good image. They still have a chance to be "good guys" without having to record and file with the state Department of Education a rejection of an IEP. For some parents, this can lead to a happy solution. You must, however, set time limits: You expect to hear within a few days whether it is possible to modify the proposed IEP, and that a meeting for that purpose can be called within the week. If the school people promise to reconvene but you can't pin them down to a specific time, you may rightfully begin to suspect that you are being stalled; you should then formally reject the plan.

Formally rejecting the plan means rejecting it in writing. On the IEP form, there is a specific line which reads "I do not accept the educational plan" with space for your signature and a space for comments. Forms may vary somewhat from state to state, but the forms are basically the same. Keep a copy of the form signed and dated by you. Three things can happen after your formal rejection of the IEP.

One is that you will get a call from the school people asking you to reconsider your objections to the proposed and now rejected IEP, and seeking to work with you to some compromise or mutually satisfactory conclusion. If you receive this kind of call, you can afford to be gracious. Yes, you would be very interested in meeting again if that would help to develop the program you believe your child needs and to implement the desired plan as soon as possible. You are willing to do much to see that your child gets the services he needs now. By using confrontation to impress the school people with the seriousness of your commitment, you have brought the school people back to the negotiating table to rewrite the IEP. When they reach out to you, they are demonstrating that they are willing to reconsider your requests and to concede to at least some (if not all) of them. It is important to meet and resolve as many differences as possible. If you get all of your requests (or the most important ones), that will be the end of your experience in confrontation. If you fail to reach agreement, you will still have reduced the number of items disagreed upon and in this way will have simplified the continuing process of confrontation.

The second thing that can happen is that you may receive a notice that you are entitled to a hearing (or mediation) to resolve differences between you and the school and to decide on the services to be provided to your child. The hearings can be informal (mediation) or formal (due process hearings). You are entitled to either or both.* The school system is also entitled to a hearing to resolve differences.

The third thing is that nothing can happen. The school people have simply filed away your rejected IEP and are proceeding with business as usual as if the IEP process had never taken place. Of course, they are in violation of the law if they have not made clear to you in language that you can understand that you have a right to a hearing. Whether you have been informed or not, you can and should initiate the hearing process. You do this by writing to your state Department of Education, informing them that you have rejected your child's IEP and are requesting an impartial due process hearing. Send a copy to your advocate and one to the school system, and keep a clear copy for your records. You can now sit back and wait for notice from your state Department of Education that the legal (due process) wheels are turning. A higher level and more difficult step of confrontation lies ahead.

Mediation†

Between your rejection of the IEP and the formal appeals process, there is a less formal procedure called mediation, which can be used to resolve differences between parents and schools. Mediation is not specified in P.L. 94-142, but it is being used by more and more states to resolve parent-school conflicts over the IEP, and it appears to be successful in a large number of cases.

In mediation, parents and school people sit down together in the presence of an unbiased third person— a mediator—whose job it is to help parents and school people reach agreement in a structured yet informal

---

*For terminology and definitions of technical issues, once again refer to Reed Martin's *Educating Handicapped Children: The Legal Mandate* (Champaign, Ill.: Research Press Company, 1979).

† The author would like to acknowledge Dr. Milton Budoff and Lawrence Kotin, Esq., for their willingness to share information about the mediation process.

setting. The mediator does not make decisions about the IEP; his role is to encourage communication and discussion, maintain some order (no shouting and people talk one at a time), and, if possible, persuade everyone to reach a mutually satisfying agreement.

"How can this third guy, an outsider, help when we have already been over everything and are just getting angrier all the time?" The mediator can help just because he is an outsider.* As you and the school people try to explain to the mediator what your problems and differences are, you will begin to see everyone's behavior improve, and any amount of snipping and sniping at each other will diminish as people on each side make their best case to convince the mediator that they are right. The mediator can ask questions and make suggestions. He can help each side understand the other better, and, from what may first appear to be two warring factions, create a group of reasonable folks willing to negotiate their differences under the watchful eyes of the impartial mediator. Sometimes, after hearing the presentations and arguments, the mediator will spend some time alone with each side to tell them what their chances are of winning an appeal:

> *Mediator:* I wanted to share with you privately some of my impressions and experience.
>
> *Principal:* You want to tell me that the IEP is inadequate, don't you? We did a lot of work on it.

---

*Make sure the mediator is an outsider. He should not be a teacher or principal in your school system, nor a relative of the superintendent of schools. These people either are paid by the school system or have a special interest in supporting the schools. Usually, the mediator is a person who is appointed or employed by the state Department of Education and who has not in any way been involved in your child's school program or IEP. Insist that your mediator be truly disinterested or impartial. Otherwise, it will be in your child's best interest to skip mediation.

Mediator: I don't doubt that. But looking at those evaluations that Mr. White keeps bringing up, I think he has a strong case for the intensive speech program he wants.

Principal: But I don't have a speech therapist in my school.

Mediator: I understand that you have problems, but those evaluations from the University Medical Center make it clear that Lynnette has a serious language handicap and needs a comprehensive language program. I have to tell you that, in my opinion, the parent would win the appeal. I expect the hearing officer would find the IEP inadequate and order a new IEP.

Principal: Well, maybe the parent won't appeal. I'm surprised he's hung in this long.

Mediator: You know I have to share the same information with Mr. White. I have to tell him that his chances of winning an appeal are very good based on the information I have.

Principal: I know you do. And that just might keep him going. He's already talking about private schools!*

Mediator: Listen, all I can do is tell you what I know. Your chances are slim. Isn't there something you can do to provide the child with the speech program she seems to need?

---

*IEPs on occasion include recommendations for private schools. When a public school system can't provide the necessary service, the administrators are required under the law to go outside of the system to purchase the educational program the child needs.

When a principal is given information and advice like this, he usually starts to think about a solution that will satisfy the parent. On returning to the group, the principal may tell the parent, "Maybe you're right and maybe we should be offering Lynnette more. Would you be satisfied if we were to hire a speech therapist?" Negotiation, guided by the mediator, follows. The principal offers something; the parent asks for more. As they bargain, talk of private schools disappears, and both parents and school people shift from counterproductive disagreement to working toward a common goal—in this case, a substantial speech program that will benefit Lynnette in her communication skills and assist her as well in reaching her other educational goals.

Sometimes, parents are told that they are probably asking for too much. For example:

Mediator: Zachary is like a lot of kids in his school. You will have a hard time making a case that he needs a private school.

Mrs. Floyd: But he's not making any progress!

Mediator: You made that clear in the discussion. It's obvious that the plan needs to be modified to meet his needs, and I think you should work on getting more out of his present school placement.

Mrs. Floyd: They've had Zachary three years now and very little has happened. It's time for someone else to do the job. I'm willing to go to an appeals hearing.

Mediator: I know you are, but I'm afraid that if you insist on a private school, you will lose. However, I think you have a strong case for requesting substantially more services from the public school and even a summer program for Zachary.

> *Mrs. Floyd:* All I want is for Zachary to learn.
>
> *Mediator:* I know that. Why not give the school people another chance today to come up with a better plan?

If the parent agrees with the mediator's advice, the mediation can continue. They can return to the group where the parent may ask the school people, "How can you provide Zachary with the services he needs?" The school people may respond with some surprising recommendations since they have also heard from the mediator that the IEP which they proposed is weak and inadequate. They may offer more individual tutoring and a new adaptive physical education program, which are high priorities to the parent. Yet they balk at the idea of a summer program for Zachary. The parent feels that with the improvements in the IEP she is willing to forego the summer program, and both parties are at last in agreement. Or the parent believes that the summer program is crucial and in spite of the positive efforts put forth by the school people, she cannot agree to the plan. She is entitled to disagree. Since mediation is only an attempt to bring the involved parties to agreement, the parent or schools always have the option to refuse the amended program.

The mediator is a kind of matchmaker, a go-between, with no power to decide the content of the IEP. Only the parents and school people can reach a decision, which must be a joint decision. If they do agree, then a formal document of agreement can be written up and signed by both school people and parents: That agreement is the new and accepted IEP. If they disagree, they must then move to a higher level of authority.

For a growing number of parents, mediation is a workable means of getting good IEPs for their children. However, you are not required to go through mediation. If you question the qualifications of the mediator chosen (he is not really an impartial party) or believe that the school people will use the mediation process to delay the development of a good educational program for your

child, then you can move from rejection of the IEP
straight to the appeals procedure. Most of the time,
mediation will help you because it is less adversarial
than appeals; your relationship with school people will
be less damaged when mediation is successful. But, for
you, mediation is successful only when your child benefits. If necessary, you, the active and committed parent,
are ready to take the next step.

Appeals

Within the educational system, appeals are the last resort,* and probably the most difficult experiences parents
can undergo. The time, emotional, and financial costs
are to be avoided if possible. However, if your child's
IEP is bad or inadequate, you must take this last step.

Your right to appeal to a higher level of authority in
the educational system is guaranteed by P.L. 94-142. If
you disagree with the school system, you are entitled to
an impartial due process hearing. That means that you
get to state your case before an impartial and qualified
hearing officer—someone who does not work for your
school system and who does not have a personal or professional interest that would bias her judgment in deciding the case. The impartial hearing officer has the power
to decide the issue of the IEP. Unlike the mediator
whose job was to assist both parties in reaching a mutually satisfying agreement, the hearing officer is not concerned with whether or not the parties agree; she makes
the decision that the IEP is adequate and appropriate or
that it is inadequate and inappropriate to the child's
special needs according to the law. Unlike mediation,
where discussion may be open and informal, the hearing
is usually very legalistic, with the hearing officer determining who talks when and what they talk about. (Hearing officers do have different styles; some will be more

---

*If you are dissatisfied with the decision reached through appeals,
you always have the right to go outside of the educational system to
the civil courts.

formal and legalistic than others. All are seeking solid information on which to base their judgment or disposition of the appeal.) And unlike mediation, your chances of ending the hearing on a friendly note with the school people are very slight indeed. Hearings tend to be adversarial; the lines are drawn—it's them or us. This is not to say that you will never be able to talk to the school people again, but, for a while, you may find it hard.

Winning an appeal will require a lot of work from you in documenting and in planning your case. You will probably need to have a lawyer represent you, because many schools are hiring lawyers to represent them at hearings. You may do a lot of work and spend a lot of money, yet lose.

"Why are you painting such a black picture of appeals?" you may be wondering. "If we have come this far on our commitment and efforts, why should we give up now? All along it's been 'Go, go, go! You can do it!' Now suddenly it's 'Take it easy! Don't jump the gun.' Why?" You're right! The description is discouraging on purpose. Sometimes when parents learn about appeals they may be tempted to rush through the development of the IEP, reject it, and go for an appeal thinking they can shorten the time it takes to get what they want for their children. Although you should never put up with any unnecessary delays (long postponements of meetings or casual cancellations), working with the school people (even when you find many disagreements) can help you to better formulate your case for rejecting the plan, for seeking mediation, and for requesting a due process hearing. If you rush the procedures, you may appear at the hearing only to be accused by the school people of not working with them to develop the necessary programs for your child while they have made good faith efforts to deal with you. If you go to an appeal which could have been avoided, you will have caused yourself some unnecessary work and possible grief.

Now that you know all that, you should also know that parents do win appeals. Sometimes they win them with the help of their personal advocates and professionals who are committed to the education and well-being of their children. Sometimes they hire lawyers to help them make their best case. They win on the merits of their case: They have done their homework, and they can back up their claims with specifics—evaluations, school reports, and other documentation.

By all means, when the IEP process and mediation have failed, you should move to appeal. If you start the appeals process, the school system just may make a last ditch effort to satisfy you because appeals are costly to school systems too. They must hire substitute teachers to free your child's teacher(s) to attend the hearing. The special education director's work piles up while he is at the hearing. The town counsel (lawyer) may be called away from "more important business to waste a day at the state Department of Education." School people do not enjoy appeals either. If there is an easier and more acceptable way, they will want to use it to avoid the appeals process.

But appeals are necessary both to resolve irreconcilable differences and to put teeth into the law. If there were no appeals process, rejected IEPs would merely be more pieces of paper to file, and school people would feel no pressure to satisfy parents' requests for services. The spectre of going through an impartial due process hearing can sometimes turn a recalcitrant school system into one that is at least willing to try cooperation.

You, the active and committed parent, are also the judicious parent, avoiding appeals when you can, but using them when they may serve your child's best interests. If you find that you need to resort to appeals, then you should seriously consider consulting a lawyer who is familiar with P.L. 94-142.

USING LAWYERS

If you find yourself involved in appeals, chances are you will need to hire a lawyer. This is the time when it is most appropriate to call on the legal profession, and this is the time when the public agency conducting the hearing (usually the state Department of Education) is required by law to provide you with information about free or low cost legal services available to parents in your area or state. If you do not receive this information, then you should ask for it by phone, or, if necessary, by letter.

Free legal services? Sounds good! Unfortunately, there are few available, and those that are available are in great demand. Even if you are very poor and entitled to publicly funded legal services, you may find that all you can get is some consultation time. The legal agency lawyers may be so overburdened that they find it impossible to represent you at the hearing, but they are generally willing to advise you, if that will help. As for low cost lawyers, keep in mind that most lawyers charge by the hour, and what is by legal standards a modest fee for representation can overwhelm the average family.

Start with an hour of legal consultation. If you are poor, it should be available; if you are of average means, one hour of a lawyer's time will not break you and may give some suggestions that could ease your way. Seek out a lawyer who has some knowledge or experience in P.L. 94-142; otherwise, you may be spending your money and time to bring the lawyer up to your level of expertise about the law. The lawyer may tell you that in his opinion you have a strong case or a weak one; that these are the important issues and arguments, the others are weak; that he believes your money will be well spent on legal fees for appeals (get an estimate of the cost to help you decide); or that the issue(s) raised in your child's case is so important to a number of children that your case could set a precedent that would benefit a whole class of children, and for this reason an advocacy organization or public interest law firm would be willing to bear the expense if you want them to represent you and your child. If you can get free legal representation, you can move ahead. If not, you must decide whether you can afford to pay for legal representation and how much.

"We've gone to the lawyer and the cost is beyond our

means. We'll just have to forget about the appeal." Not yet! You still have resources to tap—your local parent or advocacy organization, your long-distance advocate (who may come out for appeals), perhaps a nearby university law student, graduate students in special education, or even professors who may be interested in some front-line action in resolving special education problems. The more contacts you make, the greater the chances of finding help for your appeal. Search out your resources. If in the end all you have is your naive personal advocate, that person can at least be an emotional support to you. If you find that you must go to appeals without a lawyer, explain to the hearing officer why you don't have a lawyer. Unlike civil courts, educational due process hearings do not require that the parties be legally represented, and lawyers will not be appointed for either side. But it doesn't hurt your case any for the hearing officer to know that you wanted counsel but couldn't afford it.

If you have hired a lawyer, give him the best and most accurate information you can; the better the information, the stronger case he can present for you. So prepare your legal advocate as you prepared your personal advocate (review The Advocate's Advocate in chapter four, and Getting Your Advocate Ready in chapter six). You can hire the best lawyer in the world, but he will have a hard time making a case with muddy issues and scanty information. This is true for school systems as well; they can hire high-priced lawyers who will have a hard time defending a poorly designed IEP or obvious violations of parents' and children's rights.

UNDERSTANDING THE MONEY PERSPECTIVE

Since confrontation in its various forms can be a difficult and discouraging experience, wouldn't it be nice to have some kind of predictor that could tell you whether you will have a short and relatively easy disagreement or a long, tough fight ahead of you? Well, there is a rough predictor which works most of the time and which is based on a simple fact of life—money. How much are the services you want for your child going to cost the school system?

Some school people will insist that they provide all the services a child needs and that money is not a factor; other educators see that children need more services and realize that money is an important factor in determining who gets what services, how much, and how often, but they may have little control over how and how much money is spent. Even the most concerned special education director can have his hands tied by the school's fiscal policies. Any increase in costs may result in increased pressure on the school administrator to hold the line on spending.

If your requests for your child will require a modest increase in costs, chances are your struggle will be brief and not too unpleasant. If complying with your requests will result in a large expenditure, you may have to prepare for a difficult and drawn-out battle. This simple rule generally works quite well. You must, however, look at costs from the perspective of school administrators. They take into consideration three kinds of costs:

- the short-term costs
- the long-range costs
- the costs of confrontation

Short-Term Costs

These are the immediate actual costs for the new services for your child. For example:

Judy needs an extra session with the language therapist, which you estimate will cost the school system about $500 for the year.

Calvin should have regular psychotherapy (a related service)—projected cost is about $2,000.

Charlotte cannot attend school unless certain architectural barriers are removed, access ramps and accessible toilet facilities are provided, and some classes and equipment are relocated—projected cost approximately $5,000 and up.

Ross does not benefit from the school program and needs a private school day placement to meet his educational needs and tuition—$5,000 and up.

Florence's disabilities are so extensive and severe that she requires a year-round residential program— estimated cost and tuition is $14,000 and up.

Short-term costs are the school's immediate costs in providing the services and implementing the changes the parents have requested for their children. They can range from a few hundred dollars to $40,000 or more. However, there are often other hidden costs which may be of even greater concern to school administrators in reaching their decision to give the parent what he wants, or to stand fast in their refusal.

Long-Range Costs

What school people often fear is that by agreeing to provide services for your child's educational needs, they will open the floodgates and a horde of angry parents will descend on them to demand expensive services. For a school system with a bad track record for meeting children's needs, this fear may be based on real possibility—that parents who realize that their children have been denied legitimate services will be angry and demanding. But for those systems which have sincerely attempted to place children in appropriate services, this is much less of a threat.

You may have to guess at what's behind the school's refusal to comply with your request for educational services. But often the school people will help you by making certain kinds of statements.

We can't set a precedent.

If we give it to your child, we'll have to give it to everybody.

We can't send every student to private school just because a parent asks for it. Everybody would send their kids to private schools if the public schools would pay for it.

The key words to listen for are words like "precedent" and "everybody." Some of the statements are patent nonsense. You would give your right arm if your child could benefit from a special program in her own local public school. And what parents would want their children pulled away from a learning program to spend time with a speech therapist if those children did not have language problems? Do not allow yourself to be put down or put off by irresponsible statements from resistant school people.

Let's look at the earlier examples in the context of long-range costs:

Judy's parents are asking for an increase in services which the school people have already agreed upon, and it's a modest increase. There should be little fear of setting a precedent. However, if Judy were in a school system where few or no children were getting speech therapy, then giving Judy the service might have the effect of creating a large demand among a number of parents for speech programs for their children. The long-range costs could become significant.

Calvin's case is similar. If he is one of a number of students to receive psychotherapy, it is no big deal. But if he is going to be the first, the school people will be considering the costs of providing psychotherapy to ten, fifty, or more students (depending on the size of the system).

In Charlotte's case, the school, by maintaining a public program not accessible to the handicapped, is in violation not only of P.L. 94-142 but of Section 504 (civil rights of the handicapped). Charlotte's parents will point out this fact to the school people. In addition, they will explain that although the cost may seem expensive this time, the building modifications will allow services to be provided to other handicapped children. In this case, the short-term and long-range costs of the service are the same.

When we look at the requests for private school placement for Ross and Florence, we can anticipate resistance from most school administrators. The short-term costs are expensive, and the possible threat of other parents requesting private school placement can make the long-range costs appear overwhelming. This is not to suggest that all school systems will refuse to consider private placement, but you should know that this kind of request will tend to create the strongest resistance.

It is important to look for these long-range costs and try to evaluate them. When you ask for what seems to you a tiny but necessary increase in service and suddenly find yourself up against a stone wall, you should suspect that there is a serious long-range expenditure hanging over the heads of the school people; you should check out other parents in your town (or your agency or professional advocate) about the present status of the service you want. You may find that there is no speech therapist for special-needs children in your town. Depending on the size of your town, there may be one hundred or more children who need this service. Once word gets out about you, there could be a deluge of requests.* Or you could ask for a private placement for your child with fear and trembling, only to be told by a school administrator that she has been thinking about the same thing because the public school is not yet capable or ready to serve a child with needs as severe as yours, although they are working on it. Measure the potential long-range costs by collecting information about the services already available in your town. The state Department of Education may be a source. They can't tell you who is getting services, but they can and should tell you what kinds of services are being provided by schools in your town.

---

*This should not cause you to keep your request for service a secret. The more parents know about entitlement to services and get them, the more secure you can feel. You don't want to be the exception (a favor from your town!); you want to be the rule. Remember, the law is a rule for services for handicapped children.

Costs of Confrontation

Confrontation costs schools extra cash. Appeals require the presence of a number of school people (and you can request or subpoena even more). An administrator and teacher will almost always be there with a lawyer. The lawyer will generally be paid at a rate of $50 or more per hour; every teacher will have to be replaced on the job by a substitute at a rate of about $40 per day; and the administrator can plan on taking the work home for the weekend which he could not complete in the office, or being behind in the performance of his duties.

The hearing can run one, two, or more days. By multiplying your best estimate of daily costs, you can come up with a reasonable estimate of the confrontation costs to the school system. Even a one day hearing can cost the schools several hundred dollars and an extended hearing can cost thousands of dollars.

A School's Eye View

When you have reviewed the costs of the new services which your child needs, looked into the status of special education in your town to help you estimate the possible long-range costs, and made your best guess about the school's costs of confrontation, you will be better able to assess the costs from the school's point of view and to roughly predict the potential resistance of the school administrators to your request for new service(s). Let's try this predictor against the examples:

Judy. A small increase in a service which is already provided is being requested. The expected short-term cost for the service is $500. The long-range costs are small or even zero. The costs of confrontation for the school could exceed $2,000 (lawyers, substitute teachers, specialists, and some hidden costs). If finances are a concern, a school administrator will have a difficult time giving a satisfactory explanation to her superiors about how she saved the school system $500 and spent a couple of grand doing it! In Judy's case, the easiest and cheapest solution for the school is to give her a little more therapy and be done with it. The parents can anticipate that a telephoned or written rejection will result in negotiations to improve service.

Calvin. Let's assume that if Calvin were to receive the psychotherapy as part of his IEP, he would be the first student in his school system to get this service. The long-range costs could be high: It would mean annual school expenditures of tens of thousands of dollars. Since confrontation costs are not likely to exceed a few thousand dollars, there is a high probability that the school system will make a strong effort to resist the parents' request for service. Calvin's parents should prepare themselves with documentation, experts to testify for their side, and advocates, who may include lawyers, for a long, tough fight.

Charlotte. In Charlotte's case, the short-term cost is also the long-range cost. There may be other families waiting for someone like Charlotte's mother to break the architectural barrier; the parents should make an issue of the fact that the school is not only inaccessible to their daughter, but to present and future students with mobility problems, and that the public school system is violating not only Charlotte's special needs, but her civil rights as well. Her parents should get a copy of Section 504 (which guarantees the civil rights of the handicapped) and use it when talking to the school people.

The costs of renovating the school facilities will exceed the usual costs of confrontation, but renovation is a one-time cost with long-range benefits. In addition, the issue of inaccessibility is so clear that the school will be reluctant to contest the parents' appeal.

Occasionally, a school system may offer to place the child in a private school to avoid renovation costs. Some parents are willing to accept this placement, especially for severely and multiply handicapped children. But Charlotte can benefit from being in a public school program if they will only widen the doors and let her in. If Charlotte's parents persist, they have an excellent chance of settling the disagreement without recourse to the appeals process.*

Ross. His school system prides itself on its low education budget and on the fact that no student has ever "needed" a private placement—that is, the school administrators have refused to consider private placement no matter what the need. Ross's placement will cost $5,000; confrontation costs could be about $3,000 or more (the parents are determined to go through the appeals process using several expert witnesses to testify at length about Ross's needs). The difference between short-term and confrontation costs is not so great as to push the school system into a long procedure. However, Ross's mother recently learned that there are at least two children with needs similar in severity to Ross's, and that the educational programs of these children consist of several hours of home tutoring and nothing more. Ross's mother realizes that the school people are not just worried about spending $5,000 for her son; they are worried about an amount which could be $15,000, $50,000, or more, depending on how many home-tutored, handicapped children are out there. Clearly, the long-range costs are the issue here. The school system can be expected to resist this request.

Florence. The residential program which Florence's father wants for her costs $14,000. This is a heavy cost for Florence's community to bear. But this community has in past sent some students to both day and residential programs when the public school programs were not meeting the children's needs. While placing students outside the community, the school administrators planned and developed programs for those students, and, after a

---

*If there is more than one elementary or junior high school, the school administration can decide on the basis of costs which building to renovate. This can mean that your child may not go to her neighborhood school, but can at least go to school in your town instead of going across the county. You can and should be involved with the schools in assessing those costs for renovation.

year or two, were able to bring some of them back into the public schools. A community with this kind of record is not frightened by the spectre of hordes of students requiring expensive outside placements. The school people are more concerned with short-term costs and costs of confrontation in the individual cases. If they believe that they cannot serve Florence in the public schools, a push from the parents may bring forth the desired placement. On the other hand, if they feel there hasn't been enough time or opportunity for them to work with Florence, they may refuse to write the kind of IEP the parents want, and begin to prepare for the appeals.

"Some rule! Our town is going to fight to the finish over $5,000 and the other town will shell out $14,000 on request? That's quite a difference!" You're right. There is a wide difference between towns or school systems. The rule serves as a kind of yardstick which you apply to your own school system to measure or predict the likelihood of resistance (or compliance) to your special requests for your child's individual educational needs. It is a rough measure but a useful one when applied to specific cases. And your primary interest is very specific— the IEP to meet your child's needs. Understanding the money perspective from the school's point of view aids you in making a decision about engaging in confrontation, at what level, and for how long.

MAKING YOUR DECISION

While rejecting the IEP may be a new experience for you, it is something that most parents, faced with an inappropriate educational plan, can do without much difficulty or even hesitation. Deciding to appeal is a little harder. Rejecting the IEP does not require you to go to appeals, and you may not feel ready to push for a hearing. Chances are the school will do nothing with your rejection except file it, so you can take some time to reach your decision about whether to go to appeals or not. Now that you know something about the process and how to measure potential school resistance to your requests, you have to consider your personal costs. You will have expenses—financial, emotional, and physical—and you will want to be sure that the prize is worth the contest.

You can most easily predict your financial costs. These can include possible legal fees for consultation or representation at hearings, transportation, baby-sitters, and/or time away from your job. These are the hard dollars-and-cents facts you can determine from your own situation.

The other costs (energy, time, feelings) are every bit as real, but are harder to estimate. You might say, "Hey, there isn't anything I wouldn't do to get my child into the right program!" but you might be feeling, "I've worked so hard for so long; I don't think I can do anymore." If you want to go on but are feeling drained, look for ways to get support or relief for yourself. Ask yourself these questions:

- Can I get the emotional support I need from my advocate? Are there others who can help me?

- Do I need more information about my child's needs, skills, and disabilities to make a stronger case for a new IEP?

- Do I need more time? Can the hearing date be postponed if I am anxious about being ready and need more time (or the date moved up if the waiting is hard for me)?

- Do I need more preparation and practice in order to strengthen my new skills (assertiveness, self-statements) and overcome some of my personal weaknesses (timidity, short emotional fuse)?

Use these questions to determine what you need to survive the appeals process and to increase your chances of success. You are the best judge of what you can do.

Review your child's needs one more time. Are your requests for services for your child appropriate and adequate? Should you be asking for even more? Now is the time—before the appeals—to make sure you are asking for all the things you think belong in your child's educational plan. Or are you asking too much because you really want revenge on the school people for all the things they've done and haven't done? It is natural for parents to be angry with school people who they believe have neglected their children's education and welfare. However, your best chance of winning the appeal is based on your child's current actual needs. Use your best judgment to make your strongest case. As for your anger, use it to fuel your determination to keep going during the difficult moments at the hearing.

And there will be difficult moments. Confrontation at any level can be unpleasant; appeals especially can be painful. If you are convinced that the IEP you want is essential to your child's educational growth and well-being, then the prize is worth the contest. The way of a parent advocate is never easy; at times it can be tough and painful.

You need to know the worst so you can be prepared to last. If the school people change their minds suddenly and give your child the services you have been asking for, you can live with that kind of pleasant surprise. (Your aura of determination may, in fact, have helped them to change their minds.) But if you are not prepared to deal with confrontation, you can be overwhelmed by it. Knowing about confrontation (and the judicious use of it) is a kind of power to enable you to seek and achieve the IEP that meets your child's needs.

We have put confrontation towards the end of the book for a number of reasons:

- Confrontation is procedurally the last step in developing the IEP.
- It should be used by parents as their last resort in dealing with school people.
- Most parents will not need to use confrontation to get the right IEP.

For those parents who will find it necessary to engage in confrontation and for the few parents who must finally resort to the appeals process, it is important that you know the worst and prepare for it. Informed and skilled parents can and do win appeals, and their handicapped children are better served because of their caring parents' valiant efforts.

The steps you will need to take to insure continued, improved service to your child are outlined in the next chapter. You will learn how to monitor compliance with the IEP, how to deal with noncompliance, and how to sustain your active, ongoing participation in planning for your child's educational future.

Eight

The Constant Advocate: And The Beat Goes On

"It was a long haul, but it was worth it."

"I'm glad I did it, but I'm sure glad it's over."

"I've wanted Genevieve to be mainstreamed, but will she get the extra help she needs in the regular classroom?"

"How will I know whether my child gets all the services we agreed on?"

These are the kinds of feelings that parents have when the IEP is finally signed, sealed, and set up to go. You have probably put more effort, emotion, and energy into getting an appropriate IEP than you have ever put into anything else. For some of you, it was just plain hard work doing things you have never done before; for others, especially those engaged in confrontation, the whole business may have taken on the dimensions of a bad dream from which you could not awaken. Whatever you experienced, it's over and done with. The IEP is written and now you can sit back and relax, or return to whatever ordinary routine you gave up to become your child's advocate. You thought you might never see the end of the IEP process, but it's over.

Yes, developing the IEP is over; but there is still more work to do. Be assured, though, that the hardest, most time-consuming work is done. Take a break; you've earned it. In fact, you want to sit back and give the school people a little time to implement the education program before you begin your monitoring of it.

MONITORING

Monitoring is making sure that your child gets what's coming to him—the education program you and the school people proposed, discussed, disagreed on, labored over, developed, and finally agreed upon as the necessary, appropriate, and adequate IEP for your child. You certainly did not labor mightily to bring forth a piece of paper but a program: Your job is to be sure that the piece of paper becomes the real services to which your child is entitled. In order to do that, you must become the watchdog of the IEP implementation. If the IEP says speech therapy is given for three half-hour sessions each week with the speech therapist, you want to know that it is given three times every week and not only once a week because the special education director has not hired the additional therapist. Or, if your child, according to the plan, is to be mainstreamed into regular classes for sixty percent of the school day and it hasn't happened after the first week of school, you should be aware of that and hold the school system accountable for delivering those services. Read and know the specifics of the IEP so you will know when it is not being followed. In monitoring, you will realize how important the specific language of the IEP is. When you were insisting that the number and length of sessions, the location, responsible person, etc., be written into the IEP in precise language, you may have been made to feel that you were nit-picking and mistrustful. You were not; you were just being careful and thorough. Now your care will pay off.

Why Monitoring Is Necessary

"If the plan is so specific," you may ask, "why do I have to bother the school people? They can read as well and probably better than I can." You're right. It is not a question of reading ability; it's a question of the "same old pressures," such as budget, lack of personnel, and unqualified staff (see the discussion in chapter three of the pressures on school people). School people are often trying to stretch inadequate resources in an effort to keep the budget down. The child of the "good," quiet parent who does not follow through on monitoring is apt to be short-changed. The child of the parent who quotes the IEP ("It says here that my Blanche should have. . .") is likely to get all the services written in the IEP. That parent, in effect, often makes the case for the principal or special education director to bring to the superintendent or school board: He can report that "Mrs. Leary is constantly calling about the lack of the special services written in the IEP, and I don't think she's going to go away until we set them up." Usually, the squeaky parent gets the "grease" in the form of the services for her child required by the IEP.

For a few school systems, the "standard operating procedure" interferes with implementing the IEP: These schools, even when they present few obstacles in writing the IEP, have little intention of initiating any new services and routinely ignore the requests of parents to deliver promised services. They can and do get away with this since most parents either don't follow up by monitoring because they figure the plan is there and the school people will do what is required, or because they become apathetic ("I did everything I was supposed to do, and now they are ignoring the IEP. I knew you couldn't beat the system"). These systems get away with breaking the law when no one checks up on them and holds them accountable. The more successful they have been at this game in the past, the more effort required of a parent to get services. Phone calls requesting information about the start-up of the items in the program plan, and letters stating that you are ready to file a complaint against the school system for noncompliance (discussed later in the chapter) can often move a resistant system to act responsibly. The vocal and informed parent monitor can usually get the services by being assertive and relentless.

Sometimes a school will technically put all the IEP pieces in place and assure the parent that the IEP is being implemented. Jennifer's father felt good until he visited the school and saw that the reading tutorial room was located on the other side of the cafeteria walls, and learned that Jennifer was scheduled when the cafeteria was gearing for lunch, with the result that the teacher and student could only hear half of what they were saying to each other.

Another, and perhaps the most flagrant, example of "technical implementation" is illustrated in the following example of a student's language program. Richard's mother did all the right things in preparing and participating in the IEP process. Her highest priority for her retarded and language-handicapped son was language training. The school people countered her request for more time with the speech therapist with the response that there was no money. Through discussion and negotiation, a plan was agreed upon which called for the therapist to continue to see Richard but also to work closely with the classroom teacher and an aide who would implement the therapist's recommendations. The aide, under the supervision of the teacher, would be responsible for several sessions each day. Mrs. Anderson realized that this arrangement would provide her son with considerably more language instruction and practice than would an extra weekly session with the speech therapist, so she agreed to the compromise. In September she learned from the school people that the aide had been hired and the plan was underway. In November, during her parent-teacher conference at the school, she learned that the new aide's primary language was Spanish and that she lacked the necessary grasp of basic English to instruct Richard, who did not understand Spanish. Although all the pieces seemed to be in place, Richard's language program was in fact practically nonexistent. It would have been simple for the school to switch aides within the system, locating the Spanish-speaking aide with bilingual or other students who could benefit from her help, and finding another aide more capable of implementing Richard's program.

Of course, this is an outrageous example of a school's

indifference or incompetence, and it doesn't happen every day. But you should know that it does happen. Parent monitoring would not have prevented the setting up of this arrangement; however, a September visit to the classroom could have put an early end to it. Public and formal disclosure of this arrangement can move a system to apology and action ("A regrettable error! Of course, we didn't intend. . .").

Parent monitoring is essential to proper implementation of P.L. 94-142. Schools may appear to be in technical compliance but actually be violating the spirit or intent of the law. For example, a child who is "mainstreamed" into a regular class for a percentage of the school day, but who is given little or no work to do and excluded from most or all classroom activity represents this kind of violation. Presence is not enough to satisfy the law. Visiting teams from the state educational agency may not pick up some of the specific violations because they do not know the individual students. You do know one student very well. For that student—your child—you are potentially the best monitor. Good advocates never assume that the IEP is being well and fully implemented.

How to Monitor

"Okay, I accept," you say, "I will become a snoop and a nag if it will help my child. What do I need to know to monitor?" You basically already know what you need to know. By reading this book and by practicing your new or improved advocacy skills of keeping and using records, evaluating the program, speaking up in person and on the phone, writing letters, and finding and using allies, you have prepared yourself to be a good monitor. All you need is a timetable for contacts and an awareness of the kinds of contacts you should plan on making.

Phone calls. The timing of your first phone call depends on your school system's past record of providing services to your child and other students. If you have a system that is conscientious about implementing education programs, give the school people a few days to set things up. Make your first monitoring call to the teacher (or special education director) at the beginning of the second week of school. You are looking for information and assurance that the IEP is being implemented. If there are any delays in the services, such as specialists and partial integration into regular classrooms, you want to know why and for how long. If the delays seem to you to be lengthy or unreasonable, express your concern and request that the special education director or principal give immediate attention to your child's program. If all the services are in place, or one or two remaining are scheduled to start within the week, be sure to express your appreciation to the school people for doing their job, and tell them that you would appreciate hearing from them when those other services are in place.

If, however, you have a system that is notorious for ignoring IEPs, make your first call a few days before school opens. (The administrators are already working; there may also be some teachers and specialists also preparing for the new school year.) In this case, your first call serves as a reminder that you are very serious about your child's new program, and that you want no delays in its implementation. If the school people tell you, as parents of handicapped children are sometimes told, that they are too busy getting ready for the opening of school to give any time to your child's individual program, remind them that your child's program is school business and that you expect your child to have the appropriate program the day school starts, just like the other students do. Of course, for any call, you record the date, the name of the person to whom you talked, and the information you received, especially about the IEP components that are in place, the ones that are still in process, and the dates that the services will be initiated.

Your follow-up call depends on the information you receive from the school people. You may need to call the next day or the next week, or may wait a few weeks before further contact. The telephone will be one of the regular monitoring tools you use throughout the school year. You will use it to contact teachers and specialists, as well as administrators. Teachers and specialists can tell you much more about the day-to-day details of the IEP implementation than the administrators can. Of course, you should call at convenient times, which means you do not call when the teacher is with his class (you also want your child to have full benefit of the person's expertise and time). You can call the school office to ask about good times to talk to school personnel. Perhaps the person you want to reach prefers to take and return calls during a free period, in the half hour after school is dismissed, or at some other specified time. You should try to respect that preference, if at all possible.

When you call teachers and specialists, have your specific questions and the information you want to share organized and written down in advance. By preparing for your call, you make the best use of your and the school person's time. Any person can be put off by a vague and drawn-out conversation when the next class is about to start or the only other person left in the school is the janitor, who is waiting to lock up the building. On the other hand, a teacher or specialist would have a difficult time complaining about a parent's call that was three to five minutes long and focused on highly specific requests for information. You, the informed and reasonable advocate, make only reasonable demands which are hard to fault and to ignore.

Use the telephone to make periodic checks: Has the specialist been hired yet. How much time is Zelda spending in the regular class? The information you receive over the telephone should be a report of events and changes in activities. (You, the parent, are also interested in and entitled to specific information from the school people; you do not want vague, confusing, or drawn-out explanations.) But there are times when you want more than reports; those are the times when you want to see for yourself.

Visits. When you want firsthand information, you have to visit the program. The information you receive in your reports from teachers and specialists may be accurate and valid, but it is still secondhand information. Your child is also a source of information about her program, but that is secondhand information too. Your check on the accuracy of these reports is your visit to the school.

"That sounds like acting awfully suspicious to me. Why can't I just believe what they tell me?" The problems with Jennifer's classroom location and Richard's language program reveal why total trust can be dangerous. The parents were contented until they visited the school. Perhaps Jennifer's father arranged his visit because his daughter complained to him that she had a hard time hearing the teacher. In this case, information from the child led the parent to check out the program early in the school year.

Richard's mother was not so lucky since his language handicap prevented him from reporting to his mother. If he could have said, "Hey, Ma, my teacher doesn't speak much English," the parent would have investigated in September instead of being shocked in November. For parents whose children have difficulty communicating, the visits are crucial. Since their children are unable to report, the parents are minus one source of information. Early school year visits are a must. The schedule of follow-up visits depends on what a parent finds during that first visit.

"But my school discourages (or even prohibits) visits! What can I do?" The best solution to this problem is to make sure that your schedule of visits is written into the IEP. During the IEP process you can negotiate the frequency of your visits—biweekly, monthly, or quarterly (not annually or on Parents' Visiting Day or Open House). Base your case on the fact that your child cannot tell you much, if anything, about his program, and, as a responsible parent, you feel it is essential that you be scheduled for regular visits. Hold off on signing until that provision is written into the IEP.

Whatever it takes—making phone calls, writing letters,

or including visits in the IEP—you do it because first-hand observation of your child's program is an important part of your job as your child's advocate. You know that plans on paper and people in place do not always add up to an appropriate program for your child. You want to be sure that your child has the program to which he is entitled.

When you have permission or authorization and a scheduled time to visit your child's program, prepare yourself by rereading your child's IEP (You know it by heart? Read it again anyway) and chapter five on program evaluation. Write down what you want to observe and who you want to see in your order of importance. The school people may have new items and information they want to discuss with you; they have their lists too. Of course, you want to listen to their concerns and information, but you want to be sure that your list is taken care of before the visit is completed.

Perhaps you are worried that the teacher will see you as a potential troublemaker and will resent your monitoring efforts. Remember that a good teacher welcomes an informed, caring, and responsible parent. Some teachers will distrust and resent you, but maybe they can be won over if you can put them at their ease by showing them that you are there only to be sure that all the components of the IEP are in place and that the setting and support services are appropriate (see chapter five on reducing your nervousness and the teacher's). As for the few diehards who firmly believe that parents have no business inside a school, let alone their classrooms, deal with them by being very specific and very informed.

The suggestions and advice offered in the section, The Follow-up Interview: Using Your Personal Skills, in chapter five are relevant to your interactions with the teacher as you monitor the implementation of the IEP. If the teacher accepts your help as an ally who will fight for support services written into the IEP but not delivered, you will keep her off the hook when you go to the administrator to discuss the school's noncompliance:

I have visited my child's classroom and have discovered that certain components of the IEP are not being implemented. Specifically . . .

You do not say:

The teacher told me that she wants an aide and you haven't been listening to her.

If, on the other hand, a teacher feels threatened by your presence as a monitor, it will be up to you to minimize the discomfort. The following example incorporates some of the strategies suggested in chapter five (such as opening the conversation with a positive statement about the teacher's efforts), but focuses specifically on the elements of the IEP which the parent is concerned about:

> *Mrs. Lin:*   What a lovely, bright classroom you have here!
>
> *Teacher:*   Yes, it is nice. You should have seen the room I had last year. It was in the basement and was very dingy.
>
> *Mrs. Lin:*   I wish I had know that. I would have complained to the principal. These children cannot be expected to learn in second-rate classrooms. Nor is it fair to you to expect you to teach under poor conditions.
>
> *Teacher:*   Well, I asked for two years before I got a decent classroom.
>
> *Mrs. Lin:*   That's terrible. I'm glad you have this nice room now. I don't see the teaching aide that is supposed to be here. Is the aide out with another student?
>
> *Teacher:*   I have requested an aide but they have yet to give me one.
>
> *Mrs. Lin:*   With all these children, surely you are entitled to an aide! Besides, it

> says in Quentin's IEP that there is supposed to be an aide in your classroom. I'm going to take that up with the principal.
>
> *Teacher:* I don't know how much good that will do.
>
> *Mrs. Lin:* I intend to use Quentin's IEP and my observations as my argument for the necessary aide.

Note that this parent did several things to dispel the threat which the teacher might have felt from the visit. The parent commented on the nice room, acknowledged the teacher's efforts (most teachers try to make their classrooms attractive), presented herself as the parent advocate by expressing concern about past poor facilities for handicapped students, commiserated with the teacher on past (poor classroom) and present (lack of an aide) difficulties, and promised to try to improve the situation by dealing with the principal through the child's IEP rather than the teacher's complaint.

What this parent did is nothing different from what most of us have learned to do in our everyday dealings with people we want to win over to our side—offer compliments, interest, sympathy, and help. When the man who comes to repair the furnace finally arrives, you might be tempted to say, "What took you so long? You should have been here two hours ago." But if you want good service, you will probably say, "We have been waiting and we're glad you're here. Today must have been a busy day for you. Should I move these boxes out of the way to make it a little easier for you?" Put your everyday people skills to good use with the school people.

Base your conversation with the teacher on notes which you have taken during your visit; they will be related to your list of concerns and questions:

> *Mr. Frankl:* Could you show me the language program which the speech therapist de-

veloped for you to use with Tony in the classroom?

Teacher: Sorry, but the speech therapist hasn't put it together yet.

Mr. Frankl: I had hoped to talk to him next week. I think I'll start calling tomorrow.

or

Teacher: I have the program here.

Mr. Frankl: May I have a copy to take home? Perhaps there are some things I can do to help.

Teacher: You'll have to ask someone in the principal's office. They do the copying there.

Mr. Frankl: No problem. I'll ask on my way out.

When you are satisfied with the information from the teacher, you can decide when you should see the specialists and whether or not there is a need to see the principal or special education director.

Remember, you are always working from the IEP. First you look for the technical compliance. Are all the people who are to deliver the program in place? Are the hours of therapies and integration in place? Then you look for the quality of compliance. Is the classroom setting adequate? Are the program people qualified and skilled to work with your child?

If after your visit you are satisfied that the IEP is being implemented accurately and appropriately, you can go home, relax, and pat yourself on the back—the program is working. You can continue to take notes on your observations of your child and her progress to share with the school people during your next scheduled classroom visit or parent-teacher conference. (The parent-teacher conference is a chance to exchange information. It is not a substitute for firsthand observation.)

If, however, after your visit you see that there is

a poor match between the IEP and your child's daily program, you must be ready to shift gears to become, once again, the assertive, advocating parent. When the IEP is not fully implemented, the school people are in noncompliance: They are not holding up their end of the contractual IEP agreement. School noncompliance means that you must engage in confrontation strategies and actions.

DEALING WITH NONCOMPLIANCE

Parents sometimes give up when they find that the IEP they struggled to obtain is being ignored, especially if they have been through a lengthy appeals process.* They feel too tired to do more (and they are tired), or they believe that they have basically exhausted the system (they have not) and that nothing they do will make any difference. These parents are like runners in a marathon who have come twenty-five miles and falter with the finish line just a mile down the road. If you find yourself in this kind of situation, make that last effort to keep going. The end is clearly in sight.

Noncompliance, in fact, is the clearest issue you have had to deal with because you are no longer arguing about the who, what, where, when, and why of services. There is no need for more discussion about what should be in the IEP. You and the school people have already done that and signed an agreement—a legally binding contract which pinpoints the provisions of the IEP. The school is on record, in black and white, that it will provide the required services. The only question you and the school people have to consider is, "Are the services in place

---

*Actually, filing a noncompliance complaint is easier for parents who have been through appeals. The state Department of Education has a file of appeals, and someone in that agency is already familiar with the details of the case, including information on the school's reluctance to provide services.

or not?" If they are not, then the school system is violating the law and its own contractual agreement.*

Review chapter seven on confrontation for support and direction. Just as you may have told the school people that you intended to appeal and so moved them to action, you should first tell them you are considering filing a noncompliance complaint. The threat of a complaint may be enough to get those services and programs in place. As always, if nothing happens, you follow through on what you said you would do; never bluff. As a determined and responsible advocate, you say only what you mean to do and you follow through.

Filing the Complaint

When you have decided to file a complaint against your school system, you may want to use some of the resources you have already used as you worked toward and through the IEP process. Call your citizen or advocacy agency, or your personal sophisticated advocate who can tell you who to contact (name and address) in the state Department of Education with regard to your complaint. They may give you some suggestions about writing your letter of complaint, and ask you to send them a copy and to keep them informed of developments.

A letter of complaint should include the specific following information:

- the name of your town (or school system)
- your child's name
- the person responsible for implementing the IEP (the designated IEP chairperson)

---

*Of course if the school system has made good faith efforts to hire a physical therapist, but you live in Northeast Shangri-La and the nearest therapist is a hundred miles away by dogsled, you, the thoughtful parent advocate, may need to suggest other solutions, such as "Since daily physical therapy is impossible, how about having the therapist come once every four to eight weeks to spend the day with Kate and her teachers (classroom and gym teachers, and aide) for evaluation and program planning?"

- the date the IEP was signed
- the amount of time which has elapsed since the IEP was signed
- other specifics of noncompliance
- dates of meetings and hearings if you have been through mediation or appeals

The letter need not be elaborate; short and simple does the job. Here is a sample:

10 Forest Road
Your Town, State 66666
October 13, 1981

Mr. G. Howard Ford
Director, Bureau of Implementation
Department of Special Education
State Education Department
Your Town, State 66666

Dear Mr. Ford:

I wish to file a complaint of noncompliance against my child's school system.

My son, Barney, attends school in the Local Regional School District.

Last May we completed the plan for my son's Individualized Education Program and I signed it on May 25. The special education director, Ms. Davis, told me that the IEP would be in place at the start of the school year.

When I called during the first week of school in September, I was told that they were still in the process of hiring the specialists and making plans to move my child's classroom from the basement under the northeast wing. Two weeks later I called Ms. Davis, who said that the school system didn't have the money to hire the personnel specified in the IEP, and there was nothing she could do.

I understand that P.L. 94-142 guarantees that my son be given the services written into the approved

IEP, and that you are the person responsible for seeing that school districts comply with the law.

I look to you for help and will be waiting to hear from you.

Sincerely,

[signature]

Greta Black

cc.: Sen. Barry Ladd
    Drew Cody, Esq.
    Citizens for Educational
    Compliance, Inc.

Because the state Department of Education is legally responsible for seeing that school systems carry out their P.L. 94-142 responsibilities without delay, you can sit back and let the Department deal with the school system. Follow-up calls from you to Mr. Ford, Senator Ladd, and others can accelerate state action.

Once the Department has done its job and the services are in place, you will begin your monitoring. Realizing that you are dealing with a reluctant school system, you should plan to monitor your child's school program very carefully and perhaps with greater frequency than you would have done with a more cooperative school system. Not only do you want to be sure that the IEP is properly and thoroughly implemented, but you also want specific and solid information on your child's program and progress to present and use when you deal with next year's Annual Review of your child's education program.

ATTENDING THE ANNUAL REVIEW

The law requires the school system to meet at least once each year to review each child's IEP (usually on the anniversary of the first IEP), and to make revisions in the child's program if they are appropriate and necessary. All the rules and procedures of P.L. 94-142 discussed earlier in the book are still in effect, including sufficient prior notice in everyday language, the arrangement of mutually convenient meeting times, meetings conducted in language that the parents can understand, parental access to all records and reports, and opportunity for active parental participation at all meetings.

However, there is one important exception in the Annual Review procedures. In most states, program revisions are not subject to parental consent; in other words, you no longer have to sign the plan in order for it to be implemented.

"You mean, in other words, as a parent I am without any power to suggest change or negotiate services in my child's IEP?" Although you do have less power, which is why that first IEP is so important, you are far from powerless. Remember, there is a spirit to the law which is greater than technical compliance. The law intends that all handicapped children should be adequately and appropriately educated.

By insisting on your rights to information and participation, you can continue to have a strong voice in planning your child's education. All the lessons you have learned from this book (understanding how the system works, recognizing the "good" guys and the "bad" guys, keeping records, and finding allies), and the skills you have practiced (productive assertiveness, using the phone, writing letters, making positive self-statements, and drawing on your own observations of your child and his classroom) will continue to serve you. At this point, you will have become the practiced advocate. Let's look at some examples:

Mr. Donnellan listens to the school people discussing his daughter Leonore's speech therapy:

> *Principal:* Leonore didn't make much progress with the speech therapist this past year. I think we should cut it back.
>
> *Mr. Donnellan:* You remember that last year I thought Leonore should have more than three

> fifteen-minute sessions each week. But I agreed to go along with you because you said the time could be increased if Leonore needed more.

Principal: We gave her the three sessions and not much happened. There's no point in throwing any more public money away. I recommend that we reduce the sessions to once each week.

Mr. Donnellan: I believe Leonore's problem was that she didn't get enough help to make any difference. With more adequate help, she could be making more progress. Here are my recommendations. . .

In a situation like this, there are a number of responses a parent can make:

- The parent backs down and speech therapy is, of course, cut back.
- The parent announces that he plans to put his objections in writing (noting the previous year's discussion) and requests that his letter be placed in his child's school file.
- The parent has discovered, during the past year, that the language testing was done by the classroom teacher (or the school psychologist) rather than by a qualified speech therapist, and offers his opinion that, since the evaluation may have been inadequate, perhaps the original IEP is invalid.

In the second example, the threat of inserting into the school record the parent's disagreement with reference to the statements made by the school people the previous year may be enough to bring the school people around to further negotiation.

In the last example, the parent can let the school people know he is considering filing a complaint based on erroneous, false, or misunderstood information. Lack of accurate information may have violated his and his child's rights during the first crucial IEP process. The school people now face a potential appeals procedure and may prefer to deal with the parent in order to avoid it.

Even in the second, third, etc. Annual Review, a parent can, with cause, appeal the school's decision to revise the IEP. There may be many complaints a parent can use to appeal. Obviously, if a parent files an appeal after every Annual Review, the hearing officer might become suspicious of the parent (unless the school system is consistently disregarding the basic rights granted by P.L. 94-142, such as never notifying parents of meetings).

If you think you have a reasonable cause for filing a complaint against your school system, check with your advocacy or legal resources before you move to appeal to see if your complaint is strong and valid. As in the original IEP process, you exhaust your basic advocacy skills before you move to confrontation. Confrontation is always your last recourse.

In a large number of Annual Reviews, even though you do not have sign-off (or veto) power, you will find that you can still be a powerful and effective advocate.

HANGING IN

Every Annual Review requires your presence and participation if your child is to receive the full benefit of P.L. 94-142. To the parents of very young children just starting school, being your child's constant advocate may seem endless, and twelve to fifteen or more years of possible education looks like a lifetime. But it isn't: Ask the parents of a seventeen- or eighteen-year-old how fast the years go by. They will tell you that it seems like only yesterday that their children were small and they, the parents, were just starting to seek, fight, or wait for services, and now there are only a few years of education left with which to make a difference in their children's lives. Whatever age your child is, you know (or can find out) how many years of education in your state your child has left, and you will use those years to your child's best advantage.

The more you use your advocacy skills, the more comfortable you will become in your role as advocate. As school people become used to your active participation and learn that their assumptions about emotional and intrusive parents are generally unrealistic, they too will relax a bit and become more comfortable in dealing with you. They will recognize that their exaggerated fears of unreasonable and excessively demanding parents getting involved in special education have not been fulfilled. (With a few extreme exceptions, parents in fact have been demanding little of school systems, and if parents can be accused of being unreasonable, their fault lies in the direction of not asking for more, and more often.) Most school people still have little experience in working with active parent advocates; you can help them to understand that parents as advocates can be both reasonable and responsible. The educational issues will become more clear as the status and role issues are dismissed. Then one day your active participation in developing IEPs will be over. Your son or daughter will no longer be a "school-age child."

However, if your efforts have been successful, you will begin to extend your basic advocacy skills into other areas. The more seriously handicapped your child is, and, therefore, the more dependent on you, the more likely you are to generalize your advocacy skills to other important areas in your child's life. You will use these skills in dealing with physicians, assorted specialists, workshop and camp directors and others before whom you will appear, always, with just a few notes in hand on your questions, observations, references to past records, and suggestions for future service and/or treatment. You will have learned to use your eyes, ears, and common sense, and you won't want to stop. And if you are now a patient, unassertive, "no-trouble-at-all" parent (as the author once was) operating on the old erroneous assumptions about school systems and school people, you can astonish yourself by becoming an up front, outspoken, and effective advocate.

To your child, you are the constant advocate; you are always there, faithful and steady, because your child needs you.

To the school people, you must become the constant educational gadfly: "Oh-oh, she's here again! This time she's insisting on getting those records (or a meeting or a visit). What can I do?" "Give them to her and let's be done with it." Although you are not quite underfoot, your presence is always felt; you do stand fast and are an unremitting, even relentless, advocate.

Your constancy may require great sacrifices on your part, but the ends can justify the sacrifices. There may be moments when you feel close to failure. It's okay to occasionally take a little time out for a modest amount of well-placed and well-deserved self-pity. Then it's back to mustering your skills, getting yourself back on task, and forging ahead.

This book has tried to take you on a simulated but formidable journey through the special education system, pointing out along the way the perils and problems parents can face and the achievements parents can realize through the rights P.L. 94-142 grants to them and their children.

Perhaps before you read this book (or spoke to some informed parent advocate) you felt that you and your child were wandering in a maze, getting nowhere, while outside the rest of the "normal" world was passing you by. Surely there were times when you thought the world had forgotten your existence or simply didn't care. You wanted to find the way out of the maze for yourself and your child, but, alone and powerless, you feared you would remain trapped forever.

No longer are you alone or powerless. P.L. 94-142 gives you the ability to find your way through the maze. The law is your map, your compass, to keep you headed in the right direction. It reveals the most direct route to the places your child has the right to go.

Getting through the maze may still be difficult. Even with the map, it may be hard to recognize the right path; or there may be unexpected obstacles blocking it. But all the time you will know that you are making progress, getting closer to the goal.

Your goal for your child, and your child's right, is an appropriate and beneficial education, leading to a brighter future. So follow your map and get through to your destination. And may you and your child have a smooth and successful journey.

Appendix A

Resources

PARENT, CONSUMER, AND CITIZEN ORGANIZATIONS FOR HANDICAPPED CHILDREN

Organizations for Specific Disabilities

For information on local chapters which can provide you with information and assistance in your advocacy efforts, contact the national organization which best represents your child's disability.

Association for Children with Learning
   Disabilities (ACLD)
4156 Library Road
Pittsburgh, Pennsylvania 15234
(412) 341-1515; (412) 341-8077

Association for Retarded Citizens (ARC)
National Headquarters
2709 Avenue E East
Arlington, Texas 76011
(817) 261-4961

Epilepsy Foundation of America (EFA)
1828 L Street, N.W.
Washington, D.C. 20036
(202) 293-2930

International Association of Parents
   of the Deaf (IAPD)
814 Thayer Avenue
Silver Spring, Maryland 20910
(301) 585-5400

National Association for Visually
  Handicapped (NAVH)
305 East 24th Street, 17-C
New York, New York 10010
(212) 889-3141

National Easter Seal Society
2023 West Ogden Avenue
Chicago, Illinois 60612
(312) 243-8400

National Society for Autistic Children (NSAC)
1234 Massachusetts Avenue, N.W., Suite 1017
Washington, D.C. 20005
(202) 783-0125

United Cerebral Palsy Associations, Inc. (UCPA)
66 E. 34th Street
New York, New York 10016
(212) 481-6300

For other organizations concerned with specific handi-
capping conditions, consult:

*Directory of National Information Sources on Handi-
capping Conditions and Related Services.* DHEW
Publication No. (OHDS) 80-22007. Washington, D.C.:
Government Printing Office, May 1980.

This publication should be available through your local
library. You may have to tell them about it, but they
should be able to get it. (If there are any problems, call
your congressman or U.S. senator for help.)

General Organizations

These organizations have information on a broad range
of topics relating to handicapped children.

Center on Human Policy
Syracuse University
216 Ostrom Avenue
Syracuse, New York 13210
(315) 423-3851

Contact them for information on legal rights and strategies for change, and for a catalog of publications.

Closer Look
Parents' Campaign for Handicapped Children
  and Youth
Box 1492
Washington, D.C. 20013
(202) 833-4160

This is a source for information on legal rights, parent advocacy, and local parent groups, and for lists of state agencies.

The Council for Exceptional Children
Information Service
1920 Association Drive
Reston, Virginia 22091
(800) 336-3728 (toll-free except Virginia)
(703) 620-3660 (Virginia, collect calls are accepted)

They can provide information on federal and state laws, regulations, and policies.

NEWSLETTERS

Newsletters can bring you up-to-date information on problems and issues being raised in the implementation of P.L. 94-142, the results of important court suits, model projects that are improving services to handicapped children, and reports on new books dealing with parents' and students' rights under P.L. 94-142.

Closer Look
Parents' Campaign for Handicapped Children
  and Youth
Box 1492
Washington, D.C. 20013

Amicus
National Center for Law and the Handicapped
1235 North Eddy Street
South Bend, Indiana 46617

DD Protection and Advocacy Newsletter
Center for Law and Health Sciences
Boston University School of Law
209 Bay State Road
Boston, Massachusetts 02215

Exceptional Parent
Statler Office Building, Room 700
20 Providence Street
Boston, Massachusetts 02116

This is a bimonthly magazine written for parents of children with a wide range of disabilities.

BOOKS

There are many books in a number of areas which can help you become a more effective advocate for your child. Here are a few suggestions.

Legal Rights

Effective parent advocates need to know exactly what their children are entitled to by law so that they can stand up for their children's rights.

The American Civil Liberties Union handbooks

Friedman, Paul. *The Rights of Mentally Retarded Persons*. New York: Avon Books, 1976.

Levine, Alan. *The Rights of Students*. New York: Avon Books, 1977.

Rubin, David. *The Rights of Teachers*. New York: Avon Books, 1972.

Getting Yours: A Consumer's Guide to Obtaining Your Medical Record. Washington, D.C.: Health Research Groups, 1978.

This booklet could be useful if your child's medical history is an important tool in the educational planning. Contact Health Research Groups, 2000 P Street, N.W., Washington, D.C. 20036.

Kotin, Lawrence, and Eager, Nancy. *Due Process in Special Education: A Legal Analysis.* Cambridge, Mass.: Research Institute for Education Problems, Inc., 1977.

Look to this book for information about appeals and hearings in individual states.

Martin, Reed. *Educating Handicapped Children: The Legal Mandate.* Champaign, Ill.: Research Press, 1979.

This can be your basic guide to understanding P.L. 94-142.

Weintraub, Frederick; Abeson, Alan; Ballard, Joseph; and LaVor, Martin. *Public Policy and the Education of Exceptional Children.* Reston, Va.: Council for Exceptional Children, 1976.

Parent Advocacy

There are books about parents' experiences, and about organizing as parents, as well as guides for working with schools.

Biklen, Douglas. *Let Our Children Go: An Organizing Manual for Advocates and Parents.* Syracuse, N.Y.: Human Policy Press, 1974.

Brewer, Garry, and Kakalik, James. *Handicapped Children: Strategies for Improving Services.* New York: McGraw-Hill, 1979.

Des Jardins, Charlotte. *How to Organize an Effective Parent Group and Move Bureaucracies.* Chicago: Coordinating Council for Handicapped Children, 1971.

The Council's address is 407 South Dearborn, Chicago, Illinois 60605.

Turnbull, Ann P., and Turnbull, Rutherford H., III. *Parents Speak Out.* Columbus, Ohio: Merrill Publishing Co., 1978.

Assertiveness

Knowing the law is not enough. How effective you will be can depend on how well you state your case. You should read at least one or two books on assertiveness. A few are listed below, but there are many others available, some in inexpensive paperbacks.

Adler, Ronald. *Talking Straight: Assertion Without Aggression.* New York: Holt, Rinehart & Winston, 1977.

Alberti, Robert, and Emmons, Michael. *Your Perfect Right: A Guide to Assertive Behavior.* 3rd ed. San Luis Obispo, Cal.: Impact Publishers, 1978.

Charell, Ralph. *How I Got the Upper Hand.* New York: Stein and Day, 1978.

This book offers some funny, manipulative, and creative solutions to problems in everyday life. It may get you thinking about some new solutions of your own which you can shape to meet the situation.

Dyer, Wayne. *Pulling Your Own Strings.* New York: Avon Books, 1979.

Markel, Geraldine, and Greenbaum, Judith. *Parents Are To Be Seen and Heard: Assertiveness in Educational Planning for Handicapped Children.* San Luis Obispo, Cal.: Impact Publishers, 1979.

This book deals solely with P.L. 94-142.

Relaxation

To deal with your nervousness and stressful situations you may encounter, these books can help you.

Benson, Herbert. *The Relaxation Response.* New York: William Morrow, 1975.

This book is the classic. It can teach you a simple and effective technique for managing stress.

Ulene, Art. *Feeling Fine.* Los Angeles: J. P. Tarcher, 1977.

Dr. Ulene of the "Today Show" describes a number of techniques for dealing with daily stress.

Special Props

Dressing in the appropriate style can help you state your case more effectively. The following books give advice about the effects of dress on the impression you make on others.

Malloy, John T. *Dress for Success.* New York: Warner Books, 1975.

———. *The Woman's Dress for Success Book.* New York: Warner Books, 1977.

Handicaps

Books on your child's specific disability or level of involvement (mild to severe) are widely available. For example:

Doyle, Phyllis; Goodman, John; Crotsky, Jeffrey; and Mann, Lester. *Helping the Severely Handicapped Child: A Guide for Parents and Teachers.* New York: Thomas Y. Crowell Publishers, 1979.

Your library is one resource; your local organization concerned with your child's disability can also recommend some books. Being informed about the educational needs of children like your own and educational methods which have been effective will help you build your case for better services.

Appendix B

Ages of Eligibility for Special Education

The following chart lists the ages of eligibility for special education by state as of May 1, 1980. Age ranges are given for state law (labeled "Law"), the State Board of Education Regulations for Special Education (labeled "Regulation"), and the Annual Program Plans required under Part B of P.L. 94-142 (labeled "State Plan"). Ages of eligibility are the ages during which handicapped children are entitled to participate in special education; permissive ages are the ages at which special education services to exceptional children are optional—the school system has the authority to provide them if it chooses to. In general, the term "between," as used to express age ranges, indicates that the ages are inclusive, while the term "to" indicates that the upper age is actually the birthday on which the person reaches that age (students are often allowed to complete the school year rather than forced to leave on the birth date).

Ages of Eligibility for Special Education
May 1, 1980

State	Law		Regulation		State Plan	
	Ages of Eligibility	Permissive Ages	Ages of Eligibility	Permissive Ages	Ages of Eligibility	Permissive Ages
Alabama	Between 6 and 21			Preschool	6 through 21	3 – D, B, MH
Alaska	At least 3		Legal school age 3 to 19		3 to 19 inclusive	
Arizona	Lawful school age[1]				Between 6 and 21 If K – 5	
Arkansas	Between 6 and 21 If K – 5	Below 6 if SHC			6 and 21 If K – 5	Below school age if SHC
California	Between 3 and 21 C	Younger than 3	4.9 to 21 C	Birth to 4.9[2]	4.9 to 18 with exceptions[3]	Under 3
Colorado	Between 5 and 21	Under 5			Between 5 and 21 C	3-5
Connecticut	Over 5 under 21	Under 5	School age and preschool		HI – 3 to 21st birthday or C – All others 4 to 21st birthday or C	
Delaware	4 through 20 inclusive		Between 4 and 21 HI & VH – 0 to 21		Between 4 and 21	
Florida*	5	Exceptional children – 3 Below 5 D,B Severely PH TMR			13 consecutive years of instruction 5 – 18	0 to 4 18 and above
Georgia	6 to C if K – 5[4]	0 – 5 if SHC necessitates early intervention	Between 5 and 18	0 – 4 If enrolled can continue 19-21	5 to 18	0 to 4 19 to 21
Hawaii	Under 20				9/1/80 Between 3 and 20	
Idaho	School age[5]	To 21	School age Between 5 and 21		Between 6 and 18 inclusive. If K – 5, if 18 and has not graduated through 21	Between birth and 4 or 5 inclusive

State	Law — Ages of Eligibility	Law — Permissive Ages	Regulation — Ages of Eligibility	Regulation — Permissive Ages	State Plan — Ages of Eligibility	State Plan — Permissive Ages
Illinois*	Between 3 and 21	0 to 2	Between 3 and 21		9/1/80 Between 3 and 21	
Indiana	Over 6 and under 18	D – 6 mo. 3 to 5 / 18 to 21	6 to 18	3 through 5 HI – 18 through 21 6 mo.	6 to 18	
Iowa	Under 21		Between birth and 21		9/1/80 Birth through 20	
Kansas	Subject to regulations school age[6]		If K then 5 through 21 C, otherwise 6 through 21 C		Same age as non-handicapped to school year student reaches 21	Preschool
Kentucky	Under 21		School attendance age persuant to law		5 through 17	Birth to 4 / 18 to 21
Louisiana	3 to 21[7]	Below 3 – Serious handicapping condition	3rd birthday to 22nd birthday		Not less than 3 or more than 21 inclusive	SHC – under 3
Maine	5 to school year student reaches 20. If 2-year K, 4		5 to school year student reaches 20		5 until year reaches 20	
Maryland	As soon as child can benefit and under 21[8]		Birth through 20 – children under 5 will be phased in as required by law		9/1/80 Birth through 20	
Massachusetts	3 through 21		3 through 21 – 3 and 4 year olds must have substantial disabilities[9]		3 through 21	
Michigan	Under 26		Not more than 25 – if turns 26 after enrollment, may complete year		0 through 25 C	
Minnesota	4 to 21	TMR – through school yr. student is 25, if attended public school less than 9 years.	4 to 21		4 to 21	Before 4

State	Law		Regulation		State Plan	
	Ages of Eligibility	Permissive Ages	Ages of Eligibility	Permissive Ages	Ages of Eligibility	Permissive Ages
Mississippi	6 and under 21	Under 6	Under 21		9/1/80 6 through 20	3 to 5
Missouri	5 and under 21	Under 5	School age	3 and 4	5 through 20	Under 5
Montana	9/1/80 Between 3 and 21	9/1/80 0 to 2	9/80 Between 3 and 21		9/1/80 Between 3 and 21 inclusive	0 to 2
Nebraska	From diagnosis to 21		5 to 21 (school age) MH – birth to 21 C		From diagnosis to 21	
Nevada	5 and under 18	MR –3 G – 4 D & VH – under 5			5 or 6 to 18	Outside eligible age range
New Hampshire	3 to 21 C		Up to 21		3 to 21	0 to 3
New Jersey	Between 5 and 20	Under 5 and over 20	Between 5 and 20	Under 5 and over 20	Between 5 and 20	
New Mexico	School age [10]		Legal entry age until age 18	Over 18		
New York	Over 5 and under 21		Under 21		Between 5 and 21 [11]	
North Carolina	Between 5 and 18		5 through 17	Birth through 4 18 through 21	Between 5 and 17	Birth to 4 18 to 21
North Dakota	6 and under 21	3 to 6	6 to 21		6 to 21	3 to 6
Ohio*	Between 6 and 18 If K – 5	Other ages	Legal school age		Compulsory school age	
Oklahoma	4		4 eligible for a minimum of 12 years[12]		4 through 18 minimum period of 12 years	19 to 21
Oregon	Superintendent establishes eligibility		6 to 21 inclusive If K 5 to 21 If preschool 3 to 21		6 through 20 If K – 5	
Pennsylvania	6 to 21	Below 6	6 to 21 below 6 if regular programs below age 6		Policy is same as regulations and law	
Rhode Island	3 to 21		3 to 21 C		9/1/80 3 to 21	

286

State	Law		Regulation		State Plan	
	Ages of Eligibility	Permissive Ages	Ages of Eligibility	Permissive Ages	Ages of Eligibility	Permissive Ages
South Carolina	Lawful school age[13]				Between 6 and 21 HI 4 to 21	
South Dakota	Under 21		Under 21[14]		Under 21	
Tennessee	Between 4 and 21	D - 3	4 through 21 D - 3		4 through 21 D - 3 through 21	
Texas	Between 3 and 21		Between 3 and 21 inclusive. Auditorily, visually handicapped - between birth and 22		Between 3 and 21. Auditorily, between birth and 22	
Utah	Over 5 (if K) under 21		5 through 21		5 through 21	
Vermont	Under 21	Over 21 to C	Under 21		6 to 21 C If K - 5	3 to 5
Virginia	2 and under 21 VH - birth to 21		2 to 21		Between 2 and 21	
Washington	Common school age[15]	Preschool	5 to 21[16]		5 to 21 common school age	3 to 4[17]
West Virginia	Between 5 and 23	3 - 5	Between 5 and 23		Between 5 and 23	
Wisconsin	3 under 21	Under 3	3 to 21		3 to 21	
Wyoming	Over 6 and under 21. If 5 - K		School age		Between 6 and 21 If K - 5	
District of Columbia			Between 3 and 21		9/1/80 Not less than 4 or more than 21. 4 year olds when provided to regular children	

Prepared by the Policy Research Center, The Council for Exceptional Children, for The Policy Options Project (POPs)

KEY

K — Kindergarten	PH — Physically Handicapped	MH — Multiple Handicap
C — Completion of Course	TMR — Trainable Mentally Retarded	MR — Mentally Retarded
D — Deaf	HI — Hearing Impaired	G — Gifted
B — Blind	VH — Visually Handicapped	SHC — Serious Handicapping Condition

FOOTNOTES

[1]Arizona — Lawful school age is between 6 and 21.

[2]California — 3-4.9 identified as requiring intensive special education.

[3]California — Exceptions include: 3-4.9 for those identified as requiring intensive services; 19-21 if enrolled before 19 and have not yet completed a course.

[4]Georgia — 3 and 4 year old children who are physically, mentally, or emotionally handicapped or perceptually or linguistically deficient are eligible.

[5]Idaho — Services of public schools are extended to any acceptable person of school age (defined as between 5 and 21).

[6]Kansas — School age is 6 or 5 if kindergarten is available.

[7]Louisiana — Legislation has been passed extending eligibility to 25 in certain circumstances.

[8]Maryland — Effective 7/1/80 Senate Bill. No 734 provides for compensatory education over 21 in certain circumstances.

[9]Massachusetts — Substantial disabilities are defined as intellectual, sensory, emotional or physical factors, cerebral disfunctions, perceptual factors or other specific learning impairments or any combination thereof.

[10]New Mexico — School age is at least 5 and for children in special education a maximum of 21 years of age.

[11]New York — Blind, deaf, or severely physically handicapped children in state schools between 3 and 21; deaf children less than 3 years of age in approved educational facilities.

[12]Oklahoma — No set minimum age is specified for blind and partially blind, deaf, hard of hearing, or low incidence severely multiple handicapped children.

[13]South Carolina — Lawful school age is over 5 and under 21.

[14]South Dakota — Programs for children under the age of 3 years shall be provided only to those children who are in need of prolonged assistance.

[15]Washington — Common school age is between 5 and 21.

[16]Washington — 0 to 1 and 2 year old children with multiple handicaps, gross motor impairment, sensory impairment, or moderate or severe mental retardation are eligible for services.

[17]Washington — Services are permissive for children 0-2 if they have a multiple handicap, gross motor impairment, sensory impairment, or moderate or severe mental retardation.

COMMENTS

*Florida — According to Florida State Department of Education officials, there is no maximum school age.

*Ohio — According to Ohio State Department of Education officials, Ohio's mandated age range is 5 through 21.

*Illinois — Permissive ages are listed in § 10-22-38 rather than in Special Education Law.

288

Index

About the Author

Barbara Cutler got her advocacy training the hard way. Divorced and with two small children to raise, she began to search out services for her handicapped son. It took her almost ten years to realize that being a patient, no-trouble-at-all parent was not the way to get attention or services. She learned painfully, through her personal experience, that a parent has to become vocal, visible, and knowledgeable in order to be an effective advocate. Increasingly aware that an appropriate education was crucial to the development not only of her own autistic son but of all handicapped children, she simultaneously began her active advocacy "career" (contributing to the development and passage of Massachusetts's model special education law) and entered the Harvard Graduate School of Education, where she was a Merrill Fellow of the Radcliffe Institute from 1971–1973, and was awarded her Ed.M. in 1973.

In the past ten years Barbara Cutler has continued to advocate as a member of the governing boards of various service and advocacy organizations and of state councils dealing with education, mental health, and developmental disabilities. Professionally, she has directed an educational program for handicapped adolescents, coordinated programs for the Massachusetts Department of Mental Health, and is now working with Dr. Martin Kozloff at Boston University in training parents and professionals in behavioral education. She has given presentations on advocacy and education in the United States, Puerto Rico, and Canada.

Barbara Cutler lives with her two young adult sons, Robert and George, in Arlington, Massachusetts, and continues to be an active advocate for services for handicapped children and adults. Looking back, she realizes that, because of her son's disability, her career was chosen for her. She says, "I've made my personal and career decisions by dealing with the crises that parents of handicapped people learn to expect as part of their daily routine. The maze I've traveled has been harrowing, sometimes rewarding, but never, never dull. I've never regretted my decisions. Without strong parent advocates, our handicapped people could be overlooked and forgotten."